Books by John Dorfman

FAMILY INVESTMENT GUIDE   *1981*

CONSUMER TACTICS MANUAL   *1980*

WELL-BEING: AN INTRODUCTION TO HEALTH   *1980*

A CONSUMER'S ARSENAL   *1976*

CONSUMER SURVIVAL KIT   *1975*

FAMILY INVESTMENT GUIDE

FAMILY INVESTMENT GUIDE

A Financial Handbook for Middle-Income People

JOHN DORFMAN

Atheneum New York 1982

Library of Congress Cataloging in Publication Data

Dorfman, John.
    Family investment guide.
    Bibliography: p.
    Includes index.
    1. Investments—Handbooks, manuals, etc. I. Title.
HG4527.D67 1981   332.6'78'0240623   81-66020
ISBN 0-689-11208-4   AACR2

Published simultaneously in Canada by McClelland and Stewart Ltd.
Composed by American–Stratford Graphic Services, Inc.,
    Brattleboro, Vermont
Manufactured by American Book–Stratford Press,
    Saddle Brook, New Jersey
Designed by Mary Cregan
First printing October 1981
Second printing April 1982

To THOMAS A. STEWART (*aka "Pin"*)

Contents

Introduction   ix

 1 · Twenty Investment Rules   3
 2 · Before You Invest   12
 3 · Investment Basics   20
 4 · Savings and NOW Accounts   30
 5 · Certificates of Deposit   38
 6 · Money Market Funds   48
 7 · Your House as an Investment   55
 8 · Corporate Bonds   61
 9 · Government Bonds   80
10 · Preferred Stocks   89
11 · Common Stocks   91
12 · Mutual Funds   135
13 · Tax Shelters   154
14 · Real Estate, Besides Your House   166
15 · Gold and Silver   177
16 · Collecting for Profit   181
17 · Retirement Accounts, Pensions, and Annuities   200
18 · Getting Fancy: Margin, Short Selling, Options,
        Convertibles, and Commodities   214
19 · Brokers and Financial Advisers   236

Appendix I—Saving or Investing for a Specific Goal   251
Appendix II—Accumulating a College Fund   252

Appendix III—Accumulating a Retirement Fund   254
Appendix IV—Suggested Further Reading   259
Appendix V—Twenty Investment Rules in a Nutshell   260
Index   261

Introduction

This book will not make you rich quickly. No book will. No one, not even the shrewdest investor, gets rich by skillful investment decisions alone. Some rare individuals achieve instant wealth. They record hit albums, discover oil in their backyards, write best sellers. When wealth comes suddenly, it usually comes in the form of income, not a return on investments. And sudden wealth is likely to depend as much on luck as skill. This book may enhance your investment skills, but it won't bring you luck. Thus, it won't make you rich, unless you were almost rich before.

If you think you can start with a stake of a few hundred dollars, or a few thousand, and become a millionaire in short order through investments, you are fated to almost certain disillusionment. You are also fated to be fleeced. There are many opportunists in the financial world ready to take advantage of people's hopes for instant wealth. People who grab at promises of quick, extremely high returns are likely to be left holding a bag of worthless options, stock in defunct corporations, or title to land that shall remain forever undeveloped.

This is not to imply that greed is necessarily bad, nor risk, nor even speculation. It is to say that, in investing, hope and haste are two great enemies of rational decision-making.

All right, then. You're resigned to not getting rich quickly. Brace for the shocker: This book will not make you rich slowly, either.

Why? Because a savings and investment program is like many other things in life: What you get out of it depends on what you put into it. A pair of examples will illustrate the point. Ms. Smith, a young, single fashion designer, begins her savings program at the age of 24. Each year she puts $2,000 into a savings account that pays, over the long term, a 4% return after taxes. When she reaches age 65, she will have accumulated $207,638.

Mr. Jones, an executive and the father of three children, does not settle for a savings account. An extremely sophisticated investor, he manages by superb portfolio management to achieve an annual after-tax return of 10% on a blend of stocks, bonds, and funds. However, his family responsibilities and standard of living make it difficult for him to find money to invest. He therefore does not begin a systematic savings and investment program until he is 45 years old, and he invests only $1,500 a year. When he reaches age 65 he will have accumulated only $94,503.

Who is the better investor, Ms. Smith or Mr. Jones? The answer must depend on your definition. Unquestionably, Mr. Jones is more informed, has superior ability to pick investment vehicles on the basis of yield. His investments yield more than double the rate of return that Ms. Smith's do. Yet, because she was able to put more money into her savings and investment program each year, and maintain the program over a longer period, Ms. Smith achieved more than twice the accumulated sum that Mr. Jones did. The moral: Skill in picking investment vehicles is valuable, but certainly not the whole story. At least equally important are the amount you invest, and the period over which you invest. Earning power, self-discipline, and budgeting are vital if your investment program is going to succeed. These, however, are qualities to which a book on investments can make at best a modest contribution.

What this book *does* hope to do is to help you earn a higher return on the money you invest, help keep you from wasting your investment dollars, and help you pick investments that offer the best possibility of increasing substantially in value.

This book's bias is that you should take some risks with your investment money, but that they should be very carefully calculated risks. You will find information here about speculative ventures, but more often in the form of *don'ts* than *dos*. The book's focus is on the future, on deploying your limited assets intelligently to try to achieve long-term financial health for you and your family.

FAMILY
INVESTMENT
GUIDE

1

Twenty Investment Rules

You can read lots of books and magazine articles about investing. But when it comes time to apply what you've read, you may find that the ideas have slipped from your mind, like water from between your fingers.

In some cases, that's all to the good. However, most authors proceed on the belief that what they have to say is worth remembering. I'm going to go even further—perhaps out on a limb—and state at the outset what I consider to be the 20 most important investment rules contained in this book.

The elaboration is in the later chapters. But reading these rules will give you a preview of what's coming, an insight into my biases and beliefs, and a way to put the ideas in this book to easy and practical use, once you've finished reading it. (Further to that end, the 20 rules are given again in capsule form in Appendix V.)

Rule 1. Try to invest 15% of your after-tax income. This is hard to do, especially year after year. In fact, in the beginning of the 1980s the average family was saving or investing only about 5%. That's simply not enough to achieve long-term financial goals. I suggest that you save or invest at least 10%, and preferably 15%.

Accumulating Money to Invest

Where will you get the money you invest? If you plan on investing what's left over after you've paid for all your other expenses, you'll be in for a rude realization: There won't *be* anything left. Thus, the old injunction, "Pay yourself first."

Start by deciding on your savings goal for the year. Fifteen percent of your after-tax earnings would make an excellent target. Then, translate that goal into a monthly sum to be saved. Put that monthly sum into a NOW account or savings account. Whenever you have accumulated enough, you can pull out a chunk and invest it in a higher-yielding instrument.

Income After Taxes	5% Savings Level (National Average)	10% Savings Level	15% Savings Level
$10,000/year	$500	$1,000	$1,500
$833/month	$42	$83	$125
$15,000/year	$750	$1,500	$2,250
$1,250/month	$62	$125	$188
$20,000/year	$1,000	$2,000	$3,000
$1,667/month	$83	$167	$250
$25,000/year	$1,250	$2,500	$3,750
$2,083/month	$104	$208	$312
$30,000/year	$1,500	$3,000	$4,500
$2,500/month	$125	$250	$375
$35,000/year	$1,750	$3,500	$5,250
$2,917/month	$146	$292	$438
$40,000/year	$2,000	$4,000	$6,000
$3,333/month	$167	$333	$500
$50,000/year	$2,500	$5,000	$7,500
$4,167/month	$208	$417	$625

I'm not trying to spoil your fun. And I'm certainly not trying to minimize the difficulty of budgeting in inflationary times. I just want you to have a chance to fulfill your long-term needs and wants. I say "a chance" because there's no certainty about it. (Any financial adviser who claims to guarantee that you can meet long-term goals—or get rich—by following a prescribed program should be viewed with suspicion.) You could save 15% of your net income and still not be able to send your kids to Harvard or retire in style. But saving at the 15%-of-net-income level gives you a fighting chance.

Say a woman wants to send her daughter to college ten years from now. She figures her daughter's education will cost $48,000. That would take annual savings (assuming a 5% after-tax return on the savings) of $3,648. The parent can't do it, even by following my 15% rule, unless she earns an average of $24,320 a year or more. Rabbits don't jump out of hats.

But goals and dreams are still worth striving for, even if they're not guaranteed. Maybe you'd like to travel a lot, or retire in a lovely house, or buy a boat someday. If you don't make an effort to save and invest, you're not likely to achieve those dreams. If you do, the dreams have at least a chance of becoming reality.

Rule 2. Keep three months' income in a NOW account or savings account. There's no point having money in stocks, bonds, gold coins, or anything else that fluctuates in value until you have a basic pool of money to draw on for ordinary living expenses and occasional emergencies. As you know, a roof always picks the wrong time to leak, a child the wrong time to need braces, or a car the wrong time to need a brake job. If you have no savings, these events are guaranteed to happen just when your stocks (bonds, coins, whatever) are down in value. To avoid having to sell your investments at precisely the wrong time—and for simple convenience—you should have at least three months' income in a place from which you can retrieve it instantly.

Rule 3. Keep another three months' income in either a certificate of deposit or a money market fund. This comes after you've filled up your NOW account or savings account, but before you do any risk-prone investing. The reason for having this back-up fund is precisely the same reason given above in Rule 2. Why not just keep the whole six months' worth of income in a savings account, then? Because you can get a considerably higher return in a CD or money fund.

Rule 4. Don't invest until you have enough insurance. Before you put any money in the stock market or the like, check your insurance program. You should have adequate coverage in the areas of disability, health, life, car, and home. How much insurance is enough? Some answers to that question are found in Chapter 2.

Rule 5. Don't invest until your debts are under control. Chapter 2 of this book will help you figure out just what your debts are, and then apply two tests to see if they're excessive. Your monthly payments for all debts (except mortgage) shouldn't consume more than 15% of your take-home pay. And your total assets should be twice your total liabilities, before you launch an investment program.

Rule 6. Keep at least 20% of your investment money in investments that involve some risk. There's a direct relationship between how risky an investment is, and how high is the potential return. Unless you're retired, I suggest you keep at least 20% of your investment money in such medium-risk vehicles as common stocks, real estate, precious metals, and collectibles. For various reasons, my favorite among these, at least for the early 1980s, is common stocks. Unless you expose yourself to at least some risks, you preclude any chance that your investment portfolio will show major appreciation.

Rule 7. Don't put more than 80% of your investment portfolio into risky vehicles. There should be something there for ballast, something that will save your program from total disaster if the stock market, or real-estate market, or art market, or whatever risk-prone vehicle you've chosen, turns totally sour. Thus, I suggest keeping at least 20% of your investment assets in negligible-risk vehicles like certificates of deposit and money market funds, or at least in low-risk vehicles like high-grade bonds with maturity less than ten years away. (Don't count your six-month cushion in making this calculation.)

Rule 8. Use an Individual Retirement Account (IRA) or a Keogh Plan if you are eligible to. Under the new tax law passed in 1981, self-employed people can have a Keogh, and anyone can have an IRA. This is a tax shelter for the average man or woman. (It is described in more detail in Chapter 17.) Your money will grow much faster inside it than it would in a normal investment vehicle. Yet, when the Federal Trade Commission did a survey in 1978, it found that only about 10% of people eligible to start a Keogh or an IRA had done it. The money you put into an IRA or Keogh is deductible from your taxable income for the year you put it in. You don't have to pay tax on interest or capital gains as you get them, either. You owe no taxes until you reach age 59½ or later, when you start withdrawing the funds. If you don't withdraw them until you retire, you'll probably be in a lower tax bracket then than you are now.

Rule 9. If you can afford it, own your home. Home prices may not rise in the 1980s as fast as they did in the 1970s. Even so, owning your own home has substantial financial advantages. When you pay rent, you don't build up any equity; when you own your home, you do. When you pay rent, none of your monthly rent check is tax deductible—not even the portion that goes to defray real-estate taxes and mortgage interest on the building. When you own your home, you get substantial tax deductions for real-estate taxes and mortgage interest. What's more, any profit you make from selling your home will often (see Chapter 7) be tax free, up to $100,000.

Rule 10. If you're going to buy a bond, consider high-quality discounted corporate bonds, or municipals. You can get a higher yield on a bond by buying one issued by a relatively shaky corporation, but it's not worth it. If you want to speculate, better you should speculate in the stock market, or some other arena where the gains can be dramatic. The choice between corporate or municipal bonds should be made based on your tax bracket. Corporate bonds selling at a discount may be better than ones with a higher coupon rate because they'll give you more of your return in the form of capital gains, rather than interest, which is a tax advantage. If any of this is Greek now, you'll understand it perfectly after you read Chapters 8 and 9.

Rule 11. Buy stocks when they're undervalued. In my opinion, most stocks were undervalued in the late 1970s, and many continue to be undervalued as of early 1981. One good gauge of whether stocks are high- or low-priced at a given moment is the state of price-earnings ratios. In normal times, the average stock will sell for between 10 and 15 times the company's recent annual earnings per share. When most stocks are selling for more than 15 times earnings, the stock market may be getting carried away, and you may want to put at least some of your risk-prone investment money elsewhere. When stocks generally are selling below 10 times earnings, good buying opportunities for the long haul arise. It takes courage to take advantage of these opportunities, because they come at times when everyone is pessimistic about the stock market, the economy, and the world.

Rule 12. Hold stocks for the long term. If you trade frequently, you will pay a lot of brokerage commissions that eat heavily into your profits. Give your stocks lots of time. I know this runs counter to the adage, "Cut your losses, and let your winnings ride." But there's substantial evidence that the most successful strategy is simply to buy a diversified portfolio of stocks, picked as best you can, and then hold them for the long haul.

Rule 13. Prefer stocks with low price-earnings ratios. In part, the stock market is a popularity contest. A company that everyone expects to do well may sell for 20 times its current earnings per share, while one that isn't in favor may sell for only 5 times earnings. Sometimes there's a good reason why a stock is held in low regard. But opinion can be faddish, and even the experts can't predict the future. Historically, stocks with low price-earnings ratios have, as a group, outperformed those with high ratios. A high- multiple stock can get the stuffing knocked out of it if popular opinion changes. A low-multiple stock can soar if analysts reassess its prospects. A low-multiple stock gives you more ways to win.

Rule 14. Diversify your holdings. If you own stocks, you should own several, not just one or two. This lessens your risk and increases the chance of your having a big winner in your portfolio. If you don't have enough money to buy a diversified group of single stocks, then you should enter the stock market through a mutual fund.

The principle of diversification applies not just to your stock holdings, but to your total investment portfolio. A portfolio with a blend of investment instruments will, on the average, do better than one concentrated in a single vehicle, be it bonds, diamonds, options, or whatever.

Rule 15. In buying a mutual fund, look for consistency. Many mutual funds can show spectacular results for a single year. That can be due to blind luck. Or it can reflect the fact that a fund is invested in volatile assets; the very fund that looks great in a good year may be one that looks terrible in a down year. Before buying any mutual funds, you should examine the latest five- and ten-year record of a variety of funds in sources like *Forbes* Magazine's annual mutual-fund survey, or *Mutual Funds Almanac*.

Rule 16. Tax shelters should be evaluated as straight investments first, tax dodges second. It's easy, but not satisfying, to shelter your money by losing it.

Rule 17. Go light on investments in gold, silver, and collectibles. These are fine as part of a large, diversified investment portfolio. But they're too volatile to be the mainstay of your investment program.

Rule 18. Use leverage sparingly. If half of your investment is made with borrowed money, it's true that any capital gains you make will be effectively almost doubled. However, any loss you take will also be at least doubled. It makes sense to borrow money to buy a home (most people couldn't afford a home any other way, anyway). But in general, don't borrow to invest unless the interest rate is remarkably low, and the investment return remarkably certain.

Rule 19. Avoid entirely short selling, options trading, and commodities speculating. It's hard enough to know what's going to go up and what's going to go down. When you engage in these investment tactics, you're in effect saying that you not only know what's going to go up or down, but when. You are much more likely to lose.

Rule 20. In getting advice, consider the source. Brokers generally think you should trade a little more often, fund salesmen think mutual funds are the ticket to prosperity, and insurance people think annuities or cash-value life-insurance policies are swell investments. Financial advisory firms that sell only advice usually price their services beyond the reach of the average investor. So rely on reading up about investments that interest you (a number of good information sources are listed in Chapter 19) and blending together the advice of various people, all of whom have their own self-interest.

2

Before You Invest

Before you consider investing in stocks or anything else that involves a significant measure of risk, you should see that certain other matters have been attended to. There are three major prerequisites:

1 · An adequate savings cushion;
2 · An adequate insurance program; and
3 · Adequate debt management.

Let's take a look at what you should do in each of these three areas, before you begin to invest.

Your savings cushion.

No matter how sophisticated you are in financial matters, you should have some assets in a highly liquid form. In other words, some money where you can get it easily and fast. Traditionally, that meant a checking or savings account. Today, it will often mean a NOW account.

A NOW account is probably the best place to keep your ready cash. Legal nationwide since the beginning of 1981, NOW accounts are a cross between traditional checking and savings accounts. You can write checks against your NOW account, but the account also pays you interest—up to 5¼ percent interest, as of 1981. A NOW account eliminates the hassle of switching money from savings to checking when you need to pay bills. And it eliminates the drain of having some of your money sit uselessly, earning no interest, in a checking account.

Despite their advantages, NOW accounts may not be the best choice for everyone. It's possible that no bank or savings institution in your area offers them (and banking by mail removes some of the convenience). Also, some banks impose service fees on NOW accounts (see Chapter 4) that may tip the balance against your having one. If you choose not to have a NOW, substitute the words "savings account" in your mind when we mention NOW accounts in the rest of this discussion.

How much should be in your NOW account? At least three months' income (after-tax income, if you care). To have less on tap would mean that your financial plans could easily be upset by emergencies. You might then have to raise money in undesirable ways, such as selling stock at the wrong time, getting a hurry-up loan, or withdrawing money early from a certificate of deposit and having to take a penalty.

On the other hand, it's a waste for most people to keep much more than three months' income in a NOW account. Why accept a mere 5¼% on your money when you could be earning a much higher return elsewhere?

A possible exception to the three-month rule is the person whose income fluctuates sharply. If you are a salesperson working on commission, a free-lance writer or artist, or even a lawyer with major ups and downs in your income, you might prefer a larger liquid fund, perhaps up to six months' income.

In addition to the liquid fund, you should have a backup fund that can be tapped almost as easily as the liquid fund. The backup fund should be about the same size as the liquid fund, usually about three months' income. It should not be kept in a NOW account or ordinary savings account. Rather, it should be in something safe, but higher yielding. For most people, the place to keep a backup fund is in certificates of deposit or in a money market fund. These investments pay much higher interest rates than passbook savings accounts (more than double, as of early 1981), yet they involve virtually no risk. In case of emergency, the money in a certificate of deposit can be tapped easily, either through early withdrawal (in which case a penalty must be paid) or by pledging the certificates as collateral for a low-interest loan (often from the same institution that sold you the certificates). Money market funds allow withdrawals virtually on demand, though red tape or busy telephone lines may sometimes cause moderate delays in getting your money out.

Further details on certificates of deposit are in Chapter 5. You can find out more about money market funds in Chapter 6.

Your insurance program.

Before you invest, you should see that your insurance program is up to snuff. The major types of insurance most people need are disability, health, life, automobile, and home insurance.

▶ *Disability insurance.* Try to insure yourself against loss of earning power, up to 75% of current earnings. Ideally, you might think it would be good to insure even more, but disability benefits are normally tax-free, so 75% usually is enough. (High tax-bracket individuals may need less.) Anyway, few companies will sell insurance that puts you much beyond the 75% mark, for fear of encouraging fraud. (Some won't even go that far.)

You probably do not have to rely entirely on private insurance to fill that 75% target. You may already have at least part of what you need. Social Security disability benefits will fill part of the bill; a good insurance agent can help you estimate what you'd have coming from that quarter. In addition, you may already have some disability coverage on the job, or through an association you belong to. What you need to buy is enough to fill the remaining gap, up to the 75% target.

▶ *Health insurance.* The most important priority in health insurance is protection against catastrophic costs. Such protection is usually sold under the name of major medical insurance. Most people also desire to have lesser expenditures covered, both for doctor bills and hospital bills. One promising innovation in health-care financing is the health-maintenance organization, or HMO, a system in which individuals pay a fixed periodic fee and receive whatever care they need from a set of designated practitioners, usually practicing together as a group.

▶ *Life insurance.* Few people without dependents need life insurance. Nearly all people with dependents do. Simple rules (such as the often-heard five times annual earnings) are a haphazard way of calculating life-insurance needs. A good insurance agent can help you do a more sophisticated plan, taking into account Social Security benefits, living expenses for your survivors, education funds, and retirement funds. A worksheet for calculating life-insurance needs appears in *The Consumers Union Report on Life Insurance,* 4th edition, by the editors of Consumer Reports Books.

▶ *Automobile insurance.* The minimum coverages prescribed by state laws aren't enough. You should probably carry at least what the industry calls 100/300/25 coverage. That means $100,000 of liability protection for any one person you might insure; $300,000 for all such persons; and $25,000 for property damage.

▶ *Home insurance.* Whether you live in a house, an

15

apartment, a condominium, or a mobile home, you need some kind of protection for your property. One key consideration is to keep your coverage updated to adjust for inflation. Another is to be alert to the value of any special equipment or precious objects you may own; in many cases these need to be insured separately. Also, property used in the production of income is not covered by the typical home-insurance policy and should be insured separately if it's valuable.

Debt management.

Mortgages, loans, credit cards . . . Many are the ways we can get into debt, and few of us resist. Nor, necessarily, should we. But you shouldn't begin to invest until your debts are under control.

In theory, during an inflationary period, it makes good economic sense for people to borrow at rates below the rate of inflation. The idea is that the goods you buy with the borrowed money will appreciate in value—or at least that you will, by buying them early, have avoided paying even more for them next year. In addition, it's often said that you pay back the loan with "cheaper" dollars, as inflation makes a dollar worth less each year. All of that is true in theory, but there are flaws in the ointment of the argument. If your income doesn't go up with inflation, the debt you took on can be a heavy burden. Dollars may be cheaper in terms of their buying power, but unless your income is going up, they're not any cheaper for you to come by. Also, your purchases may not turn out as well as you'd hoped. If you borrow to invest, the money you borrowed at 10% may earn you only a 7% return instead of the 15% you were hoping for. If you borrow to buy goods, the goods you buy may go down in value. The painting you bought may be by an artist who goes out of fashion. The car you bought may develop gas line leaks and be worth less at trade-in time than you expected. If inflation abates, it won't cost more next year to buy the same goods, but you'll be stuck with a high-interest loan.

Some debt is perfectly acceptable. Hardly anyone, for example, can afford to buy a house without getting a mortgage loan. And a house (see Chapter 7) can be a good investment, as well as a place to live. The important thing is that the debt be kept within reasonable bounds.

The two crucial tests of whether your debts are under control are the monthly-payment test and the net-worth test.

To give yourself these tests, you first have to know precisely how much debt you have. The chart on page 18 will help you find out.

Once you've filled in the debt scoreboard, it's easy for you to give yourself the monthly payment test. Not counting your mortgage payments (if any), your total monthly payments on all of your debts should never exceed 20% of your monthly income after taxes. Even 15% is a sign that you're nearing the danger point. If you find yourself in the 15% "yellow zone" or the 20% "red zone," remedial steps are in order to bring your budget into better shape. Until you've taken those steps, you should avoid any involvement in risk-prone investments.

The second test of whether your debts are under control is the net-worth test. Your net worth is the sum of your financial assets minus the sum of your financial liabilities. I suggest you postpone investing until your assets equal twice your liabilities. The table below, which you can photocopy and update from time to time, makes it easy to calculate your net worth.

Your Debt Scoreboard

Type of Debt	Interest Rate (APR*)	Outstanding Balance	Monthly Payment
MORTGAGE(S)			
First mortgage	_____	_____	_____
Second mortgage	_____	_____	_____
CREDIT CARDS			
Card #1			
_____	_____	_____	_____
#2 _____	_____	_____	_____
#3 _____	_____	_____	_____
#4 _____	_____	_____	_____
#5 _____	_____	_____	_____
#6 _____	_____	_____	_____
#7 _____	_____	_____	_____
#8 _____	_____	_____	_____
#9 _____	_____	_____	_____
#10 _____	_____	_____	_____
LOANS			
Loan #1			
_____	_____	_____	_____
#2 _____	_____	_____	_____
#3 _____	_____	_____	_____
#4 _____	_____	_____	_____
#5 _____	_____	_____	_____

* Annual Percentage Rate

Your Net Worth			
Assets		*Liabilities*	
Savings, checking, or NOW accounts	_____	Credit-card balances	_____
		Personal loans	_____
Certificates of Deposit	_____	Mortgage(s)	_____
Bonds	_____	Other	_____
Stocks	_____		
Mutual Funds	_____		
Real estate, including market value of home	_____		
Collectibles	_____		
Equity in pension plan	_____		
Cash value of life insurance	_____		
Other	_____		
Total Assets:	_____	Total Liabilities:	_____
	Net Worth:	_____	
(total assets minus total liabilities)			

3

Investment Basics

Not many people would try sky-diving without getting some instruction first. Yet some people invest their money on hunch, on whim, on hot tips from their uncle or their broker, without any real idea of the basic principles behind investing.

This chapter is intended to teach you—or remind you of—some of those basic principles. We'll look first at some of the reasons why certain investments offer a higher potential return than others. Next, we'll examine the reason why you should see that your investments are diversified, rather than keeping all your eggs in one basket. Finally, we'll talk very briefly about what kinds of financial records you should keep.

Why investments aren't all created equal.

Why is it, some people wonder, that a passbook savings account pays between 5% and 6% interest, while a certificate of deposit may pay double that or more, and shares of common stock may provide a bonanza (or a disaster)? What makes the returns of some investments high, others low. Why are some steady, some volatile?

The answers to these questions lie in three notions that sound abstract but really aren't: risk, liquidity, and size.

All three can affect your investment return. Probably the most important is risk.

If you lend ten dollars to a friend who says she will pay you back the next day, you do not expect to get interest on the loan. One reason for that is that you have assumed very little risk.

By contrast, suppose you place a ten-dollar bet on a horse. Substantial risk is assumed, for you well know that picking the winner from a field of eight to twelve horses is difficult. However, you may be willing to assume the risk, because there is a possibility that you will get a return substantially above ten dollars.

When a bank lends money to a major, highly successful corporation, the interest rate charged may be the so-called prime rate—a relatively low interest rate that reflects the bank's near certainty that it will be paid back.* When the bank loans money to a fledgling company, it is likely to charge a higher rate. The increased return to the bank compensates for the increased likelihood that the business might fail and the bank might lose its investment.

As you see, there's a very direct connection between risk and return. When risks are high, investors will demand a higher return (or potential return) before they are willing to commit their money. When risks are low, investors will accept a more modest—but more certain—return.

In 1981, savings accounts—the safest thing going—provided a rate of return of about 5½% (5¼% at commercial banks and on NOW accounts) before taxes. That's low, but the risk is essentially zero. In early 1981, corporate bonds were providing a current return of about 14%. One reason for the dramatic difference: The buyer of a bond risks losing his (her) money if the company goes broke. To extend the

* Actually, one of the financial world's worst-kept secrets is that banks often lend to their best customers at rates below the prime.

point, the bonds of shakier corporations in early 1981 yielded considerably above 14%. Many of the bonds issued by Chrysler Corporation, for example, were yielding between 16% and 19%. That's because investors wouldn't be willing to buy the bonds of a company that had a higher risk of going broke unless they were compensated by a higher return.

To summarize: When one investment carries a higher potential return than another, it's usually because the higher-yielding investment is more risky.

A second factor affecting investment yields is liquidity. The word sounds forbidding, but the concept is simple. An investment is liquid if you can withdraw your invested money when you wish, rapidly and with ease. An investment is illiquid if, once you've put your money in, you are forced to wait a long time or go to a great deal of trouble before you can get your money out again. Many investments fall between the extremes. Thus, different investments have varying degrees of liquidity.

Suppose you had a choice between Investment A and Investment B. Both pay the same rate of return, say, 10% a year. However, Investment A requires that you agree to keep your money invested for ten years to earn your 10%, while Investment B requires only that you keep it in for a year. Which is the better investment? Under most circumstances, Investment B is better. However, if Investment A raised its rate of return to, say, 12%, you might reconsider. Thus, a higher rate of return compensates you for tying up your money, or, in other words, for accepting a lack of liquidity.

Pretend you're a bank executive. If you can attract deposits that you know will be available for you to invest during an entire year, those deposits are worth more to you than deposits that may be around for a shorter time. Several years is better still. That's why banks and savings institutions pay higher interest rates on long-term certificates of deposit than on shorter-term ones or savings and NOW accounts.

Liquidity isn't always a matter of contractual agreement, as is the case with certificates of deposit. It can be a matter of the mechanics of buying or selling a given commodity. Stocks, for example, are liquid, but not nearly so liquid as a savings account, because it takes time for a sales transaction to be processed and the proceeds to reach the seller. It also costs money, in the form of a brokerage commission.

Moreover, the time when the owner of stock needs cash may happen to be a time when the stock market is down, and the stockholder doesn't wish to sell. The same holds true for real-estate investments, where the mechanics of sale are even more time-consuming. Neither stocks nor real estate has a guaranteed rate of return, but both involve a potential for high returns. This potential may compensate the investor both for the high degree of risk assumed, and for the loss of liquidity.

A third factor affecting investment returns is the size of the investment. Suppose, again, that you are a banker. A company with a new process for making solar heaters comes to you asking for financing. You think the proposal is promising, and want to lend the requested $3 million. The money you lend the company must come, of course, from deposits with your bank. Accumulating this large a sum from many small deposits is cumbersome. Naturally, you'd like your bank to attract some large depositors. How to do it? An obvious answer is to pay a higher rate of interest on deposits exceeding certain thresholds, such as $10,000 or $100,000. And this is precisely what banks do.

For the individual investor, the thresholds most often encountered are $1,000 and $10,000. Many bonds, for example, are sold in minimum denominations of $1,000 each. Some high-yielding certificates of deposit are available only to savers who are depositing $10,000 or more at a crack.

So there you have the story of investment returns in a nutshell: risk, liquidity, and size.

I've already said something about liquidity in Chapter 2, namely that you should have on hand relatively liquid funds equivalent to six months' income. About half of that should be extremely liquid (i.e., NOW account or savings account), and half at least reasonably liquid (certificates of deposit or money market fund). About size, there's not much I can say. But I would like to say something more about risk.

No one can tell you how risky your investment portfolio should be. That's a decision only you can make. And you have to make it in light of a number of variables.

One is your age. For years, investment advisers have urged young people to take more risks, and older people fewer. By and large, that's reasonable advice. When you're retired, or near retirement age, you can usually afford to take very few investment risks. Or at least you should aim to have 20 years' worth of income in relatively safe investments before you dabble in anything more speculative. When you're young and earning a good income, you can afford more risks, and are likely to want to take more, in the hopes of building up some substantial wealth.

Another is your occupation. If your income is uncertain or sharply fluctuating, you might be wise to invest somewhat more conservatively.

The number of dependents you have matters, too. A single person can afford to take more chances than someone with a spouse, a mortgage, and three children.

But at least as important as age, occupation, or your number of dependents is your own temperament. There are people who cannot sleep at night if they own stock. Those people are better off not owning stock, even if they end up with a lessened return on their investment portfolio. There are other people who depend for a major part of their enjoyment on the ability to discuss the hot little growth stock they uncovered. Who would deny them this thrill? Your own happiness and peace of mind are important, and no investment is really suitable for you unless you feel comfortable about it.

That said, there are certain guidelines about risky investments that deserve your serious consideration. With the exception of retirees, I believe that everyone (who can afford to invest at all) should have at least 20% of their portfolio in investments that involve some pinch of risk. Reason: Higher risk, on the average, means higher return. If you have no risk-prone investments at all, you're passing up your best chances for a big profit. Converse: I think you should think seriously before putting more than 80% of your investment dollars into risky assets. Just in case those gloom-and-doom prophecies forever being uttered by the Bozos of the best-seller list come true, you should have something left.

The most important thing about risk, whether you accept my advice or not, is that you should make a conscious decision about how much you want to assume, and you should know what percentage of your investment portfolio is in risk-prone investments. The chart below will help you do just that.

Your Investment Portfolio

With this chart, you can easily see at a glance how risky your investment portfolio is, compared to how risky you'd like it to be. Then you can work gradually to bring the portfolio into the shape you'd like it to be in.

Type of Investment	Dollar Amount	Percent of Assets	Desired Percent of Assets
NEGLIGIBLE RISK			
1. Savings, checking, or NOW accounts	_____	_____	_____
2. Certificates of Deposit	_____	_____	_____
3. Money Market Funds	_____	_____	_____
LOW RISK			
4. Pensions	_____	_____	_____
5. Annuities	_____	_____	_____
6. High-grade bonds maturing in 10 years or less	_____	_____	_____
7. Other	_____	_____	_____
MEDIUM RISK			
8. Bonds not included in Item #6	_____	_____	_____
9. Mutual Funds	_____	_____	_____
10. Common stocks	_____	_____	_____
11. Real estate	_____	_____	_____
12. Precious metals	_____	_____	_____
13. Collectibles	_____	_____	_____
14. Other	_____	_____	_____

HIGH RISK			
15. Options	————	————	————
16. Commodities	————	————	————
17. Other	————	————	————
Totals:			
NEGLIGIBLE RISK	————	————	————
LOW RISK	————	————	————
MEDIUM RISK	————	————	————
HIGH RISK	————	————	————
Total Portfolio:	————	100%	100%

Note: If you own a house, this chart will look considerably different if you count your home equity (the difference between estimated market value and the balance remaining on the mortgage) than if you don't. You may find it enlightening to analyze your portfolio both ways. If you include it, count it under Item #11 as a real-estate holding.

Diversification.

Some investments do very well, others poorly. With stocks, for example, an occasional high flier will double in a year; by the same token, an occasional dud will lose half its value or more. By definition, the majority of stocks will do about as well as the stock-market averages.* The same holds true, generally, for other forms of investment. Investment returns, in other words, distribute themselves along a sort of bell curve.

This fact has important implications for the individual investor. If you choose to put most of your assets into one

* The broad stock-market indexes, not necessarily the Dow-Jones Industrial Average.

single investment, you might hit the jackpot and gain a very high return. Or you might suffer a financial disaster and lose almost all your money. Your "portfolio" (consisting in this case of only one investment) is extremely volatile.

But suppose you decide to diversify your portfolio. The more separate investments you make, and the more diverse they are, the greater is the chance that the performance of your portfolio will duplicate the performance of the investment market as a whole. Diversification, then, lessens the volatility, and the risk, of your investment program.

This does not mean that diversification is an unmitigated good. Naturally, if you have only a certain total to invest, each investment in a diversified portfolio will be smaller than a single, all-your-eggs-in-one-basket investment would be. That lowers your risk of a disaster, but by the same token it reduces your chances of a spectacular gain.

Another potential problem with diversification is the possibility of having to pay repeated sales commissions. Using the example of stocks again, you must pay your broker a commission each time you buy or sell. If you have a portfolio of five stocks rather than one, you've paid five commissions, and reduced your potential profits by the amount of those commissions.

The desire to achieve diversification without excessive transaction cost is one reason for the popularity of mutual funds. When you buy shares in a mutual fund, you are buying a portfolio that is already (at least to some extent) diversified. And you pay, at most, one commission. Mutual funds are discussed in detail in Chapter 12.

One more claim may be made for a diversified portfolio, especially of stocks. Each stock can lose no more than 100% of its original value, but it can potentially gain more than 100%. By having several holdings, you increase the chance that one of them will prove to be a strong or spectacular gainer.

The same principle applies on a grand scale. Let's say you're wealthy enough to diversify your investment portfolio into real estate, gold, and artworks, as well as stocks. A good performance in one sector may carry the whole portfolio to a good level of investment return, despite weak or middling performance of other sectors.

Keeping records of your transactions.

For tax reasons, it's wise to keep a file of all your investment transactions. If you buy and sell securities very rarely, the file will remain lean enough so you probably will never need to weed it out. If you do feel the need for paring, hold onto records of transactions for the most recent eight years.

Ordinarily, the Internal Revenue Service will not audit a return more than three years after it's filed. But there are some exceptions. One exception comes into play when a taxpayer uses income averaging, a useful method of minimizing taxes in high-income years. When income averaging is used, a potential is created for the IRS to demand documentation of transactions as far as eight years back (the standard three-year period plus the five-year period over which income was averaged).

It's a good idea to do an annual review of your investment portfolio, to make sure its elements are in the balance you wish, and to assess the performance of each of your investments. Filling out the chart, "Your Investment Portfolio," each year may be a helpful device in your annual review.

29

4

Savings and NOW Accounts

Your savings or NOW account is the accumulation tank for your investment program. When the tank fills up to a certain point, you can remove funds to deploy them into higher-yielding investments.

It's now common to disparge savings accounts. In early 1981, for example, they were paying only 5¼% to 5½% interest, while money market funds were paying around 16%. Under those circumstances, it's said, you have to be crazy to keep much money in a savings account.

The fact is, your savings (or NOW) account is a very important part of your investment program. Failure to keep an adequate cushion in your savings account could cause you considerable grief in your more sophisticated investments. You'll recall that I recommended you keep three months' worth of income in a savings or NOW account (and another three months' worth in certificates of deposit or a money market fund). Without such a cushion, you may be forced to sell stocks, bonds, real estate, gold, silver—or whatever else you've invested in—precisely at the wrong time, when its price is down. To avoid such calamities, a savings cushion is imperative.

What's more, the gap between savings-account yields and

yields on other safe, liquid investments (notably money market funds) is likely to narrow. Between now and 1987, the federal government is phasing out the interest ceilings on savings accounts which have forced small investors to take less than they would get for their savings in a free market. Furthermore, short-term interest rates were at an all-time peak in early 1981, which had swollen the yields (and the popularity) of the money funds. A decline in those yields seemed likely.

Granted, a savings or NOW account will never be the place where you get the best possible return on your money. (Nor should it be. The accounts give you practically absolute safety, and yield rises with risk.) But don't let that deter you from maintaining an adequate savings cushion.

Save regularly. When your account balance is $500 or $1,000 greater than your savings-cushion requirement, withdraw that amount and invest it in something with a potential for a significantly higher return.

Look back at Chapter 1, at the chart called "Accumulating Money to Invest." It will suggest how much per month you ought to be putting in your savings account.

Since it offers near-total safety and liquidity, a savings account is also a logical place to plop proceeds from the sale of investments, if you plan to reinvest the proceeds within a couple of weeks. (However, it's not the only place for such money. A lot of brokerage houses pay interest at savings-account rates on customer balances. If the balance is large enough, some brokerage houses will park the money in a money market fund for you, even if it's only for a few days.)

Ideally, your three-month savings cushion should remain untouched. If you do drop below the three-months' income level, your first priority is to refill your savings account, and that should take precedence over any new investments.

31

(However, you shouldn't liquidate investments for this purpose, unless you were planning to sell anyway.)

If your savings and checking account are one (i.e., if you have a NOW account), you'll probably want, as a practical matter, to have an extra $500 to $1,000 in the account so that paying ordinary bills won't cause you to dip below your three-months' level. When you get a raise in pay, add to your cushion so that it reflects your new standard of living (and so that it will be equal to three months' after-tax earnings at your new pay scale).

Suppose you make $25,000 a year, which works out to $20,000 after taxes. Your aim would be to put about $250 a month (15% of after-tax earnings) into savings, until you'd built up a $5,000 savings cushion. Once that was accomplished, you'd keep putting the $250 a month into savings. When the savings account reached $5,500 or $6,000, you'd take out $500 or $1,000 at a time and put it in certificates of deposit or a money market fund. (Some money funds require a larger minimum deposit, in which case you'd have to adjust your timing, but the idea remains the same.) When you had $5,000 in savings and another $5,000 in CDs or a money fund, you'd be ready to put some money into something riskier, like stocks, in hope of a greater return. But you'd still keep putting that $250 a month into your savings account, and would withdraw money to invest in stocks (or whatever) only when your savings account balance reached $5,500 or $6,000.

If your annual income is more or less than $25,000, you have to adjust the numbers in the example. But you'll find the procedure to be a useful one.

Picking a savings account.

Your savings account should probably be a NOW account. Legal nationwide since the beginning of 1981, a

NOW account combines the traditional savings and checking account, and pays (as of 1981) 5¼% interest. The advantages are that you earn interest on all of your money (instead of having some funds in a checking account earning zero interest), and that you avoid the hassle of transferring funds from savings to checking. The possible disadvantages are that it may be tempting to deplete the account (since you can write checks against it), and that there may be fees associated with a NOW, usually imposed if you drop below a specified minimum balance. For most people, the advantages outweigh the disadvantages. But you should check fees carefully, and shop around for the bank that imposes the fewest fees.

Banks compete against each other, and you can use that competition to your advantage. But you have to be discriminating in what you look at. Bank ads draw your attention mainly to image ("we're your friends," "we care about you," and similar drivel) or to "free gifts." The gifts, in reality, are interest substitutes. As interest rates on savings accounts are deregulated, you'll see some banks and savings-and-loan associations dispensing with gifts, and offering increased interest instead.

Don't pick your bank by its scales, teddy bears, or watches. Far more important is the way the bank calculates the balance in your account.

▶ *Balance method.* Stop people on the street, and they'll be able to tell you what rate of interest they get on their savings—usually 5¼% or 5½%. But if you ask "5½% of what?" they'll look at you as if you were balmy. "My balance, of course," they would reply.

But the fact is, there are lots of ways of calculating your balance. The most favorable of these is the day-of-deposit to day-of-withdrawal method. If at all possible, you should keep your savings account in an institution using that method. Here's why.

Suppose you engaged in the following chain of transactions, starting from an initial January 1 balance of $1,000 in an account paying 6% interest. On January 10 you deposited $2,000; on February 6 another $1,000. On March 3 you withdrew $1,000; on March 20 another $500; and on March 30, $500. You then made no further deposits or withdrawals until after July 1. Interest was compounded quarterly and credited to your account April 1 and July 1. (This pattern of deposits and withdrawals is called the Pinson pattern. It was designed by Jackie Pinson Martin, when she was doing graduate research about ten years ago under Dr. Richard Morse* of Kansas State.)

The question is: How much interest did you earn? It depends how your bank calculates your balance. Under the day-of-deposit to day-of-withdrawal method, you'd get $75.30. Interest is credited each day on the amount you have in the account.

Under the worst method, the low-balance method, you'd get first-quarter interest only on $1,000, because that was the smallest amount you had in the account at any time during the quarter. Your interest for the six months would come to only $44.93.

Other methods are the first-in, first-out method ($52.44 using the Pinson pattern example), and the last-in, first-out method ($58.44). As you can see, the choice of balance-calculation methods makes considerable difference in how much interest you earn—more than enough difference to let you buy your own toaster, or whatever it is a bank is "giving away."

* Morse is the nation's leading scholar on savings-account practices, and the leading exponent of Truth in Savings legislation.

Some other factors to consider are compounding practices, grace days, and service charges.

▶ *Compounding.* Some people find the term "compound interest" mysterious, but it's not. It simply means earning interest on your previous interest. And it can make a big difference. Take $1,000 and park it for 50 years at 5%. If you withdraw the interest as it accrues, you end up with only $3,500. If you leave the interest in to compound, your initial sum grows to $11,467.

Some banks make a big deal about how often your interest is compounded: gimmicky stuff, like "compounded every minute." It hardly matters. Daily compounding is better than quarterly, and quarterly is better than semiannually. But it doesn't add up to much in dollars and cents. Far more important is how your balance is computed.

▶ *Grace days.* At some banks, you can make a deposit as late as the tenth of the month, and earn interest on that money from the first of the month. There are also withdrawal grace days, sometimes called "dead days," that allow you to withdraw funds as much as three days before the end of a quarter and still earn interest as if the money had been on deposit the whole quarter. Grace days may be a sign of a pro-consumer orientation. In any case, they can boost your yield a shade above the stated rate.

▶ *Taking it away.* Some banks levy a charge against your savings account if you make what they call "excess" withdrawals. Some charge you a penalty if you close out your account "prematurely." And some don't pay any interest unless you maintain a certain minimum balance. All of these practices, whether adequately disclosed to potential customers or not, penalize the saver by the lessening of the effective interest yield.

Worst of all is a stipulation that a bank won't pay interest on your account unless a specified balance (which can range from $1 to $100) is left in the account until the end of a quarter. Under such a rule, you would receive no quarterly interest at all on a $5,000 day-of-deposit to day-of-withdrawal account if you closed it one day before the quarter ended.

With all of these variables in mind, you'll be able to make an informed choice as to where you should keep your savings. To help in the selection, here's a Savings Account Checklist.

SAVINGS ACCOUNT CHECKLIST

Name of bank:
Name of officer providing information:

Type of institution:
- ☐ Commercial bank
- ☐ Savings and loan association
- ☐ Mutual savings bank
- ☐ Credit Union

Is account covered by federal deposit insurance?
- ☐ Yes
- ☐ No

Interest rate paid on passbook (or NOW)
    account: _____

Method by which your balance is computed:
- ☐ Day-of-deposit to day-of-withdrawal:
- ☐ Last-in, first-out (LIFO)
- ☐ First-in, first-out (FIFO)
- ☐ Low-balance method

Frequency of compounding interest: _____

Grace days for deposits (if any):   _____

Dead days for withdrawals (if any):   _____

Penalty for "excess" withdrawals: _____

    Number of withdrawals permitted per period   _____

    Length of period   _____

Penalty for premature closing of account: _____

    Minimum time account must stay open to
      avoid penalty   _____

Minimum balance required to receive interest: _____

Free services (if any) offered to savings-account
    holders: _____

    Minimum balance required to receive these
      free services: _____

5

Certificates of Deposit

All right, you've managed to sock away three months' worth of take-home pay in a savings account. You're ready to launch step two of your investment program—accumulating a backup fund in vehicles that are safe, but higher yielding than passbook savings.

For the small investor, one of the most obvious places to put this secondary cushion of assets is also one of the best: certificates of deposit available at your local savings institution or bank. Certificates of deposit are also called CDs, time deposits, savings certificates, investment certificates, or high-interest passbooks.

A certificate of deposit is similar to a savings account with one notable difference. You agree to leave your money in the account for a specified length of time, and in return the bank rewards you with a higher rate of interest. The longer the period, the more use the institution can make of the money, so the higher the interest rate. (The higher rate also compensates you for your loss of liquidity; see Chapter 2.) In early 1981, the most popular kinds of certificates were paying 12% to 14% interest—more than double the rate on savings accounts. For a person with $5,000 to put in the bank, the difference amounted to at least $350 a year.

The interest rate on a certificate is guaranteed, and your

entire investment, up to $100,000, is protected by federal deposit insurance, just as savings accounts are. (This assumes that your bank or savings institution is insured by either the Federal Deposit Insurance Corporation or the Federal Savings and Loan Insurance Corporation. Almost all institutions are covered nowadays, but it wouldn't hurt to spend half a minute checking on yours if you're not sure.)

There are four major kinds of certificates available today —six-month certificates, thirty-month certificates, traditional time deposits, and jumbo certificates. Tax-sheltered certificates have also been proposed. You're most likely to be interested in either a six-month or a thirty-month certificate.

Six-month certificates.

Since they appeared on the scene in 1978, six-month certificates have been gobbled up like potato chips by savers and investors. You need at least $10,000 to buy one, unfortunately, unless you live in New York City or a few other places where banks will loan you (at low interest) a significant part of your initial stake. The lure is the yield. As of early 1981, for example, six-month certificates were paying about 14½% interest. At that rate, you put in $10,000, and come out six months later with about $10,725. Not bad at all.

It should be noted that interest rates in 1981, when this book went to press, were at record high levels. Interest rates may well have dropped by the time you read this. (For the sake of the economy, I hope they have.) In any case, you can find out the current rate on six-month certificates by checking the financial page of your newspaper, or by checking with local banks. The rate paid on six-month certificates is identical with that on six-month U.S. Treasury bills. Be-

cause of a few technical wrinkles, the Treasury bills themselves are a slightly better deal. But the certificates are almost as good, and much simpler to get.

Each week, U.S. Treasury bills (including six-month
ones) are auctioned. The price for any given week determines the yield on six-month certificates that are sold in the
next seven days. But once you purchase a six-month certificate, you have locked in the stated interest rate for the next
six months.

As you understand from the chapter on Investment Basics,
investors normally demand a higher interest rate on longer-
term investments. Thus, a thirty-month certificate should
normally have a higher yield than a six-month certificate
(just as a thirty-year bond should normally have a higher
yield than a five-year note). You can draw a line on a graph
to illustrate this relationship. On the horizontal axis, the
short term is on the left, the long term on the right. The
vertical axis shows the yield, or interest rate. Ordinarily, you
expect the line to slope gently upward, from left to right.
This line, by the way, is called by economists the "yield
curve."

Once in a while, in times when interest rates are high, the
yield curve does a funny thing. It turns the wrong way;
short-term investments yield more than longer-term ones.
That peculiar state of affairs prevailed during most of the
period from 1979 to early 1981. The reason for the oddity
is that, when interest rates are quite high, many people expect them to come down before too long. So they'll accept a
somewhat lower rate on a longer-term investment, for the
sake of locking in that return before rates fall. When this
book was written, interest rates were inverted from their
normal state, and six-month certificates paid higher interest
than thirty-month ones.

To go with the oddity, here's an irony. Banks and savings

institutions pushed hard on regulators for the privilege of offering six-month certificates. They wanted to be able to offer savers something that would give them a reason, once again, to keep money in the bank. (The banks and savings institutions were losing their depositors to the money market funds.) But the banks' glee turned to consternation when interest rates began to soar in 1979. They wanted to be able to offer savers a good deal, but not *that* good a deal. Soon the initial trumpet blast of advertising for the six-month certificates muted to a squeak. It made no difference. Investors in droves continued to snap up the certificates.

In March of 1979, the government took two steps to make the certificates a shade less attractive (and less costly to the issuing banks). First, bank regulators announced that there would be no compounding of interest on the certificates. Second, they stated that during times when the interest rate on the certificates was above 9%, savings institutions would not be allowed to offer an extra quarter point of interest on them. Despite these two relatively minor changes, the six-month certificates remain well worth considering—particularly as a place to keep your backup fund.

Thirty-month certificates.

These are the small saver's ticket to a portion of the pot of gold. Six-month certificates require a minimum investment of $10,000, but thirty-month certificates usually require a minimum of only $500 or $1,000. Until recently, the small saver was penalized by a lid on the interest that thirty-month CDs could pay; the top was 12%, whereas six-month CDs, floating with the rate on Treasury bills, paid more. In 1981, however, the lid was removed, and now thirty-month CDs can pay interest in line with the interest on thirty-month Treasury notes—interest comparable to that on six-month CDs.

The interest on a thirty-month certificate may be paid monthly, quarterly, semiannually, yearly, or all at the end, depending on the practice of the individual bank and—in some cases—the investor's choice. Some banks give you a choice, others don't. Some banks give you a broader choice if you're depositing a relatively large amount (e.g., $5,000) than if you're putting in a smaller amount. However you elect to have the interest paid, it doesn't affect your taxes at all. You're deemed by the IRS to get your share of interest each year, and the bank will send you a tax statement accordingly.

Thirty-month certificates were created in January, 1980, mainly in response to complaints from small savers that they were being unfairly excluded from a chance to earn the kind of investment returns available to buyers of six-month certificates. The thirty-month certificates have proved popular, and will be more popular now that the lid is off the interest that they can pay. They are a very attractive investment and a good place to keep your backup fund. You will have to forfeit some of your interest if you are compelled to redeem one of these certificates before thirty months have passed. And you are locked into the interest rate at which you made your deposit. This can be an advantage or a disadvantage, depending on what happens to interest rates during the two and a half years your money is on deposit. If you invest at 15% and the interest on Treasury notes goes up, you will be stuck at 15%; but if you invest at 15% and T-note rates go down, you'll come out ahead of the game. The gamble is probably worth taking; interest rates are at present so high that it is difficult to imagine them rising so much more that the cost of being "stuck" would be great. It's more likely that they will fall or stay about where they are. And, of course, the thirty-month certificates are insured by the Federal Deposit Insurance Corporation, which means they are virtually totally safe.

Traditional time deposits.

Only a few years ago, time deposits were quite popular. Today, inflation, and the advent of the six-month and thirty-month CDs tied to U.S. Treasury bill rates have caused investors to pass them by. For the record, the lineup, as of early 1981, looked like this.

Type of Deposit	Bank Rate	Savings Institution Rate
Regular (passbook) Savings Account	5¼ %	5½ %
3-month (90-day) certificate	5¾ %	6%
1-year to 2½-year certificates	6%	6½ %
2½-year to 4-year certificates	6½ %	6¾ %
4-year to 6-year certificates	7¼ %	7½ %
6-year to 8-year certificates	7½ %	7¾ %
8-year or longer certificates	7¾ %	8%

Later in 1981, however, the ceilings were taken off time deposits of four years or more, making them more attractive than they had been. Gradual removal of the other ceilings was planned. When you are planning where to put your backup fund, ask at your bank about current rates.

Jumbo certificates.

These are certificates of deposit in amounts of $100,000 or more. Banks like to sell them, since they get a lot of money at one crack, saving administrative expenses. To attract these jumbo deposits, banks often pay a very nice rate, up around 15% to 16% during much of the period from 1979 to early 1981. There are no governmental interest rate ceilings on certificates of $100,000 or more. It's strictly between the bank and the depositor.

If I had $100,000, there are things I'd rather do with it than park it at the bank. However, if you have $100,000 to plop down at a time, you probably aren't bothering to read this book anyway.

Tax-sheltered certificates.

In 1981, Congress authorized tax-sheltered "all savers' " certificates. The one-year certificates pay 70% of the interest rate available on Treasury bills. The interest, up to $1,000 a year ($2,000 on joint returns) is tax exempt. The certificates were authorized only through the end of 1982.

One motive for this proposal was to help the nation's ailing savings and loan associations, which have been losing depositors' money to the money market funds. Another motive was to help ordinary savers, hard pressed by inflation and taxes.

The chart, "How Important Is Tax Exemption to You?" from Chapter 9, will help you evaluate the merits of these certificates. As a rule of thumb, they deserve consideration only if your tax bracket is 30% or higher.

Those penalties.

Almost the only risk in buying savings certificates is the risk that you might have to withdraw your money early and incur a penalty. You've probably heard radio or TV ads tout savings certificates but warn of a "substantial" penalty if the money is withdrawn early. Well, it's only proper that the ads tell you about the penalties (and bank regulators make sure they do) but the penalties aren't really so terrible.

Federal regulations prescribe the minimum penalty a bank has to charge. It can charge a stiffer penalty if it wants to. The only way to be sure about an early withdrawal penalty is to check your contract or ask your bank.

Most banks do stick with the minimum penalty prescribed by law, for the sake of customer relations. On certificates issued after June 1, 1980, that penalty is loss of three months' interest on certificates with a maturity of a year or less, and loss of six months' interest on certificates with a maturity of more than a year. The penalty can be taken out of your principal, if necessary. (Before June, 1980, it could only be taken out of the accrued interest.) The penalty is normally based on simple interest, not compound interest.

Naturally, you wouldn't buy a savings certificate if you knew there was a large chance you'd need the money before it matured. But if you're pretty sure you will be able to leave the money in, it pays to take the plunge.

Let's say you're thinking of putting $5,000 into a thirty-month certificate, but the penalty worries you. Consider this. If you leave the money in a passbook account for a year, you'll have only about $5,275 at the end of the year. If you put it in the certificate and have to withdraw it early (only a year from purchase, with a year and a half still to go until the certificate's maturity), you'd forfeit six-months' interest. But you'd still have six months of interest left. Even at 12% (the old rate), you'd have had $5,300 after the penalty. You'd still be ahead.

Shopping for a certificate.

If you want to buy a certificate of deposit, check with a local commercial bank and a local savings-and-loan associa-

Penalties for Early Withdrawal

A lot of investors are confused about the penalties for early withdrawal of certificates of deposit. It's no wonder they are, since the minimum penalties have been changed twice by federal regulators. Thus there have been three sets of minimum penalties, through early 1981.

Investors should also be aware that the government specifies only the minimum penalty that banks must impose. Each bank or savings institution may, if it wishes, write a stiffer penalty into its certificate agreements. Check on the penalty before buying any certificate of deposit.

Date Certificate Issued*	Penalty	Does Interest Rate Revert to Passbook Rate?	Can Penalty Be Taken Out of Your Original Investment?
Before July 1, 1979	Loss of 3 months' interest, and reversion to passbook rate on the remainder of interest	Yes	No
July 1, 1979— June 1, 1980	Loss of 3 months' interest (6 months' interest on certificates with maturities of more than a year)	No	No
After June 1, 1980	Loss of 3 months' interest (6 months' interest on certificates with maturities of more than a year)	No	Yes

* If you renew or extend an existing certificate, the date of extension or renewal determines the minimum penalty. Banks may, if they wish, substitute a later penalty for the one that applied before July 1, 1979, but they are not required to do so.

tion to see what certificates are currently available, and what interest rates they provide.

Before buying a certificate, find out whether the institution is paying the maximum rate permitted on that type of certificate. As of 1981, you should insist on getting the maximum. If a bank or savings-and-loan doesn't offer it, go elsewhere. However, that situation might change over time, so if you're offered less than the maximum, shop around and compare.

Before buying a certificate, check to make sure that the penalty for early withdrawal is the minimum penalty.

If you are buying more than one savings certificate (at once or over time), try to stagger their maturity dates so that you will have some coming due periodically. That way, you'll be less likely to have to cash one in early and take a penalty. You will also get an investment return that is smoothed out, rather than sharply fluctuating with changes in prevailing interest rates.

6

Money Market Funds

If you borrow $50 from a friend, you may scrawl an IOU on the back of an envelope. If you borrow $5,000 from a bank, the IOU will be somewhat more formal, and will include a provision for your paying interest on the loan. When your bank borrows $500,000 from another bank, the contract may be more elaborate, but the idea is the same.

A money-market instrument is simply a big, short-term or intermediate-term IOU. (An IOU that will take more than ten years to pay back is usually called a bond. Bonds are discussed in Chapter 8.) The money market is simply the place where these debts are bought and sold. The IOUs bought and sold in the money market include bills, notes, jumbo certificates of deposit, and commercial paper. These will be explained, with merciful brevity, in a moment.

There are two ways to invest in short-term and intermediate-term debt securities. One is by buying money-market instruments directly. The other is by putting your money into a money-market mutual fund that pools investors' money to buy money-market instruments.

Money-market instruments.
If you have $10,000, $25,000, or $100,000 to invest, and want to get a good fixed return on your money, there are

48

plenty of institutions that will be glad to borrow your money. Broadly, they fall into three categories:

First, the government. The federal government, to cite the chief example, borrows money by issuing U.S. Treasury bills. Treasury bills are issued in denominations of $10,000 and up, with maturities of three, six, nine, or twelve months. (The *maturity* is simply the end of the contract period; you get your money back, plus accrued interest, and the IOU is cancelled.) As of early 1981, Treasury bills were yielding about 14½. If you wanted to tie up your money a little longer, you could buy a Treasury *note,* with a maturity of anywhere from one to ten years. As of early 1981, Treasury notes were yielding about 13%. This was bass-ackwards from the way things usually work. Ordinarily, the longer-term notes will yield more than the shorter-term bills. However, in times of high interest rates, things sometimes get reversed. As I said in the last chapter, that's because a person who expects interest rates to drop may accept a somewhat smaller yield to lock in that yield for a while.

A fair number of individual investors do buy Treasury bills, or T bills, as they are popularly known. If you may be interested in buying them, you can get detailed information by contacting the Federal Reserve bank nearest you. There are Federal Reserve district offices in Atlanta, Boston, Chicago, Cleveland, Dallas, Kansas City, New York City, Philadelphia, Richmond, St. Louis, San Francisco, and Washington, D.C. These offices also can be a useful source of information about a variety of fixed-return investments, and some districts publish a monthly newsletter following developments in fixed-income securities.

T bills are sold through weekly auctions, and interest is paid implicitly (through a discount to the buyer at the time of purchase) rather than explicitly. This technicality makes them a slightly better deal than six-month bank certificates, even though the two pay the same interest rate.

T bills are all issued simply to the bearer, so they must be guarded carefully: Losing them is like losing cash (only worse).

While T bills are the most popular short-term government instrument among individual investors, both the Treasury and other government agencies also issue other short-term IOUs.

A second type of institution that will pay an investor for the short-term use of his cash is a corporation. When a corporation issues a short-term IOU, it's called *commercial paper*. If you loan your money to a corporation this way, you normally get no collateral, just the company's good word that you'll be paid. For this reason, you would need to pay especially close attention to the rating a company's paper has for financial soundness. Three independent rating companies—Moody's, Standard & Poor's, and Fitch Investors Service—grade commercial paper in terms of investor risk. Here are the grades they use.

These rating systems, like most rating systems used in the

Grades for Commercial Paper

Fitch Investors Service: F-1 = highest grade; F-2 = investment grade; F-3 = good grade; F-4 = not recommended.

Moody's Investors Service: Prime-1; Prime-2; Prime-3; Not Rated.

Standard & Poor's: A-1 = highest investment grade; A-2 = high investment grade; A-3 = medium investment grade; B = medium grade; C = speculative; D = expected to default.

---

financial world, should be considered as written in a special language. "Good" can mean "bad" if there are several grades above good. Investors should look at the relative rankings, and not pay much attention to the words given as a translation of the grades.

Very rarely is commercial paper sold in denominations smaller than $25,000, and amounts of $100,000 or more are more common. If you are wealthy enough to take advantage of commercial paper sales, you may get a return which ranges from just above that of T bills to about 5% above that yield. It is a high-stakes calculation in which, as usual, higher yields correlate with higher risk. Maturities are usually short, but you'd better not need your money back early: You usually can't get it before maturity. If you're one of the rare individuals who can play in this league, be aware that commercial paper is sold both directly by issuers, and by dealers (brokers and investment bankers); ask your broker for a referral.

The third type of institution that will pay you for a hefty chunk of cash is a bank. As mentioned in Chapter 5, banks issue large-denomination certificates of deposit, or CDs, at rates above those they pay on the smaller CDs available to ordinary savers, and sometimes substantially above the rate paid on T bills. Denominations usually begin at $100,000.

Some drowsy readers may wonder why we've spent several paragraphs on investments beyond the reach of most investors. The answer is that there is an indirect way that the average investor can tap the substantial yields of such vehicles as T bills, commercial paper, and big bank CDs. It's through a money market fund.

Money market funds.

The money market funds take the deposits of small investors and pool them to buy the types of high-yield, short-term instruments we just discussed. To invest in a money market fund, you need ordinarily plunk down only $1,000 to $5,000. Shares in a money market fund offer several advantages.

· The main advantage is the relatively high yield, which varied from about 9% to 16% during much of the period from 1979 to early 1981.
· Interest is often credited daily.
· You can usually withdraw your funds when you choose, without penalty.
· The fee for administration usually reduces your yield by less than 1%, still leaving you with a yield considerably above what you might ordinarily be able to obtain on your own.
· As with any mutual fund, you automatically obtain a substantial degree of diversification, and hence a lowered risk.
· Normally, there is no cost for buying or selling shares.
· Some money market funds let you write checks against your fund holdings (in amounts of $500 or more).

Against these advantages you should weigh certain potential pitfalls. First, the yield you get on a money market fund is not fixed or guaranteed. It changes every day, and such changes aren't reported in the daily financial pages of most newspapers, so you may have to contact the fund if you want to find out what your current yield is at a particular time.

Second, some funds that offer what look like extremely attractive yields do so by carrying a comparatively risky portfolio. If you want to know how risky a fund's portfolio is, one good indication is the grade of any commercial paper it holds.

Third, money market funds, since they invest in fixed-return investment vehicles, can be hurt by rises in interest rates. If a fund holds mainly instruments that yield 10%, and prevailing rates rise to 13%, the value of the fund's holdings is diminished proportionately. (Why should any buyer pay in full for an asset that yields less than a competing one does? Each relatively low-yielding vehicle thus diminishes in its market value.) The decline may be reflected either in the fund's price per share, or (for funds that choose to hold the share price constant, as many do at $1 per share) in the yield. In fairness, it should be noted that this pitfall affects money market funds less severely than bond funds, which are more vulnerable to interest-rate shocks because they invest in securities with longer maturities.

Fourth, the high yields the money market funds have offered in the late 1970s and early 1980s can't be expected to last forever. Historically, short-term interest rates are more volatile than long-term ones. And historically, short-term rates are lower than long-term ones, which hasn't been the case in 1979 through early 1981. This period of very high interest rates, like the period 1968–69 and 1973–74, may prove to have been the exception, not the rule. So the rate paid by the money market funds could well decline to levels where the funds offer no special advantages over, say, bank certificates. Yet this isn't necessarily a serious drawback, since the investor in a money market fund can withdraw money without much trouble.

Weighing the pros and cons, money funds certainly deserve consideration as a possible place to keep some of your money—particularly the money in your backup fund (see Chapters 1 and 2).

Choosing a fund. Choosing a money market fund is a bit easier than choosing stocks, or real-estate parcels. You can't go as far wrong. But there are differences among funds. In choosing a fund, here are some factors to look at.

- The current interest rate paid on shares.
- The degree of risk assumed in order to gain that interest rate. A bankruptcy or near-bankruptcy in the fund's portfolio could lower your return.
- Services offered, such as the ability to write checks against your account.
- Minimum investment required.
- Presence of a toll-free telephone line to call the fund, preferably one whose circuits aren't always busy.
- Procedure for withdrawals.
- Average maturity of the instruments in the fund's portfolio. This information appears once a week in certain papers, like *The New York Times* and *Wall Street Journal*. (So does the current yield.) When interest rates are rising, it's good for a fund to hold very short-term investments, so it can take advantage of the new, higher rates quickly. When interest rates are falling, a fund is better off when it's invested in instruments with somewhat longer maturities.

When you've become interested in a particular money market fund, you can get its address from advertisements or by checking a reference source at the library, such as *Mutual Funds Almanac* (published by the Hirsch Organization) or *Investment Companies* (Wiesenberger Services). Write directly to the fund for a prospectus and application form.

7

Your House as an Investment

Do you invest in real estate? No?

Do you own a home? Yes?

Then, like it or not, you're investing in real estate. Of course the way home prices have gone during most of the 1960s and 1970s, you probably like it. Houses have been good investments.

I don't think investment factors should be primary when you decide whether to buy a house or not. There are a number of pluses and minuses of home ownership that have nothing to do with finances. On the plus side, there's the pleasure of having a place of your own, one that you can fix up precisely to your taste, one that gives you privacy and freedom. On the minus side, there's the constant maintenance a house seems to demand, and the unexpected hassles and repairs. It would be silly, I think, to base your decision about where to live on investment strategy alone.

However, you should know the financial implications of your decision to rent or buy. For the most part, the financial consequences of condominium ownership are the same as the financial consequences of home ownership.

The most obvious financial aspect to owning a home (or condo) is that it can go up in value, giving you, when you sell it, a substantial capital gain. The average house sold for about $17,500 in 1960, about $30,000 in 1970, and about $65,000 in 1980. Clearly, home ownership has been rewarding. Whether it will continue to be equally so in the 1980s isn't clear; high mortgage rates caused home prices to dip in 1980–81, and in some areas (such as California or Washington, D.C.) prices had already been bid up to a point where a decline seemed if not inevitable, at least possible. The price of the average home, of course, doesn't tell you what will happen to yours. It depends on a lot of variables: trends in your neighborhood, the state of local schools, zoning changes, the building of highways or airports nearby, the entrance or exit of major employers in the area, and so on. You could do substantially better or worse than the averages.

Even if the value of your home rises, however, you won't necessarily be in a position to cash in on the rise. A house is one of the least liquid of investments. You wouldn't want to sell your house at the drop of a hat, or the sign of an uptrend in real-estate prices. What's more, you couldn't if you wanted to. Selling a house is time consuming, and usually costly as well, since you're likely to pay 6% of the sale price in real-estate brokerage commissions. If your $40,000 house rises in value to $80,000, what does that mean to you? Quite possibly, very little. If you plan to stay in the house for many years to come, there's no real way you can count the gain as anything but a paper profit. If you sell, but buy a new house in the same neighborhood, chances are that the cost of your new house will have risen as fast as the value of your old one. Even if you're moving across the country, you may find that your new house costs as much or more as the one you left behind. End of profit.

In this connection, we should observe a few points about current U.S. tax law. Suppose you buy a home for $60,000, put $20,000 of improvements into it, and then sell it a few years later for $110,000. Most home improvements (but not all—check IRS literature) can be added to your "cost basis" for tax purposes. Assuming all of your $20,000 in improvements qualify, it's as if you had bought the house for $80,000. Your capital gain is then $30,000. Under current income-tax rules, only 40% of a capital gain is taxable, so you'd pay taxes only on $12,000. If your tax bracket is 28%, the actual tax you'd pay would be about $3,360.

However, you wouldn't necessarily owe any tax at all. Suppose you bought another house (or condominium) to replace the one you were living in. If the replacement house is purchased within 18 months of the sale*, a new set of rules takes effect. If your replacement house costs more than your proceeds from selling the original one, you owe no tax immediately. However, your $30,000 capital gain could affect the tax you'd pay when the replacement house was eventually sold. For example, suppose your replacement house cost $120,000, and that in the distant future you sell it for $165,000. At that time, the $30,000 gain on your first house gets added to the $45,000 gain on the second house, so you could be taxed on a $75,000 gain. (However, you may get out of this, too, as we'll see in a minute.)

If your replacement house costs less than the proceeds on the one you just sold, you'll owe some tax, but it may be very little. Take the case of a woman who bought a house years ago for $30,000 and recently sold it for $100,000. She then moved into a $75,000 condominium. In this case, her capital gain would be $70,000. But she would have to pay taxes immediately on at most $25,000—the amount by which the proceeds from the sale exceeded the cost of her new residence.

Here's better news yet. Once in your lifetime—and only once—you are entitled to an exclusion of up to $100,000

* If you're building a new home, the clock doesn't run out until 24 months after the sale.

on capital gains from the sale of all your previous homes. (That is, all of them on which you were carrying forward deferred capital gains.) This lifetime exclusion can only be taken after you reach the age of 55. It applies only to houses sold after July 26, 1978, and only when you've owned and occupied the house for at least three of the previous five years.

That means that when you're nearing retirement age, you can reap a capital gain of up to $100,000 tax free. It's a major advantage for home ownership as opposed to other forms of investment.

It may be tricky, though, figuring out when you should take your one-time exclusion. You can use it only once, even if you don't use the full $100,000 exclusion. The key questions to ask yourself are: 1. "Do I plan to move again?" and 2. "What would my tax liability be now if I saved the big exclusion for later?" If you're planning to stay put, and would face a substantial tax liability if you don't use the exclusion, then by all means use it—even if you're using only part of the $100,000.

Of course, capital-gains tax considerations don't matter at all if your house falls, rather than rises, in value. Most people nowadays don't give this possibility too much thought, but it can happen. A 1978 article in *Forbes* Magazine had some pointed comments on this subject.

"Most people," *Forbes* wrote, "have been conditioned to expect housing prices to rise faster than inflation." However, "when most people think anything—at least about business —most people are usually wrong." *Forbes* noted that home prices declined in 1970. More importantly, it cautioned that the bubble of constantly rising prices could burst. It quoted Charles Kirkpatrick, a market analyst, as saying that the recent rapid rise in house prices cannot be rationally explained by population density, family-income factors, inflation rates, or other factors. Said Kirkpatrick: "Whenever you have something that is increasing in price at an enormous rate and is being fueled by an even more rapidly increasing debt, and everyone is convinced that the price can't go down, and that the increased cost of that debt is immaterial because the projected price is superior to that cost, you've got yourself a mania very similar to the stock market back in 1929." He foresaw large declines in the price of houses, perhaps as much as 65% or 75%, because "the percentage declines after manias are enormous." *Forbes* couldn't swallow that prediction, saying that more likely we would simply see a period in which houses will appreciate more slowly in value.

There are some economic incentives to owning a house, even if the house doesn't appreciate in value at all. Given the alternatives of renting or owning, owning is clearly the economically preferable alternative under the present tax structure. When you rent an apartment, your monthly rent check pays for your living quarters, and that's the end of that. Your economic return is minus 100%, and you get no tax deductions, either.

By contrast, let's look at what happens when you own a house and have a mortgage loan. First of all, you get some return on your money, in the form of gradually increasing equity in the house. Let's say you buy a $60,000 house, putting $20,000 down and taking a mortgage loan for $40,000. Over the next 25 years or so, you might pay out about $400 a month in mortgage payments, for total payments of $120,-000. A whopping $80,000 of that goes for interest on the loan, while $40,000 represents your equity in the house, which is yours to keep. For the person who pays $400 a month to rent an apartment, all $120,000 goes down the drain (speaking purely in terms of investment return). You might say that the return for the owner—disregarding any capital gains—is a 66% loss, while the return for the renter is a 100% loss.

But in fact the homeowner comes out more than $40,000 ahead of the renter in this example, because there are also income-tax considerations in home ownership. If you own your home, you get to deduct from your gross income the interest you pay on your mortgage loan. In this case, the interest over 25 years is $80,000 or so; if the homeowner is in the 33% bracket, the tax savings from the deduction amounts to more than $26,000.

Further, the homeowner can deduct property-tax payments, while the renter cannot deduct that portion of the rent that reimburses the landlord for tax payments on the building.

All in all, given that you have to live somewhere, you are economically better off owning your dwelling than renting it. You may not be able to afford to. Even if you can afford to, you may not want to, because of your personal tastes or temperament. But to the extent that you can afford it and want to let economics play a part in the choice, there is no question which way you are better off.

8

Corporate Bonds

With this chapter, we leave the calm lagoon of the safest investments, and venture out into the realms of what many people mean when they talk about investing—the purchase of securities. Stocks and bonds are the bread-and-butter items of investing.

If stocks are the relatively tangy butter, bonds are the comparatively staid bread. But both can involve substantial risk.

Bonds are for relatively conservative portfolios. The conventional wisdom is that stocks are for younger people, bonds mainly for people who are at, or approaching retirement age. With lots of *ifs, ands,* and *buts,* the conventional wisdom is pretty much right.

When you buy a bond, you know exactly how many dollars you'll be paid each year in interest. You also know that if you buy a bond and hold it until its maturity date, assuming the issuing company does not go bankrupt, you will get your initial investment back in full—no more, no less. What you don't know when you buy a bond is how its market value will fluctuate between the time you buy it and the maturity date. If you sell your bond early, you could be forced to take a loss (or you could achieve a gain).

When a corporation wants to raise money, it can do two

things. It can sell stock, giving a number of people part ownership of the company and a share of future profits. Or it can borrow money. When a corporation borrows from a bank, it's called a loan. When a corporation borrows from the public, it's called a bond issue.

The company that issues bonds (which are normally issued in face amounts of $1,000 and up) guarantees that, at a stated date in the future (the maturity date), it will pay the bearer of each bond precisely the amount stated on the face of the bond (the "face amount"). So if you buy a newly issued 25-year, $5,000 bond, you know that, unless the company goes kaput, you will be getting back your $5,000 25 years from now. In the meantime, you get the stated interest rate, called the *coupon rate* because in the old days people actually clipped coupons off the edge of the bond and sent them in, to be rewarded with their interest payment by return mail. (Nowadays, companies simply mail the interest checks to bondholders twice a year.)

But bonds needn't be kept by their original owners. They can be bought and sold by brokers and securities dealers, and (through these intermediaries) by the public. Thus, you can sell your bond early, or buy a bond previously held by someone else. A bond may go through many hands before it finally comes up for redemption. So the business of investing in bonds involves not only the collection of interest, but the possibility of a capital gain or loss when you sell.

The trick to making capital gains in bonds is to buy them when interest rates are high, and sell them when interest rates are low. (You'll see why in a minute.) However, you cannot predict interest rates very well, and neither can anyone else. Besides, if it's capital gains you want, stocks are a better vehicle to try to achieve them. So, if you buy bonds at all, buy them as an income investment. And buy them only if you're reasonably sure you could afford to hold onto them until maturity if necessary. That way, you won't be forced to sell a bond at a loss.

At bottom, a bond is simply an IOU. In that sense, it's similar to the money-market instruments discussed in Chapter 6. The word bond, however, is normally used only for IOUs whose maturity date is at least ten years from the time of issue.

Bonds can be issued by government (federal, state, or local) and by private corporations. In this chapter we look at corporate bonds, those issued by private enterprises. In the next chapter, we'll discuss U.S. government and municipal bonds.

When you buy a bond, you're loaning your money, for a considerable period of time, to the corporation or government entity of your choice. In doing so, you run several risks, the chief of which is the risk of not getting paid back if the outfit you loaned to goes bankrupt. In the early 1960s, a boom time, many people had forgotten this risk was meaningful. Since then, occasional bankruptcies (Penn Central, W.T. Grant) and near bankruptcies (New York City, Chrysler Corporation) have provided a grim reminder. Every bond carries some risk, remote or otherwise.

Rating the risk.

The greater the risk, the less incentive anyone would have to buy a particular bond, if everything else were equal. So, to sell their bonds, cities or corporations that are on relatively shaky financial footing have to pay higher yields than do their competitors. The extra yield compensates the investor for assuming the greater degree of risk.

But how is the individual investor to assess the financial soundness of, say, Galveston, Texas, or the American Motors Corporation? As a practical matter, individual investors don't have the expertise to do so. They rely primarily on the ratings issued by the independent bond-rating services. The two giants of the bond-rating business are Moody's and Standard & Poor's. The chart below shows how the two services rate corporate bonds.

CORPORATE BOND RATINGS

Moody's	Standard & Poor's
Aaa	*AAA*
Best quality . . . interest payments are protected by a large or by an exceptionally stable margin and principal is secure.	The highest rating assigned . . . to a debt obligation. Capacity to pay interest and repay principal is extremely strong.
Aa	*AA*
Judged to be of high quality by all standards. Together with the Aaa group they comprise what are generally known as high-grade bonds. They are rated lower than the best bonds because margins of protection may not be as large . . . or fluctuation of protective elements may be of greater amplitude. . . .	Have a very strong capacity to pay interest and repay principal and differ from the highest rated issues only in small degree.
A	*A*
Possess many favorable investment attributes and are to be considered as upper medium-grade obligations. Factors giving security to principal and interest are considered adequate but elements may be present which suggest a susceptibility to impairment sometime in the future.	Have a strong capacity to pay interest and repay principal although they are somewhat more susceptible to the adverse effects of changes in circumstances and economic conditions than bonds in higher rated categories.

64

Moody's	**Standard & Poor's**
Baa	*BBB*

Bonds which are rated Baa are considered as medium-grade obligations, i.e., they are neither highly protected nor poorly secured. Interest payments and principal security appear adequate for the present but certain protective elements may be lacking or may be characteristically unreliable over any great length of time. Such bonds lack outstanding investment characteristics and in fact have speculative characteristics as well.	Regarded as having an adequate capacity to pay interest and repay principal. Whereas they normally exhibit adequate protection parameters, adverse economic conditions or changing circumstances are more likely to lead to a weakened capacity to pay interest and repay principal for bonds in this category than for bonds in higher rated categories.

	BB
	B
	CCC
Ba	*CC*

Judged to have speculative elements: Their future cannot be considered as well assured. Often the protection of interest and principal payments may be very moderate and thereby not well safeguarded during both good times and bad times over the future. Uncertainty of position characterizes bonds in this class.	Regarded, on balance, as predominantly speculative with respect to capacity to pay interest and repay principal in accordance with the terms of the obligation. BB indicates the lowest degree of speculation and CC the highest degree of speculation. While such bonds will likely have some quality and protective characteristics, these are outweighed by large uncertainties or major risk exposures to adverse conditions.

Moody's	Standard & Poor's

Moody's

B

Generally lack character-
istics of the desirable investment. Assurance of interest
and principal payments or of
maintenance of other terms
of the contract over any long
period of time may be small.

Caa

Of poor standing. Such issues
may be in default or there
may be present elements of
danger with respect to principal or interest.

Ca

Speculative in a high degree.
Such issues are often in default or have other marked
shortcomings.

C

Lowest rated class of bonds
. . . issues so rated can be
regarded as having extremely
poor prospects of ever at-
taining any real investment
standing.

Standard & Poor's

C

The rating C is reserved for
income bonds on which no
interest is being paid.

D

Bonds rated D are in default,
and payment of interest
and/or repayment of principal is in arrears.

NR

Indicates that no rating has
been requested, that there is
insufficient information on
which to base a rating or that
S&P does not rate a particular type of obligation as a
matter of policy.

Stick to high-grade bonds, at least for the first bond or two you buy. That means triple A or double A. Sure, you can hike your yield by taking on more risk. But isn't that really kind of silly? To me, speculating in bonds is a bit incongruous, like an elephant imitating a chorus girl. If you're willing to take on some risk, why not do it through common stocks or other investments that have the potential to rise 50%, 100%, or more? Bonds have their place. But that place is in the conservative part of your portfolio, not the speculative part.

If you are irresistibly drawn to the high yields on lower-quality bonds, then buy them not individually but through a junk bond fund. These are mutual funds that invest in a diversified group of high-risk, high-yield bonds (and sometimes other debt securities). Buying risky bonds through a fund is a lot less risky than buying them on your own because the diversification protects you against getting wiped out by a single bankruptcy.

The ups and downs of bonds.

Suppose that in the late 1970s you plunked down $5,000 for a corporate bond paying 9% interest. Three years after you bought it, you discovered that you seriously needed cash, so you decided to sell your bond. Then, to your horror, you discovered that the bond would be worth only $3,462 on the open market! To sell, you'd have to take a major loss.

The example is anything but hypothetical. It has happened to plenty of people who always thought that bonds were safe investments.

Relatively safe they are, *if* held to maturity. But an early sale can result in gains or losses, because bond prices fluctuate with interest rates. This fluctuation has nothing to do with how good a company issued your bond. You cannot protect against it by buying the bonds of AAA-rated cor-

67

porations like General Motors and AT&T. When interest rates fall, the market value of your bond goes up. When interest rates rise, the market value of your bond goes down.

Why? An example will make it clear. Suppose the universe contained two giant corporations. One of them, Amalgamated Enterprises, sells an issue of 20-year bonds which pay 7% interest. Your neighbor, Sam, buys a $5,000 Amalgamated bond. You don't. Six months later, Conglomerate Industries offers an issue of 20-year bonds paying 8%. You buy a $5,000 Conglomerate bond. Now, consider Sam's situation. He would prefer to be getting an 8% return, as you are. He wants to sell his Amalgamated bond, get back the $5,000 he paid for it, and then buy a Conglomerate bond. But he can't sell his Amalgamated bond for $5,000, because no one would be foolish enough to buy it from him. Why should people take a 7% yield when they can get an 8% yield? Certainly you wouldn't buy Sam's bond—unless Sam lowered its price. If Sam would sell you the Amalgamated bond for, say, $4,375, you might well consider it. At that price, Sam's bond would yield the same current return, 8%, as the Conglomerate bond.

The sketch here is oversimplified. But it makes a point that is perfectly true in the bond market. When interest rates rise, bonds issued at the old, lower interest rates lose a portion of their face value. In early 1981, there were a lot of bonds around that could be sold for only 66% to 75% of the amount printed on their handsomely engraved fronts. Some bonds were fetching even less.

Of course, the reverse is also true. If interest rates fall, then a bond you purchased at the old, higher rates becomes worth more than its face value.

How concerned should you be, as an individual investor, with the outlook for interest rates? It depends. If you buy a bond, knowing with absolute certainty that you are going to hold onto it until it matures, then what happens to interest rates in between needn't trouble you much. At maturity, you'd cash in your $5,000 bond for exactly $5,000.

If there's a significant chance that you will sell your bond before it matures, then it matters quite a bit to you whether you'd sell it at a profit or a loss. So interest rates are of keen interest to you.

Most people who buy bonds fall in between. They buy the bond as a long-term investment, not planning to cash it in early. However, they recognize the possibility that an unexpected need for cash could force them to change their plans.

But how is the individual to predict the movement of interest rates? Even the experts disagree on what interest rates will do over the next three months, year, or two years. Over a long period, such as the life of a 20-year corporate bond, uncertainty is compounded. About the only certain thing is that interest rates will go up and down a good deal over such a period.

The moral, then, for the individual investor is this: Don't commit money to an investment in bonds unless you are reasonably sure you can afford to leave the money in. If you buy a bond without an adequate cushion of more liquid investments, you may be forced to sell at the wrong time, taking a loss. (That's why you should have at least three months' income in some form of savings account, and at least an equal amount in bank certificates of deposit, or in a money market fund.)

If you have money that you want to invest at a fixed return, and you feel apprehensive about committing it for the long term, don't buy a bond. A money market fund may be a much better alternative, because you can withdraw your money from such a fund at will. Ordinarily, a money market fund will pay a somewhat lower interest rate than a bond will. (This varies depending on current economic conditions; in 1979 through early 1981, short-term interest rates were very high and money market funds had yields a bit above those of high-grade bonds.) But it may well be worth accepting a slightly lower return to avoid the risk of selling out at a loss.

If you're confident that you will be able to leave the money in as long as necessary, then you are in a position to start shopping seriously for a bond.

The yield on a bond.

There are three important ways of measuring the investment yield on a bond. You shouldn't buy a bond until you understand all three, and know what yield a particular bond offers by all three measures.

The first interest rate you need to know about is the *coupon rate*. A $1,000 bond with an 8% coupon rate constitutes a promise by the issuing company to pay you $80 in interest a year. On a $5,000 bond with an 8% coupon rate, you get $400 of interest a year. It's obvious why the coupon rate is important. However, it's just the beginning.

The second interest rate you need to know is the *current yield*. If you buy a bond for exactly $1,000 (or exactly at *par,* so that you pay exactly the face amount of the bond, be it $5,000, $10,000, or whatever), then the current yield is the same as the coupon rate. If you buy a bond selling below par—for example, if you buy a $5,000 bond for $4,500— then the current yield is above the coupon rate. A $5,000 bond with a 9% coupon rate selling for $4,500 has a current yield of 10% a year. If you buy a bond selling above par, the current yield is less than the coupon rate. For example, if you pay $5,500 for a bond with a 12% coupon rate, the current yield is 10.9%.

You might think that these two ways of measuring yield

would tell you everything you want to know, but they don't. Remember, the bond you bought either above or below par will be redeemable exactly at par when it matures. That means the value of your bond will either slowly rise or slowly decline as maturity approaches. And that affects your yield. So, we have a third measure called *yield to maturity*.

Suppose we return to the examples we used above. Let's say there are five years until the bonds mature. If you pay $4,500 for a $5,000 bond that matures in five years, and has a coupon rate of 9%, then you'll get $450 in interest each year for five years, plus a capital gain of $500 at maturity. That's a total return of $2,750, or $550 a year, which means the yield to maturity is about 12.2%.

Take our other example, where you pay $5,500 for a bond with a 12% coupon rate. If it matures in five years, you have a capital loss of $500, partly offsetting your interest income of $600 a year. So, while the coupon is 12%, the current yield is only 10.9%, and the yield to maturity is only about 9%.

On any given day, almost all bonds of similar quality (riskiness) will have about the same projected yield to maturity. If you look at the bond page in the newspaper, you'll see that coupon rates are all over the lot. Current yields vary too, but somewhat less. And if you do some arithmetic with the figures in the paper, you'll find that the yield to maturity varies very little from bond to bond. What variation there is mainly reflects the level of risk, as measured by the quality grades of the rating services. Professional bond traders are always alert for bargains. When any difference in yield to maturity crops up, they'll move to take advantage of it. In so doing, they'll very quickly wipe out that difference.

Coupon rates and current yields of bonds are shown in the daily financial pages. Yields to maturity are not. All three measures are important, since you normally can't be certain when you buy a bond whether you are going to hold it to maturity or not.

Even if two bonds have the same yield to maturity, one may be a better investment than the other for tax reasons. Discount bonds (bought below par) can be better deals than bonds bought above par. Reason: A good part of your return on a discount bond comes, not in the form of interest, but in the form of capital gains. And capital gains are taxed more lightly than interest is. (As of early 1981, only 40% of long-term capital gains are subject to income tax.)

Reading the bond page of a newspaper.

Most major newspapers use a similar format for reporting on current prices and trading activity in the bond market. The examples below are from the March 1, 1979, issue of the *Wall Street Journal*.

Bonds	Cur Yld	Vol	High	Low	Close	Net Chg
Ford 8⅛90	9.7	8	93½	93½	93½	....
Purex 4⅞94	cv	25	71	71	71	+½
StOIn 10.55s89	10	62	101⅛	101	101⅛	....

These listings provide the following information. Ford has bonds maturing in 1990 with an 8⅛ percent coupon rate. They were selling on March 1, 1979, at a price of $935 per $1,000, or 93½% of par, and thus were yielding a current yield of 8.7%. Their price was unchanged from the day before. Trading volume* was $8,000.

Purex has convertible bonds (that is, bonds that under some circumstances can be exchanged for common stock) maturing in 1994. The coupon rate is 4⅞%. Because con-

---

* Trading volume is based on the bonds' face amount, not current value.

vertible bonds have special characteristics, the current yield is not shown in the bond tables. (Convertible bonds are discussed in Chapter 18.) $25,000 worth of the bonds were bought and sold, at a price of $710 per $1,000 or 71% of par, up from $705 the day before.

Standard Oil of Indiana has bonds with a coupon rate of 10.55%, maturing in 1989.* Because the bonds were priced above par, the current yield was slightly less, 10%. Bonds totaling $62,000 changed hands at prices ranging from $1,010 to $1,011.25. The closing price, the higher of the two, was unchanged from the day before.

Be a knowledgable bond buyer.

There's more to buying bonds than checking the risk rating and knowing the yield. Bonds differ in some key provisions. Here is some background to help you understand exactly what you're buying.

▶ *Callability*. When a company issues a bond, in some ways it makes a "heads we win, tails you lose" bet. If interest rates go up, you'll have a loss in the market value of your bond, as we've seen. But if interest rates go down, the company may take your bond away from you. (It might then proceed to issue new bonds at the lower interest rate.) When a company takes your bond away, it "calls in" the bond, or "calls" it for short. Most corporate bonds are callable. (Some U.S. government bonds are also callable. Municipal bonds usually aren't.)

When a corporation calls in your bond, it pays you the full face amount of the bond (no great bargain, since at that moment your bond probably has a market value greater than its face amount). It also pays you any interest due you up to

* The "s" in between the 10.55 and the 89 is meaningless. It derives from the Wall Street custom of calling a particular issue of bonds "the 9½s" if that's their coupon rate. In the newspaper, the only function of the "s" is to serve as a divider.

that point. And it may (depending on the provisions of the individual bond) pay you what's called a *premium,* which is a sweetener to make you feel better about the financial slap in the face you've just received. The premium is often one year's interest.

Let's say you buy a bond yielding 14% in 1981. It's a $5,000 bond selling at par, and providing you $700 a year in interest. Then let's suppose interest rates drop so that in 1988, most corporate bonds are yielding only 8%. The company calls in your bond. Under the bond's call provision, you receive a premium of $700, plus your $5,000 back. You will nevertheless be irked, because if you reinvest the money at the presumptive 1988 interest rate of 8%, you will get only $400 a year in interest. It will only take 2½ years at that rate to offset the effect of the $700 premium. (Of course, if your bond is called and you get no premium, that's even worse.)

There are a couple of ways you can protect yourself against calls. One is to buy a noncallable bond in the first place. But most corporations won't issue a bond that's flat out noncallable. The best you're likely to get is partial call protection.

Many corporate bonds can't be called for the first five years, or the first ten years after they're issued. If you buy a bond with that provision, at least you're protected against a very early call.

You can also buy a bond that has a provision against *refunding.* Refunding is the refinancing of debt by a company which calls in some high-interest bonds, and immediately issues some new bonds at the lower interest rate then prevailing. Since a desire to refund is one of the main reasons companies call bonds, a no-refunding provision does give the investor considerable call protection. But it's not total protection, since there *are* other reasons a company might call bonds (such as to reduce total debt).

Yet another way you might escape the hassle of having your bond called is to buy a bond selling well below par. Such a bond would be one with a low coupon rate, so it's not likely the issuing company would want to call it. The yield to maturity might be just as good as that of a higher-coupon bond, but a larger part of that yield would consist of capital gains, rather than income. Many sophisticated investors follow this strategy, but you should be aware of a couple of pitfalls. First, check to make sure the bond's low price is due to a low coupon rate, and not to poor quality (i.e., a low rating). Second, be aware that fluctuations in the market value of deeply discounted bonds (those selling well below par) are more extreme than fluctuations in the value of the average bond.

Some people might argue that all this precaution to avoid having your bond called is excessive. What's so bad, they ask, about getting a chunk of money back during a time of falling interest rates? After all, when interest rates are falling it's often a good time to invest in the stock market.

Granted, there's truth to that argument. But the stock market doesn't *always* do well when interest rates are falling. (It doesn't *always* do anything.) Besides, not everyone is in a position to invest in stocks, however attractive they may look.

Overall, it pays to give serious consideration to the degree to which the bond is protected against calls.

▶ *Security for repayment.* If you go to a bank for a car loan, the bank may require you to use the car as collateral for the loan. If you fail to meet your payments, the bank gets the car. But it's also possible to get an unsecured loan (no collateral), usually at a higher interest rate.

A parallel situation exists in the world of bonds. A bond can be secured or unsecured. *Mortgage bonds* are secured by a contingent lien on the company's property. The situation here parallels the car loan, where the car is the collateral. The bondholders collectively have the company's physical plant and facilities as collateral. Sometimes the same collateral is used for more than one bond issue, so there can be first mortgage bonds and second mortgage bonds.

Collateral trust bonds are also secured, but not by physical property. The company issuing such bonds put financial assets (such as stocks or other bonds) into a trust, which serves as security to make sure bondholders get repaid.

Unsecured bonds are called *debentures*. When you buy a debenture, you get no specific security. You depend, instead, on the company's earning power to make sure you'll get repaid. Years ago, financial analysts considered this a very important consideration. Today, it's widely viewed as less important. The debentures of large, financially sound companies are considered less risky (and hence pay lower yields) than the first mortgage bonds of shakier outfits. Nonetheless, you should know whether the bond you're buying is secured or unsecured. If it's the latter, you will want to be especially careful in checking out the financial soundness of the company.

To refine things a bit further, there are gradations of debentures. Companies that have already issued debentures may issue *subordinated debentures*. If the company has to be liquidated, holders of subordinated debentures must, in effect, wait in line behind holders of more "senior" debentures (but ahead of stockholders) to get paid back. In some cases, there are also degrees of subordination.

From the mere fact that a debenture is subordinated, you can't tell whether it is a risky investment. But you should certainly check.

One type of bond you should avoid is the *income bond*. Ordinarily, bondholders must be paid their annual interest whether the company has made or lost money that year. But with an income bond, the company is obliged to pay interest on its bonds only in years when it can afford to.

Bond-buying recommendations.

Bonds are for people who want high income with relative security over the long term. If it's capital gains you're after, there are better places to look—stocks, mainly. If you want total security or close to it, stick with a money market fund. But if you're nearing retirement age and want high income with only a moderate amount of risk, bonds may be a good choice for you.

If you're going to buy a bond, stick with one of the highest grades—AAA or AA. It's poor judgment to try to hype your return by buying a bond from a riskier company.

If you decide to buy a bond, your most basic choice is between a corporate bond and a government bond. Let your tax bracket make this choice for you. If you're in a high bracket, municipal bonds are typically your best bet; this is explained in the next chapter. If you're in a medium to low bracket, the higher yield on a corporate bond may be worth the extra tax you have to pay.

Picking a bond isn't like picking a stock. It's not crucial what company's bond you buy; they're semiinterchangeable. To put it another way, when you buy a corporate bond, you don't care how well the company does, so long as it isn't in any danger of bankruptcy.

So, if you want to buy a bond, tell your broker that you're interested in an AAA or AA issue with some call protection. Let him or her suggest some alternatives.

The broker may very well suggest that you buy into a new bond issue. There are two possible advantages to this. One is that if your brokerage house is part of the issuing syndicate, you'll pay no brokerage commission (it's absorbed by the issuing company). The other is that you may get a very small dollop of extra interest, since bonds in the process of being issued may be priced favorably to facilitate a rapid sale.

But there's also an argument for buying an older, discounted bond. If you buy a bond with a low coupon rate by current standards, more of your gain from the bond will be a capital gain, and only 40% of long-term capital gains (under 1981 federal tax law) are taxable. So, if your broker offers you a new issue, discuss the pros and cons of this point with him or her.

Once your broker has suggested one or more corporate bonds for your consideration, take the time to check on the bond's rating, its call provision, and the way it's secured.

If you own (or are about to own) more than one bond, diversify. Don't own all bonds from the same company. And try to stagger the maturity dates of your bonds, so that you won't be too much at the mercy of temporary market fluctuations if at some point you need to sell some of your bonds.

Corporate bond funds.

One way for the average investor to invest in bonds is through a corporate bond fund. This is a type of mutual fund that buys a large pool of bonds, and sells shares in the pool to individual investors.

The nice thing about the bond fund approach is that it provides you with diversification right off the bat. You needn't worry too much about a default, because you're holding (by proxy) the debt of many corporations instead of just one. You gain a measure of call protection, since, though some of the fund's bonds may be called, not all of them will be.

If you buy a bond fund, *don't* buy one that imposes a sales charge, or "load." If you do, you're likely to forfeit 8½% of your investment money right off the top. Buy instead a no-load bond fund. Check the management fee, and buy the fund only if that fee is less than 1% of assets under management per year.

Check carefully on the quality of the bonds in the fund's portfolio. It's easy to jack up the yield on a bond portfolio by investing in risky issues. However, this may not be what you, as an investor, had in mind. If you do wish to consider a "junk bond fund," as they're known, be aware that your higher yield is purchased with additional risk, and consider how this risk fits into your total investment portfolio.

A variation on the idea of a bond fund is the *unit investment trust*. These are fixed packages of bonds assembled as a pool and sold to investors on a basis similar to that of mutual funds. However, unlike a mutual fund, a unit investment trust does not offer continuing management. The bonds in the pooled portfolio at the start are the bonds that will remain there until the end, when the bonds mature (or default). One attraction of this arrangement is that you might save a bit on the management fee. However, you should watch carefully the initial sales fee. And you should be aware that there might be a tendency to "hit and run" on the part of some unit trust organizers. That is, they might load up the unit trust with low-quality, high-yield issues. The high yields can make the shares easy to sell initially, and if some issues default, the organizers may no longer be around to hear the complaints.

9

Government Bonds

A lot of us are no richer than we used to be, but we make more money. The extra money makes no difference at the supermarket or at the gas station, where prices have gone up as fast as our salaries, if not faster. But it makes a big difference on taxes. Our "higher" salaries have pushed us into higher tax brackets. So, a great many people are now paying a bigger percentage of their incomes in taxes than they used to. As a result, tax-exempt bonds, once mainly for the rich, now deserve consideration by middle-income investors. Tax-exempt bonds means government bonds. But you need to resurrect your eighth-grade civics to understand which bonds are exempt from which taxes.

As President Reagan has recently reminded us, there's a separation of powers between the states and the federal government. The states can't tax the income on bonds issued by the federal government. And the federal government can't tax the income on the bonds issued by the states. Lump in with the "states," the counties, municipalities, and various agencies of each. The bonds issued by states, counties, municipalities, and their agencies are collectively known as *municipal bonds.*

Municipal bonds are almost always exempt from federal income taxes. You don't even have to report the income you get from them on your federal tax return. They are also, in most cases, exempt from state and local income tax in the state where they were issued. Thus, municipal bonds issued by, say, Springfield, Illinois, would be exempt from Illinois income tax but not from New York income tax.

Bonds issued by the U.S. government are not exempt from federal income tax. But they are exempt from state and local income tax. In some places this is a moot point (because there is no state or local income tax); in others it's a trivial virtue. But in some high-tax localities (e.g., New York, Massachusetts or Wisconsin) it's a point worth considering.

Corporate bonds, discussed in the previous chapter, offer no tax exemption. However, they pay a higher rate of interest than municipal bonds of comparable safety. The ratio varies over time, but often you'll find the pretax yield on corporates is about 40% more than on municipals.

It traditionally works out that you're better off with corporates if your marginal tax bracket (i.e., your highest bracket—the one you pay on your last portion of income) is below 30%. But if your tax bracket is 30% or more, municipals deserve a look. The higher your tax bracket, the more appealing municipal bonds look.

If you're not sure about your bracket, check the chart, "What Tax Bracket Are You In?" Once you know your top bracket, you can use the chart, "How Important Is Tax Exemption To You?" It will help you determine whether you're better off in municipal bonds or corporate bonds.

There's a relatively simple formula you can use to figure the equivalent taxable yield for a municipal bond. Divide the municipal bond yield by 1.00 minus your tax bracket expressed as a decimal. For example, let's say you're in the 30% tax bracket. For you, the equivalent taxable yield to an 8% municipal bond is 8.00/1.00–.30, or 8.00/.70, which is 11.43%.

What Tax Bracket Are You In?

Some people really don't need to worry much about the tax implications of their investments. Others let tax considerations push them unnecessarily toward ill-considered tax shelters: shelter at any cost. Still other people who really would be well-advised to seek out tax-exempt investments have not done so because they don't realize how big a chunk of their investment return is going to Uncle Sam. As a first step, the investor should know his or her own tax bracket. The brackets shown below are as of 1980. To see if yours has changed, you can check Schedule X, Y, or Z in the instructions accompanying your most recent federal tax return.

Sample Brackets (1980)

If your taxable income was:	and you were: married (filing jointly)	single	single head of household
$10,000	19%	24%	22%
$15,000	22%	29%	27%
$20,000	28%	34%	31%
$25,000	32%	40%	36%
$30,000	36%	45%	41%
$35,000	39%	50%	45%
$40,000	45%	50%	48%
$45,000	48%	55%	52%
$50,000	50%	60%	55%
$60,000	53%	62%	58%
$70,000	55%	64%	59%
$80,000	58%	66%	62%

If you heed the call of your tax bracket and decide to take the plunge into municipals, what are some of the factors to keep in mind? The dominant considerations are the same as those for buying corporate bonds. Check the risk rating from Moody's or Standard & Poor's. Stick with highly rated (AAA or AA) bonds. After all, if you wanted to speculate, you could be buying stocks, or silver, or oriental rugs.

Once again, as with corporate bonds, you needn't pick an issuer the way you would pick a stock. When you buy a stock, you're hoping in a sense to pick the best possible company. When you buy a bond, once you've set your safety standard, the available choices are semiinterchangeable. So long as the municipality doesn't get anywhere near bankruptcy, you have no strong reason to be concerned about the details of its financial situation.

Instead, you can select an issuer based on the yield, the time to maturity, the amount of call protection you have, and the way the bond is secured.

The yield is calculated in the same ways as for corporate bonds. To start with, there's the coupon rate. Beyond that, there's the rate the bond is currently paying. And beyond *that,* there's the yield to maturity. You should know all three yields before buying. With municipal bonds, unlike corporates, there are no tax advantages in buying a discount bond—your income is already tax exempt. In fact, there is a small tax disadvantage to buying municipals at a discount, since capital gains on tax-exempt securities are taxable (though at the relatively low capital-gains rate).

The time to maturity is important, because it bears on your ability to keep the bond as long as necessary to assure yourself against loss of capital. Municipals fluctuate in value with interest rates, just like corporates. So an early sale could result in a capital loss, if interest rates have risen in the meantime. Buy only bonds you're reasonably confident

How Important Is Tax Exemption To You?

Once you know your tax bracket, you can use the table below to figure out how important a feature tax-exempt status is for you in selecting an investment. This knowledge is especially important if you are investing in bonds or bond funds, since both taxable and tax-exempt bonds are widely available.

| If your tax bracket is: | then a tax-exempt yield of | | | | | |
| | 5% | 6% | 7% | 8% | 9% | 10% |
	is the equivalent of a taxable yield of:					
19%	6.17%	7.41%	8.64%	9.88%	11.11%	12.35%
24%	6.58%	7.89%	9.21%	10.53%	11.84%	13.16%
28%	6.94%	8.33%	9.72%	11.11%	12.50%	13.88%
32%	7.35%	8.82%	10.29%	11.76%	13.24%	14.71%
36%	7.81%	9.38%	10.94%	12.50%	14.06%	15.62%
40%	8.33%	10.00%	11.67%	13.33%	15.00%	16.67%
45%	9.09%	10.91%	12.73%	14.55%	16.36%	18.18%
50%	10.00%	12.00%	14.00%	16.00%	18.00%	20.00%
55%	11.11%	13.33%	15.55%	17.77%	20.00%	22.22%
60%	12.50%	15.00%	17.50%	20.00%	22.50%	25.00%

you could afford to hold to maturity, if necessary. If you own (or are buying) more than one bond, try to stagger the maturities to give yourself better protection against market fluctuations.

Call protection is generally better with municipals than with corporates. Many municipals aren't callable at all. But you can't assume this without checking. Discuss the point with your broker.

The security provisions for municipal bonds are different from those for corporates. The highest degree of safety lies in buying *full faith and credit* bonds, also called *general obligation* bonds. These are backed by the taxing power of the issuing government body.

Slightly more risky are *revenue bonds*. With these, bond issue money is used to build a facility (like a toll bridge or power plant) that generates revenue, which in turn is used to repay the bondholders.

A third type of security arrangement is that of *assessment* bonds. These are bonds used to finance civic improvements, which are paid for out of a specific tax assessment. They're a tad riskier than full faith and credit bonds because only one type of tax is available to finance them.

Whatever the security arrangement (full faith and credit, revenue, or assessment), it should be reflected in the risk rating given a particular bond issue by Moody's or Standard & Poor's.

U.S. government bonds.

An alternative to buying corporate or municipal bonds is buying U.S. government bonds. For the most part, this alternative should be taken only by people to whom safety or patriotism are more important than investment yield.

U.S. government bonds are very safe indeed. But because of the correlation between risk and return, yield is generally lower on U.S. debt securities than on comparable securities issued by corporations or municipalities.

Nevertheless, some U.S. government securities may be of interest to certain investors. Here is a brief description of a few selected U.S. government bonds.

▶ *U.S. Treasury bonds.* In early 1981—a time of high-interest rates, by historical standards—U.S. Treasury bills (maturity a year or less), U.S. Treasury notes (maturity two to ten years), and U.S. Treasury bonds (maturity longer than ten years) were generally paying between 12% and 14%, with the short-term obligations paying more. That was atypical; usually long-term interest rates are higher than short-term ones. The return on Treasury bonds (about 12%) was about one percentage point less than the return on triple-A corporate (industrial) bonds. That's fairly typical, since corporate bonds involve at least a pinch more risk than U.S. government bonds do.

Treasury bonds are usually callable, starting five years before maturity. They pay you interest twice a year. You can buy Treasury bonds, for as little as $1,000, directly from a Federal Reserve Bank. These bonds represent a conservative investment with fairly good call protection.

▶ *U.S. savings bonds.* Traditionally, U.S. savings bonds have been a terrible investment. Lately, they've been upgraded to mediocre.

There are two kinds now being issued—series EE and series HH. As of early 1981, series EE bonds had a maturity of nine years, and yielded 8% a year if held to maturity. If you cash them in early, you get your full principal back, but you're credited wtih interest at a lower rate. HH bonds mature in 10 years, and pay 7½% annual interest if held for the full term. The interest of both types of savings bonds is exempt from state and local tax, and needn't be reported as income on your Federal tax form until the bonds are cashed in.

▶ *Fannie Maes* are the colloquial name for the debt securities of the Federal National Mortgage Association (FNMA). The FNMA was set up by Congress in 1938 to help reduce instability in the mortgage market; it is a quasi-governmental organization that buys and sells government-guaranteed mortgages from and to banks, insurance companies, and other financial institutions.

Fannie Mae issues several types of debt securities (and common stock as well). Some of the debt securities are backed by the full faith and credit of the U.S. government, others aren't. Fannie Maes have large minimum-purchase requirements (for example, $25,000 on mortgage-backed bonds), and offer yields roughly comparable to those of Treasury bonds.

▶ *Ginnie Maes* are the colloquial name for the debt securities of the Government National Mortgage Association (GNMA). Ginnie Mae is an arm of the U.S. Department of Housing and Urban Development. It issues several types of debt securities; the one of greatest interest to individual investors is the *modified pass-through certificate*. It works like this. A lender assembles a pool of mortgages and uses them as collateral for the certificates. Investors get a "pass-through" of the mortgage interest and a portion of the principal each month. It's a "modified" pass-through because Ginnie Mae promises to pay you whether the mortgage borrower pays on time or not. You get your payments monthly, not semiannually as with most bonds, which can be convenient for investors with fluctuating incomes. The rate of interest you get is fixed when you buy a Ginnie Mae. It often works out to be a bit above the yield on Treasury bonds, and during some periods has been higher than the yield on top-grade corporate bonds. This is true despite the fact that the investment is considered very safe. (No U.S. government agency has ever defaulted on a bond payment.)

Newly issued Ginnie Maes sell for $25,000 and up. However, you can buy into a partially paid-up pool for less. Recently it's also become possible to buy Ginnie Maes through mutual funds, or through broker-run trusts, in much smaller amounts (as little as $1,000 to $3,000). Watch the sales charges, though.

Ginnie Maes tend to be a little less volatile in the long run than most other bonds, because your principal is being eased back to you a bit at a time.

Municipal bond funds.

As with corporate bonds, you have the option of buying municipal bonds singly, or buying into a pool of municipal bonds assembled by a municipal-bond mutual fund. For small investors, the mutual-fund approach makes sense, since it provides diversification from the outset. This lessens the risk of default (or alternatively allows you to raise your yield by taking on slightly higher risks than you would if you were putting all your money into a single bond).

Income from a municipal bond fund, as from a single municipal bond, is exempt from federal income tax. Some funds are arranged so that the investor can purchase a package of bonds issued in his or her home state. In that case, the income will usually be exempt from state or local taxes, too.

If you are interested in a municipal bond fund, never purchase one that requires you to pay a sales charge, or "load." The typical load is 8½%, which takes a big chip out of your working capital. If you opt for a fund, choose a "no-load" one.

10

Preferred Stocks

Preferred stock is stock doing a convincing imitation of a bond. It has many of the disadvantages of a bond, without all of the advantages. While the common stockholder can participate fully in the good fortunes of the company by receiving increased dividends, the holder of preferred stock can receive no more than a fixed and stated dividend. In that sense, preferred stock is a fixed-return investment.

However, the fixed return is not guaranteed. The company's board of directors can either pay or not pay the preferred stockholders' dividend, depending on how good the company's profits were in a given year. If the dividend is not paid, the company cannot pay any dividend to common stockholders either.

Suppose that you own preferred stock and miss your dividend one year. Does the company have to make it up to you when it can afford to? The answer is yes if, and only if, you hold *cumulative preferred stock*. A company must pay back its dividend backlog or *arrearage* on the cumulative preferred before it can pay any dividends on common stock.

Preferred stock is "preferred," then, in the sense that preferred stockholders get paid their limited dividend before common stockholders get paid their unlimited one. It is also preferred in that the claims of preferred shareholders come before those of common stockholders (but after those of bond owners) if the company is liquidated.

Preferred stock in many ways resembles a perpetual bond, that is, a bond without a fixed maturity date. Like bonds, shares of preferred stock have a par value (often $25, $50, or $100 per share). Like bonds, many issues of preferred stock are callable. If a company does call in its preferred stock, it must pay you at least the par value for each share, and often a small redemption premium as well.

What about market fluctuations? Here we come to another disadvantage of preferred stock. Its market fluctuation is greater than that of a bond. In the case of a bond, knowledge that it can be redeemed at par at a future date provides an anchor that contains fluctuations. In the case of preferred stock, there's no such anchor, since there's no set maturity date.

Since 1958, the yields on preferred stocks have moved in close concert with bond yields. In most years, bond yields have been somewhat higher. Preferred stock is a bit easier to buy and sell than bonds are, and it usually pays interest four times a year, as against twice a year for bonds. But these are piddling advantages.

At this point, you may be wondering why preferred stocks still exist. The answer: They can be attractive investments for corporations, because of the tax laws. If you happen to have your own incorporated business, you might want to look into preferred stocks with your financial adviser. Otherwise, you would probably do best to forget about preferreds.

11

Common Stocks

Common stocks deserve a prominent place in the portfolios of most investors. While the 1970s were not great years for the stock market, there are some reasons to think that the 1980s may be.

Common stocks are a different breed of animal from the investments discussed in the chapters up to now. When you buy a fixed-income investment like a bond, you are loaning out your money. You expect to get it back, plus interest at a stated rate. You do not have any say in running the enterprise to which you loaned the money.

When you buy shares of common stocks, you become, at least technically, a part owner of the enterprise that issued the stock, and you expect to participate in its good or bad fortunes. You do not expect for sure to get your money back: Though you certainly hope to make a profit, you realize that you are assuming the risk of a loss, if the company fares poorly. Nor do you expect to receive interest at a fixed rate. Rather, you hope that as company profits rise, the dividends it pays to shareholders will rise. You are promised nothing, but hope for a great deal.

If you're a typical stockholder, the percentage of the company's stock you own is so infinitesimal as to make your say, for all practical purposes, moot. However, a few small shareholders do take advantage of their rights to attend companies' annual meetings, or place items on the agenda. If you're a large shareholder, owning a major chunk of a company's stock, your voice in company affairs becomes very real indeed.

The yield from a stock.

The profit you can make from investing in common stock comes from two sources: the dividends you may receive and the capital gain you get if you eventually sell the stock at a price higher than what you bought it for.

▶ *Dividends* are your share of company profits, as determined by the board of directors. A dividend is declared each quarter by the board, and is totally discretionary. The fact that a company has been paying a dividend of $1.00 per share each quarter for the past eight years does not guarantee you that the board will not decide to omit the dividend altogether next quarter. In practice, however, most companies attempt to keep their dividends from fluctuating too sharply from one quarter to the next or from one year to the next.

There are a number of things companies can (or must) do with profits besides pay dividends to stockholders. First, the company must pay its corporate taxes. After-tax earnings can be distributed to shareholders or plowed back to fund company expansion, research and development, or thicker rugs for the offices. Some shareholders believe that the right thing for companies to do is to pay out every nickel to the holders of common stock. Other shareholders can see that it may be in their long-range interests for a company to put some of its profits into future expansion and development. In fact, companies vary widely in their attitudes about dividend payout. Some companies, especially new and rapidly growing ones, pay no dividend whatever and plow everything back into internal growth. Other companies, especially long-established ones in relatively stable industries, pay a large percentage of profits to shareholders, year after year. Companies that are losing money, of course, usually have no money available for the payment of dividends. If you're considering an investment in common stock, one factor at which you will want to look closely is a company's philosophy in regard to dividend payments.

A starting point of obvious interest is the *dividend yield* on a stock. This is a percentage figure, in some ways comparable to the interest rate on a fixed-return investment. To calculate the dividend yield, you divide the annual dividend (either for the past year, or the expected dividend for the coming year) by the price of the stock. Here are some samples of dividend yields that prevailed in early 1981. They are shown solely to illustrate the magnitude and range of dividend yields, not in praise or denigration of any stock.

The yield table makes it obvious that there is a tremendous range among companies in dividend yield. The next logical question is: Why not simply pick a stock paying the highest dividend yield? Answer: While such stocks may be well suited for conservative investors, they are often not the stocks with the greatest potential for capital gains. High dividend yields are often associated with companies that have reached or neared the limits of their growth, perhaps in stable or highly regulated industries. Since such companies can't lure investors with hopes of dramatic capital gains, they have to pay a higher dividend rate to attract investment capital. Utilities are the classic example of such stocks, and you may note that the two stocks paying the highest dividend yields in the chart on page 94 are utilities.

A high dividend yield in a company with stable earnings and a consistent dividend payout record results in an investment not too dissimilar in its effect from a high-grade bond. For years, conventional wisdom dictated that the portfolios

Samples of Dividend Yields

The yields shown below were those prevailing in early 1981 on ten common stocks. They are shown solely to illustrate how dividend yields range. A high yield does not necessarily indicate a good stock, nor a low yield a bad one. Yield is only one of several considerations in buying a stock.

Stock	*Dividend Yield, Early 1981*
Borden	7.0%
Borg-Warner	5.9%
Boston Edison	13.6%
Braniff International	none
Briggs & Stratton	6.1%
Bristol-Myers	3.6%
British Petroleum	0.9%
Brockway Glass	7.1%
Brooklyn Union Gas	10.6%
Bruno's	2.5%

of conservative investors should consist in large part of bonds and utility stocks. Then, in the early 1970s, Consolidated Edison shocked the investment world by omitting payment on a quarterly dividend. Investors were sharply reminded that a stock is not a bond.

If yield alone is what you seek, and you are not concerned much about capital gains, then the relative safety of bonds may tip the scales toward buying a bond rather than a stock. The dividend yield on stocks is normally below the yield on bonds. In early 1981, for example, the average stock that paid dividends yielded about 4½%. The average high-grade corporate bond at the time had a current yield of 14%. That's bigger than the usual difference, but it certainly makes the point. And it's logical for bonds to yield more than stocks do (in dividends alone), because stocks offer an additional lure to investors: the prospect of major capital gains.

▶ *Capital gains.* Stocks are not unique in offering the potential for capital gains. You can get a capital gain by buying a painting for $300 and selling it ten years later for $600. You can get a capital gain by buying a home for $52,000 and selling it eight years later for $74,000. You can, as we saw in the last chapter, even get a capital gain from a bond, for example by buying a $5,000 bond for $4,500 and redeeming it a few years later at par.

The stock market, though, is the most popular arena for investors seeking capital gains. One reason is that stocks are fairly easy to buy and sell. Another is that, unlike the case with bonds, there's no fixed limit on what you can make in the stock market.

Every dabbler in the market dreams of finding "the next Xerox," the next IBM, the next Wang, or whatever his (her) image of an explosively successful growth stock may be. Xerox will do nicely for an example. If you'd bought 100 shares at $10 a share early in the 1960s, your $1,000 investment would have grown to more than $16,000 by 1972.

We all know one person who's done sensationally in the stock market. One of my relatives, for example, made such a killing in Mohawk Data that he retired early, and bought his daughter a house (with no mortgage). The trouble is, we all know just one—not seven or twenty-five. And it never seems to be us.

Guess what? Stocks that rise tenfold or more in a decade aren't commonplace. If you do buy one, it will probably be by luck as much as skill. (My relative, incidentally, didn't want the Mohawk Data stock; it was forced on him by his employer.) Also, what rises with meteoric speed can plummet pretty fast too. Take for example . . . well, Xerox. In late 1977, its price was about $40 a share, down 75% from its 1972 peak. The $1,000 investment that had ballooned to $16,000 had shrunk back to $4,000.

You can't count on a killing. But an expectation that stands a good chance of being fulfilled is that you can match the performance of the market averages. Over the half century from 1925 to 1975, stocks yielded an average return (dividends plus capital gains) of about 9% a year.

Phooey, you say. You can get more than that in a bond. Ah, now you can. But the 9% return stocks provided over that 50-year period was during a time when bonds yielded less than a 4% return. During much of that period, the rate of inflation was insignificant.

Will stocks, which performed poorly in the 1970s, once again become a vehicle in which you can outrun inflation? Will they return, for that matter, to providing a substantially better total return than bonds? My own opinion is that they will. In the long run, for financial markets to function properly, they have to give a greater reward to capital at risk than to money simply lent at a fixed rate.

In my view, stocks should be treated as long-term holdings. You have to be prepared to ride out the bad times. Better yet, add to your holdings during bad times. But whatever you do, don't sell then. This emphasizes, yet again, the need for you to have a cushion of savings before you invest. Otherwise, you'll be forced to sell precisely when things look bleakest, as many people did during the great market valley of 1974. For the shrewd, and prepared, investor, 1974 was a great time to buy stocks—as are most years in which people are convinced that the economy is hopeless and stock prices will be depressed indefinitely. For example, 1979 was that kind of year. In 1979, *Business Week* ran a cover story on "The Death of Equities" (i.e., common stocks). A person who bought stocks on the day that story ran would have done very well in the market for the ensuing year. The courage to act contrary to prevailing opinion is a large part of the secret of achieving capital gains.

Before leaving the subject of capital gains, let's have a word about taxes. As of 1981, federal income-tax law provided that long-term capital gains (gains from the sale of assets held more than a year) were subject to tax on only 40% of the gain. This gives stocks a major advantage over fixed-return investments. To take a simple example, consider a stock that has gone up 10% a year in price for five years, and pays no dividends. You bought it for $1,000 five years ago, sold it yesterday. Your gain is $610, of which only $244 is taxable. If you're in the 32% bracket, you owe $78 in taxes, and get to keep $532.

Contrast that with a fixed-return investment (like a certificate of deposit) that also returns 10% a year, but in the form of interest rather than capital gains. The interest is taxable each year, so the effective rate of growth for your investment is slashed to 6.8% (again assuming you're in the 32% bracket). The after-tax gain is only $389.

As a buyer of stock, you came out $143 ahead of the

certificate buyer, even though both of your investments could be said to have "gone up" the same amount.

Is all of this fair? Yes. By taxing capital gains at a lower rate, the government encourages investment in businesses that create new jobs. Not everyone agrees, though. Your state, for example, may require you to report on your state income-tax form the full amount of your capital gains, not just the amount reported on the federal form.

Can you beat the averages?

It is the goal of every investor who buys stock to rack up gains better than those of the market averages (such as the Dow Jones Industrial Average, the Standard & Poor's 500, and the New York Stock Exchange Index). If the stock market as a whole has produced a long-term yield of 9% a year, many investors figure that they can get a return of, say, 14% or 15%.

And, of course, some do. If you made a chart of the investment yield obtained by various investors, it would form a bell curve. At the left-hand extreme of the chart would be a few investors who suffered disastrous losses; at the right-hand extreme, those who made marvelous gains. The big lump in the middle would represent the majority of people, whose results were about the same as the market averages.

Pure chance would dictate that if you invest in the stock market long enough, some year you will be among those who outperform the averages. By the same token, pure chance would dictate that in some years you'd do worse than the averages.

Can shrewdness, expertise, or hard work help you consistently outperform the averages? For a number of reasons, the answer is unclear. Let us look first, not at the reasons, but at the record. The record shows that professional money managers do not consistently produce results better than the market averages. This assertion, astounding when first heard, has been supported with a good deal of evidence. Here are three examples.

1. *Mutual funds, as a group, have not outperformed the market averages.* Mutual funds are organizations that pool the money of small investors and invest it under professional supervision. The people who pick stocks for mutual funds can be presumed to be among the best-informed individuals in the securities industry. Yet their record can be charitably described as mediocre. For example, in the period of late 1968 to mid-1978, according to *Forbes* Magazine, the average mutual-fund share lost 2.1% of its value every year. (That's without taking inflation into account.) During the same period, the Standard & Poor's 500 Stock Average was also down, but only by an annual average of 1.3%.

These figures do not reflect the offsetting effect of dividend income. (By the way, the average mutual fund from mid-1977 to mid-1978 returned 3.6% in dividends. The dividend yield of the average stock in the Standard & Poor's 500 was 5.3%.)

Mutual funds have done better since 1978. Most of them have been outperforming the market averages, some of them by very substantial margins. Does this mean that the funds have wised up, and will consistently outperform the averages in the future? I don't think so. In the long run, I expect the funds to do just about as well as the market averages. In the very long run, I expect *everybody* to do just about as well as the averages. (Except for me, of course. Like everybody else, I expect to beat the averages.)

2. *In any given year, some mutual funds do better than the averages, but their performance is inconsistent.* The laws of pure chance dictate that about half of all investors will do better than the averages in any given year. A quarter will beat the averages two years running, and an eighth three

years running, by pure luck. To demonstrate consistent expertise, then, much more is required than two or three good years. Yet very few mutual funds can show a consistent record of outstanding performance.

One study of the performance of 39 funds over a ten-year period, conducted by Eugene Fama of the University of Chicago, found dramatic inconsistencies in performance from year to year. One fund was first in performance for three of the ten years—and thirty-fifth, thirty-sixth, and thirty-eighth in three other years! Another fund made first place twice, last place once. A third fund made first place twice and last place twice. Over the ten-year period, the average ranks for these three funds were 15.7, 17.2, and 23.2.

3. *Randomly selected portfolios have performed as well as or better than expertly selected ones.* Probably the best-known portfolio selected by throwing darts is the so-called Forbes Dart-Board Fund. In 1967, three *Forbes* Magazine executives selected a portfolio of 28 stocks by throwing darts at a stock-market page from *The New York Times*. They invested a hypothetical $1,000 in each stock, and reported annually on the results. As of March, 1979, the Dart-Board Fund had grown in value from $28,000 to more than $43,000, a performance far exceeding the performance of the market averages—or of mutual funds—during that period. Pure luck? Perhaps. But the *Forbes* executives are not the only people who have tried such experiments. In 1967, Paul Samuelson, the Nobel-Prize-winning economist, testified before the Senate Banking and Currency Committee that mutual funds, as a group, had not outperformed the stock-market averages over long periods of time. Senator Thomas McIntyre of New Hampshire, intrigued by Samuelson's testimony, constructed his own dart-board portfolio, then checked to see how he would have done had he bought that

portfolio ten years ago. He found that he would have done better than most mutual funds had done.

You may say that these three pieces of evidence merely prove that mutual funds can't beat the averages, not that you can't. Perhaps so. But you must admit it's intriguing that the professional money managers who run the mutual funds, who are paid to try to beat the averages and who spend full time doing so, have great difficulty doing it with any consistency.

Now that we've seen some evidence that it's hard to beat the averages, let us consider some reasons why it's so. These reasons are usually grouped together under the name of either of two closely related theories, the *random-walk theory* and the *efficient-market theory*.

Suppose the stock of Innocence Corporation is selling for $30 a share, when an acquiring company announces that it intends to offer shareholders of Innocence stock $37 a share for their shares. The stock does not continue to trade at $30 a share, while shareholders await the formal offer. Instead, the price is almost immediately bid up to the vicinity of $37 a share. The market is *efficient* in absorbing new information, and reflecting it in a stock's price.

This goes not only for tender offers but also for earnings reports, confirmed or unconfirmed reports of new processes, new products, labor strife, pending lawsuits, oil strikes, price hikes, regulatory actions, favorable publicity, or the state of the mole on the neck of the chief executive. Every iota of infromation is quickly digested by the market and reflected in the price of the stock.

Perhaps the first three or four people to learn of these developments may gain some advantage from it (though only if their information is correct, and the market views the development in the same light as they do). However, no investor, no matter how well-informed, is likely to be among the first three or four people to know something significant of this sort more than once or twice in a lifetime. (The people most likely to know, corporate insiders, face legal penalties if they act on the information.) So by the time the typical investor (even the well-informed one) gets the news, the effect of this information has *already* been reflected in the price of the stock.

In its extreme and simplified form, the efficient-market theory can be boiled down as follows. Stocks of companies with good future prospects are already priced relatively high (in ratio to current company earnings) to reflect those good prospects. Stocks of companies with poor prospects are already priced relatively low (in relation to current company earnings) to reflect their presumably dim future. As a result, the individual investor might as well flip a coin or throw a dart. His or her chances of making money are about as good in one stock as in another. It depends on pure chance (or what mathematicians call a *random walk*). However, to the extent that the stock market as a whole tends to move up over time, the odds are weighted in the investor's favor.

This theory sounds like heresy. But it certainly cannot be dismissed as nonsense. The efficient-market theory is quite consistent with the findings we described earlier regarding the inability of professional money managers to beat the market averages.

The random-walk theory goes a bit further than the efficient-market theory, although the two are closely allied. Random-walk theorists are likely to point to the significant role that chance, luck, and unpredictable events play in business affairs (as in human affairs in general). It is not so much that things happen randomly, but rather that people simply are not capable of predicting complex, long-range events with accuracy. A few examples may help make the point. Who predicted, and properly assessed the potential impact of the Russian grain deals of the early 1970s? The Penn Central bankruptcy? The Arab oil embargo of 1973? These were major events, and, with hindsight, we can say that anyone should have seen them coming. But hindsight is one tool uniformly denied to the forecaster.

Even securities analysts specializing in the study of particular industries cannot make reliable profit projections for companies in those industries. Burton Malkiel and other researchers at the Princeton University Financial Research Center studied company earnings projections made by 19 major brokerage firms, financial analysts, and investment officers. Both one-year and five-year forecasts were poor. Poor in what sense? In the sense that you would have gotten more accurate predictions by assuming that earnings of every company would rise 4% a year. You also would have gotten more accurate results by using several other of what Malkiel calls "naive forecasting models," or "placebos."

Does this mean that the financial analysts were stupid? Not at all. Does it mean that forecasting the future is difficult and sometimes impossible? It certainly does.

Price-earnings multiples.

In the world of stocks, the future often counts for as much as, or more than, the present. The price of a stock is determined, in large part, not by what the company has done, but by what people think it is going to do.

It's not too hard to see why predicted growth counts for a lot. Consider dividends first. If you take a mature company whose business is neither growing nor shrinking appreciably, and assume that its dividends will hold relatively constant, then you can make a calculation something like this. Mature Industries pays an annual dividend of $2 a share. If you buy 100 shares, you will get about $200 a year in dividend income, or about $2,000 over ten years. Now contrast that with what happens if you buy Fast-Growing, Inc., which also currently has a $2-a-share dividend, but whose profits are growing at the rate of 20% a year. Assuming the company chooses to increase its annual dividend at the rate of 10% a year, ten years worth of dividends on 100 shares would amount to about $3,500. It's obvious, then, that the stock of a fast-growing company is worth more than the stock of a company with stable earnings. But how *much* more? That's a tricky question.

The $3,500 you expect to get in dividends over the ten-year period works out to $35 a share. Does that mean it would be worth your while to pay $35 a share for the stock now? No, it doesn't. If you pay $35 a share now, you would be giving up interest on $3,500. You can make a reasonable guess about how much interest you're foregoing, based on your guess about what long-term rates will be on certificates of deposit, money market funds, bonds, and the like. Let's say you decide that your "opportunity cost," the rate of return you'd be giving up, is 10%. In my judgment, that's both a reasonable and a convenient figure to use. Anticipating that we would agree about this, I've provided you with a little chart showing how much a dollar you expect to get in the future is worth today (its "present value"), assuming you discount at a 10% rate of interest.

Based on dividends alone, the stock of Fast-Growing, Inc., is worth about $13.65 a share to you. That's the present value of $35 realized 10 years from now. (This is simplifying a bit, since you don't have to wait ten years to get some of that $35, but we'll ignore that to keep the math simpler.)

But dividends are only part of the picture. Let's look at the other part, capital gains. Obviously, a fast-growing company is more likely to produce capital gains than a slow-growing one. In other words, the stock of a growth company is more likely to rise in price than the stock of a stable or declining company.

104

Present Values at 10% Interest	
Number of years until you get your hands on $1.00	*Present value of that $1.00*
1	$0.91
2	$0.83
3	$0.75
4	$0.68
5	$0.62
6	$0.56
7	$0.51
8	$0.47
9	$0.42
10	$0.39
15	$0.24
20	$0.15

Predicting the performance of a stock's price is even harder than predicting future dividends—which, as we've already seen, is hard enough. However, even if investors don't realize it, they are making some kind of conscious or unconscious price predictions when they decide to invest in a stock. Let's suppose that you expect the stock of Fast-Growing, Inc., to sell for $100 a share by ten years from now. Does that mean you should pay $100 a share for it today? Of course not. Once more, you would be forfeiting interest on your savings in order to buy the stock. Once more, the prudent price to pay (assuming your prediction is accurate) would be the present value of $100. Checking the chart you can see that it works out to about $39 a share.

Well, then, you are all set to see whether Fast-Growing, Inc., constitutes a good buy. The dividends you anticipate are worth about $13.65 a share; the capital gains you anticipate are worth about $39 a share. Together, they mean that the stock is worth about $52.65 a share, *if* your predictions are right.

Should you buy the stock? Why, what an easy question! Certainly you should, if the price is below $52.65 a share. If the price is above $52.65, you shouldn't.

Of course you get different answers depending on the assumptions you make. If you decide that only a 12% annual return would satisfy you, you can use present value tables at 12% interest. Assuming you kept your estimates of a company's future performance unchanged, you'd then find fewer stocks giving off "buy" signals.

In the real world, you wouldn't necessarily go through these numerical calculations, because the process suggests an exactitude in prediction that you know isn't really possible. As we've seen, even the experts have a lot of trouble predicting company earnings and dividends. Predicting what a stock will sell for a few years in the future is even harder. So the kind of exact (or semi-exact) mathematics we've used here must be taken with several grains of salt.

The numbers we've used, though, have been intended to make a point that does apply directly to the real world. The market does make an estimate (intuitive or exact) of a stock's growth potential, and it reflects this growth potential in the price of the stock. There is a widely available number that will give you a good idea of what conventional wisdom is regarding the future prospects of any stock. That number is the *price-earnings multiple*.

The term is complicated only at first glance. Actually, it's simple. The price is simply the selling price of the stock, right now. The earnings are the company's reported profits for the latest 12-month period.* The ratio of the price to the

---

* Sometimes people use the estimated earnings for the upcoming 12 months, or a figure that's half reported earnings, half estimated earnings.

earnings is the price-earnings multiple, often called the PE ratio, or, simply, the multiple. The table on page 108 shows some multiples prevailing in 1981 on a few sample stocks.

The multiple works like a public-opinion poll. It tells you how much faith investors, as a group, have in a company's growth prospects. In the chart above, the three highest multiples (49 for McMoRan, 36 for Yankee Oil, and 33 for Sabine) were for companies involved in exploring or drilling for oil and gas. Companies in that line were the darlings of Wall Street in early 1981, and the high multiples reflected glowing expectations of growth. The lowest multiple in the chart was for Occidental Petroleum, whose prospects seemed dim in early 1981 to many people. Occidental had a potentially costly lawsuit hanging over its head in regard to Love Canal, where its subsidiary, Hooker Chemical, had been accused of pollution abuses leading to health problems. Other relatively low multiples were for Quaker Oats and Nabisco, both established companies in what were widely perceived as no-growth or slow-growth industries.

One important way of using multiples is to look at the multiples for competing companies in a particular industry. In recent years, General Motors has had the highest multiple in the auto industry (which wasn't saying much), while Delta has consistently had one of the highest multiples in the airline industry. Anyone considering an investment in the auto industry or airline industry would naturally want to know why this was. Thus, a look at multiples within an industry can be a useful jumping-off point for research about what's happening in that industry.

The investor should understand that a company's multiple will change over time, and not just because the company is doing better or worse. A multiple reflects the state of investors' faith, not only in a particular company, but in a particular industry as well. It also reflects investors' faith (or

Some Sample Price-Earnings Multiples

The multiples shown below were those that prevailed on 26 selected common stocks on January 21, 1981. Multiples can change over time, as explained in the chapter. Think of the multiple as an index of expectations. A high multiple indicates that investors expect a company to show rapid earnings growth; a low multiple indicates that investors as a group expect a company to show slow earnings growth or none.

Stock	*Price-Earnings Multiple*
Atlantic Richfield	9
Braniff	NA
Control Data	8
duPont	9
Esmark	19
Ford	NA
General Motors	NA
Humana	22
IBM	11
Johns Manville	9
K Mart	9
Eli Lilly	14
McMoRan	49
Nabisco	7
Occidental Petroleum	3
Parker Pen	9
Quaker Oats	7
RCA	8
Sabine	33
Texas Instruments	13
UAL	NA
Varian	10
Walgreen	8
Xerox	8
Yankee Oil	36
Zenith	12

NA: Not applicable; multiple cannot be calculated because company had a loss for preceding 12 months.

lack of it) in the performance of the stock market as a whole. When a company like General Motors sells at only five times earnings, as it did in 1979, the cautious valuation reflects lack of confidence in the stock market and the auto industry at least as much as lack of confidence in the company.* By the same token, when the stock of a company like Mc-Donald's Corporation sells (as it did for a time in 1972) at 60 times earnings, the faith being expressed is not only in one well-run hamburger chain. A multiple like that is likely to occur only during a time when investors are also optimistic about the stock market in general.

Here are a few examples of how drastically multiples can change. McDonald's sold for 60 times earnings in 1972, 20 times earnings in 1975, and 10 times earnings in 1979. IBM sold for 34 times earnings in 1972, 14 times earnings in 1977. General Motors sold for 10 times earnings in 1972, 13 times earnings in 1974, and 5 times earnings in 1979.

You may notice that the spread between high and low multiples has declined in recent years. During times of rapid growth, some stocks begin to sport very high multiples; these are known as glamour stocks. Some people expect glamour stocks to show rising profits every year. When the market, or economic conditions, turn sour, glamour stocks may come crashing down, in large part because anything so high up has a long way to fall. In contrast, the so-called cyclical stocks, in which earnings fluctuations are expected, usually have lower multiples to begin with, and their multiples vary less from year to year.

For analytical purposes, you can also calculate a multiple for the stock market as a whole, or for a stock index. For example, the average multiple for the Standard & Poor's in-

* Caution was warranted. In 1980, all the U.S. automakers, including GM, lost money.

Historical Price-Earnings Multiples for Various Industries

Industry	Average Multiple, Jan. 1970	Average Multiple, Sept. 1972	Average Multiple, Dec. 1975
Aerospace	10	15	6
Airlines	16	19	12
Aluminum	12	27	10
Automobiles	9	11	16
Automobile parts	10	13	13
Banks	12	13	6
Beverages	23	30	12
Chemicals	13	18	15
Coal	31	18	8
Construction supplies	16	15	10
Containers	15	13	6
Copper	10	13	19
Cosmetics	30	32	16
Drugs	34	35	18
Electric equipment	20	23	13
Foods	16	15	10
Forest products	19	18	13
Home furnishings	15	18	12
Hotel and motel	36	37	11
Machinery	12	17	9
Metal fabricating	14	16	9
Office equipment	33	32	14
Oils	12	17	8
Paper	14	20	10
Publishing	22	20	7
Railroads	9	10	9
Railway equipment	13	16	6
Real estate	24	20	1
Restaurant	29	26	17
Retail trade	15	15	10
Rubber	11	10	9
Shoes	13	15	10
Soap	16	27	14
Steel	12	15	5
Textiles	11	12	12
Tobacco	12	14	10
Utilities			
Electric	12	11	8
Gas	11	12	7
Telephone	16	15	9
Vending	19	21	8

* Source: First Boston Corporation.

110

dex of 425 industrial stocks was about 16 in early 1970, 21 in late 1972, 7 in late 1974, and 12 in late 1975.

What signals do these multiples give to individual investors? It depends whether you're talking about the short run or the long run. High multiples suggest that investors generally are sweet on stocks; high multiples in a particular industry suggest that investors think things look bright for that industry. Short-term buying opportunities might be good. But I don't advocate buying stocks for the short term. It's too easy to go wrong. Also, taxes and commission costs (to brokers for buying or selling stock) eat significantly into any short-term profits. Stocks should be bought for the long haul. For the long-term investor, high multiples are a sign to stay away. If you pay many times earnings for a stock, you're in effect going out on a limb. Comes the time when multiples generally decline, your stock would be hard put to hold its lofty price. Or, look at it this way. The multiple of a high-multiple stock testifies that the stock's price reflects glowing expectations. The stock would have to do *even better* than the prevailing great expectations for you to make a significant amount of money.

Low multiples convey exactly the opposite message. Investors are down on the stock, or the industry, or the stock market in general, or all three. Short-term profit opportunities are unlikely. But for the long-term investor, low multiples spell opportunity. The best time to buy stocks is when multiples are below traditional levels. A good time to buy stocks in a particular industry is when multiples for that industry are below traditional levels (see chart). This assumes, of course, that you do your homework and understand why investors are sour on the industry at the moment. Your judgment and research may tell you the industry is likely to bounce back—in which case, one or more stocks in that industry might represent good buys. But industries, like individual companies, do fade away. You presumably would not have wanted to buy stock in a horse-drawn carriage maker once cars came into vogue, even if the carriage makers had low multiples by traditional standards.

When you buy a stock with a low multiple, you have two chances for achieving gains. The company's earnings might rise, carrying the stock price up with them. Or earnings might not rise dramatically, but an upward movement in multiples might cause the same earnings to command a higher price. You hope, of course, that both will happen. In any case, when investing in an arena as difficult as the stock market, it certainly makes sense to give yourself two chances to win.

Volatility.

When the stock market goes up, some stocks go up more than others. When the stock market goes down, some stocks go down more than others. Often, they are the same stocks. Certain stocks tend to be *volatile*, or susceptible to dramatic price movements. Others tend to be more stable, and trade within a narrower range.

Wall Street has a Greek word commonly used to discuss, or measure, volatility. The word is *beta*. Stocks with a high beta are comparatively volatile, those with a low beta are comparatively stable.

Beta can be expressed numerically. First, you need a guideline, a base against which to measure an individual stock's volatility. The movement of the Standard & Poor's Stock Index is frequently used as the base. Suppose that whenever the price of the index moves $1.00, the price of Smith Jones & Co. moves $1.50. In that case, Smith Jones would have a beta of 1.5, which is considered a very high beta.

By contrast, suppose that whenever the index moves

$1.00, the stock of Stodgy, Inc., moves only $0.66. Stodgy would then have a beta of 0.66, which is a very low beta.

In actual practice, of course, betas aren't as simple to compute as the example indicates, because a stock's volatility isn't uniform. Any figure presented as a stock's beta must be derived from some sort of averaging process. Traditionally, this was done by looking at the stock's price movements, compared with index movements, over several stock market uptrends and downtrends.

The only trouble with this way of constructing beta figures was that it didn't work very well. The past price volatility of a stock didn't prove to be a reliable indicator of its future volatility.

Some researchers responded to this situation by trying to devise more sophisticated ways of estimating a stock's beta. Best known among these researchers has been Barr Rosenberg, a professor of business administration at Berkeley. Rosenberg has attempted to improve the usefulness of betas by calculating them using not only a stock's past performance, but certain other characteristics of the stock as well. For example, a stock with 500,000 shares outstanding can be expected to be more volatile than one with 5 million shares. The stock of a company that carries a lot of debt can be expected to be volatile. Same with stocks in industries with pronounced boom-and-bust cycles. Rosenberg builds these and similar factors into his models for calculating a stock's beta. These models (or similar ones) are then used by investment advisory firms to assign particular beta values to particular stocks. The beta figures, along with other market research, are usually sold by the advisory firms to clients.

Occasionally, beta estimates are published in periodicals available to individual investors. For example, the June 12, 1978, issue of *Forbes* Magazine carried a chart, prepared by

BETAS FOR 100 LARGE STOCKS, LISTED NUMERICALLY AND ALPHABETICALLY

The numerical listing is reprinted from *Forbes* Magazine, June 12, 1978. The data were calculated by Wilshire Associates.

Numerical Listing

Stock	Fundamental Beta	Stock	Fundamental Beta
AT&T	0.54	Public Svc Elec & Ga	0.80
Gulf Oil Corp	0.62	Standard Oil Co Cal	0.81
Royal Dutch Pete Co	0.63	Mobil Corp	0.82
General Tel & Elec	0.64	Kraft Inc	0.82
R J Reynolds Inds Inc	0.65	Shell Oil Co	0.83
Phil Elec Co	0.65	Unilever N V	0.83
Pacific Gas & Elec	0.66	IBM	0.84
Exxon Corp	0.67	Merck & Co Inc	0.84
Commonwealth Ed	0.68	Eli Lilly Co	0.85
Amer Home Prods	0.69	Texas Utils Co	0.85
Standard Oil Co Ind	0.70	General Mills Inc	0.85
Southern Calif Edison	0.70	3M	0.89
Texaco Inc	0.71	PepsiCo Inc	0.89
Ralston Purina Co	0.71	General Foods Corp	0.89
Johnson & Johnson	0.72	Atlantic Richfield Co	0.90
Southern Co	0.72	Sun Inc	0.90
Procter & Gamble Co	0.73	Union Oil Co Calif	0.91
Kellogg Co	0.73	BankAmerica Corp	0.92
American Elec Pwr	0.74	Getty Oil Co	0.94
Duke Power Co	0.74	Bristol Myers Co	0.94
Philip Morris Inc	0.77	Pfizer Inc	0.94
Schlumberger Ltd	0.78	Halliburton Co	0.95
Beatrice Foods Co	0.78	Revlon Inc	0.96
Phillips Pete Co	0.80	Emerson Elec Co	0.97
Warner-Lambert Co	0.80	Continental Oil Co	0.98

Stock	Fundamental Beta	Stock	Fundamental Beta
J P Morgan & Co	0.98	Con Edison	1.17
GM	0.99	U S Steel Co	1.20
Cities Svc Co	0.99	CBS Inc	1.20
GE	1.01	Dow Chem Co	1.23
Caterpillar Tractor	1.01	Alcoa	1.23
Coca-Cola Co	1.03	NCR Corp	1.24
Avon Prods Inc	1.03	ITT	1.26
Schering-Plough Corp	1.04	Westinghouse Elec Co	1.26
Sperry Rand Corp	1.04	Federated Dept Store	1.27
Ford Mtr Co	1.05	K mart	1.30
Eastman Kodak Co	1.06	International Paper	1.30
Abbott Labs	1.07	Weyerhaeuser Co	1.31
Colgate-Palmolive Co	1.07	Digital Equip Corp	1.32
E I du Pont	1.08	Deere & Co	1.32
Baxter Travenol Labs	1.09	Continental Corp	1.34
Burroughs Corp	1.10	Hewlett-Packard Co	1.35
Citicorp	1.11	RCA Corp	1.35
Dresser Inds Inc	1.11	Motorola Inc	1.38
Georgia-Pac Corp	1.13	McDonald's Corp	1.40
Boeing Co	1.14	Monsanto Co	1.45
Xerox Corp	1.15	Texas Instrs Inc	1.47
Union Pac Corp	1.15	Connecticut Gen Ins	1.49
Sears, Roebuck & Co	1.17	Aetna Life & Cas Co	1.50
J C Penney Inc	1.17	American Express Co	1.52
Union Carbide Corp	1.17	Travelers Corp	1.56

Alphabetical Listing

Company	Fundamental Beta	Company	Fundamental Beta
Abbott Labs	1.07	Continental Oil	0.98
Aetna Life & Casualty	1.50	Deere	1.32
Alcoa	1.23	Digital Equipment	1.32
American Electric		Dow Chemical	1.23
Power	0.74	Dresser Industries	1.11
American Express	1.52	Duke Power	0.74
American Home		DuPont	1.08
Products	0.69	Emerson Electric	0.97
American Telephone &		Exxon	0.67
Telegraph (AT&T)	0.54	Federated Department	
Atlantic Richfield	0.90	Stores	1.27
Avon	1.03	Ford Motor	1.05
BankAmerica	0.92	General Electric	1.01
Baxter Travenol Labs	1.09	General Foods	0.89
Beatrice Foods	0.78	General Mills	0.85
Boeing Co.	1.14	General Motors	0.99
Bristol Myers	0.94	General Telephone &	
Burroughs Corp.	1.10	Electronics	0.64
Caterpillar Tractor	1.01	Georgia-Pacific	1.13
CBS	1.20	Getty Oil	0.94
Cities Service	0.99	Gulf Oil	0.62
Citicorp	1.11	Halliburton	0.95
Coca-Cola	1.03	Hewlett-Packard	1.35
Colgate-Palmolive	1.07	International Business	
Commonwealth		Machines (IBM)	0.84
Edison	0.68	International Paper	1.30
Connecticut General		International	
Insurance	1.49	Telephone &	
Consolidated Edison	1.17	Telegraph (ITT)	1.26
Continental Corp.	1.34	Johnson & Johnson	0.72

Company	Fundamental Beta	Company	Fundamental Beta
Kellogg	0.73	Schlumberger	0.78
K Mart	1.30	Sears Roebuck	1.17
Kodak	1.06	Shell Oil	0.83
Kraft	0.82	Southern California	
Eli Lilly	0.85	Edison	0.70
McDonald's	1.40	Southern Co.	0.72
Merck	0.84	Sperry Rand	1.04
Mobil	0.82	Standard Oil of	
Monsanto	1.45	California	0.81
J.P. Morgan	0.98	Standard Oil of	
Motorola	1.38	Indiana	0.70
NCR	1.24	Sun Inc.	0.90
Pacific Gas & Electric	0.66	Texaco	0.71
J. C. Penney	1.17	Texas Instruments	1.47
PepsiCo	0.89	Texas Utilities	0.85
Pfizer	0.94	3M (Minnesota	
Philadelphia Electric	0.65	Mining &	
Philip Morris	0.77	Manufacturing)	0.89
Phillips Petroleum	0.80	Travelers	1.56
Procter & Gamble	0.73	Unilever	0.83
Public Service		Union Carbide	1.17
Electric & Gas	0.80	Union Oil of	
Ralston Purina	0.71	California	0.91
RCA	1.35	Union Pacific	1.15
Revlon	0.96	U.S. Steel	1.20
R.J. Reynolds		Warner-Lambert	0.80
Industries	0.65	Westinghouse	1.26
Royal Dutch		Weyerhaeuser	1.31
Petroleum	0.63	Xerox	1.15
Schering-Plough	1.04		

Wilshire Associates, showing betas for the 100 stocks with the largest total market value. The betas ranged from a low of 0.54 for the American Telephone & Telegraph Co. (AT&T) to a high of 1.56 for Travelers Corporation.

What does beta mean to you? In the long run, historically, portfolios with a high average beta have outperformed those with a lower average beta. Based on history, a portfolio with a high beta (say, 1.1 to 1.3) has yielded a long-term annual return of about 10% to 13%. A portfolio with an average beta (say, 0.9 to 1.1) has yielded between 8% and 12%. A portfolio with a low beta (below 0.9) has yielded between 7% and 10%.*

In other words, volatile stocks have, over the long run, produced a better long-term yield than stable ones. There's logic to this: Investors are being compensated for assuming risk.

But risk there is. Your particular high-beta stocks might do poorly. When the stock market gets knocked for a loop, volatile stocks are knocked down harder than others.

Obviously, it is not appropriate for people to keep all their assets in high-beta stocks—but, then, it's not appropriate for people to keep all their assets in stocks in the first place. As I've said before, most investors should look at stocks as long-term investments, and shouldn't put in money that they can't leave in for the long haul. If that is your philosophy, and if you're confident you can carry it out in practice, then high-beta stocks may be a more logical investment for you than low-beta ones.

Another caution: If you do choose to buy high-beta stocks, by all means diversify. It's an inordinate risk to put all your investment eggs into a basket composed of one or two vola-

* These figures include both dividends and capital gains, and are derived from a chart in Burton Malkiel's 1973 book, *A Random Walk Down Wall Street*. The data are from the period 1957–1972.

tile stocks. But then, diversification is a good idea whether the stocks you buy are volatile or stable ones.

We must close our discussion of volatility on a regretful note. Expert estimates of stock betas are not easy to come by —at least not yet. Individual investors using publicly available sources of information may well have to settle for a crude idea of probable volatility, based on a stock's past price movements. Records of past price gyrations are easy to come by, and many investment reference books include graphs comparing a stock's price movements with the movements of broad market indexes.

One way, of course, to obtain a diversified, high-beta portfolio is to invest in a mutual fund specializing in such stocks. More on that in the next chapter.

Picking individual stocks.

All right, some of you are saying, enough of these general principles, price-earnings ratios, and betas. How, pray tell, do I make smart picks of individual stocks?

The smart-aleck answer is that you don't, won't, and can't. In the long run, your picks will probably do as well as the averages. (The fewer stocks you hold, the more likely you are to do better or worse. The more diversified your portfolio, the more closely it will move with the averages.)

You want to beat the averages, nevertheless. Here are a few suggestions that may possibly help you.

▶ *Research the industry, not just the stock.* Pardon the crude analogy, but if you were betting on a horse race, you would look at the records of all the horses in the race, not just the particular horse you were considering betting on. Most industries, despite the imperfect functioning of anti-trust laws, *are* horse races. If you plan to put your money on Burroughs, you should also know something about IBM. If you contemplate investing in Chrysler Corporation, you

119

should understand what distinguishes it from Ford or **GM**. Also, even if you pick the outstanding stock in an industry, you may wind up unhappy if the outlook for the whole industry is dim. Failing to research the industry, not merely the company, is a common mistake of individual investors.

► *Look at sales.* Follow the company's annual sales for at least the past five years. Do they go up every year? If not, why not? What is the annual rate of increase for sales? How does the track record compare with that of competitors?

► *Look at earnings.* Almost no one omits this step, I admit. But do it carefully. First, track the earnings over at least a five-year period. Growing? If so, how fast? If not, why not? Look at both earnings in total dollars and earnings per share. If the two show varying patterns, find out why. Again, compare the growth pattern with that of competitors.

► *Look at profit margins.* Sometimes earnings can be going up while profit margins (earnings per dollar of sales) are going down. If this is the case, you may not be happy with the stock for as long as you expect. What exactly is the company's profit margin? What's the trend? How does the trend compare against—yes, you guessed it—that of competitors?

► *Look at cash flow.* Why should you look at anything as esoteric as cash flow? That's the company's internal business, isn't it? In a word, no. You should look at cash flow because it provides a useful cross-check on the validity of the earnings figures you analyzed earlier. There are a variety of accounting techniques that have the effect of enlarging reported earnings. But "paper earnings" may not be enough; companies also need cash, to pay for salaries, taxes, dividends, and reinvestment.

► *Check the "extraordinary items."* Apparent large jumps or dips in earnings can often be understood if you check on any extraordinary items (which are called precisely that) that

120

affected earnings. Essentially, an extraordinary item is a one-time event. For example, an airline might report a big boost in profits for a single year if it sold 50 of its planes during the year. The long-term implications of that step, however, might be unfavorable. Conversely, a conglomerate might report a loss, or diminished profits, in a year when it shut down an unprofitable division. But the company's long-term prospects might be enhanced by the step. Before buying a stock, you should know whether any extraordinary items have been reported for the last few years, how earnings would have looked without these items, and what the long-term implications of the actions in question seem to be.

▶ *Check for "qualifications."* Corporations with 500 or more shareholders must have their income statements and balance sheets audited by outside, independent auditors. Whether auditing firms are as independent as they should be is a complex and somewhat controversial question that we will not explore in depth. In any case, the auditor's report appears as part of the company's financial statement, and is usually *unqualified*. That means the auditors say the company's figures are fine: The figures "fairly present the financial position" of the company and are "in conformity with generally accepted accounting principles consistently applied."

With no wish to be nasty, we note that generally accepted accounting principles can cover a lot of ground. So, when an auditor actually tacks a qualification onto a report—saying, in effect, that the company's statement is *not* just fine and the auditor has doubts—investors should pay careful heed. Sometimes the auditor believes that a company has overstated the value of goods it owns or expects to receive. Sometimes the auditor believes that a company has understated a present or potential liability, such as that from a pending lawsuit. In any case, it behooves you to check any qualifications and under-

121

stand them. If your broker or financial adviser can't explain to your satisfaction what the fuss is about, avoid the stock.

► *Consider the dividend record.* Stocks with a consistent record of dividend payments are safer than stocks without such a record. They're safer in two ways. First, companies that regularly pay dividends are probably not running into the red (or at least not too far into the red) during downswings in the business cycle. Second, the dividend helps buoy up the total yield for the investor. Take a stock selling at 40, and paying an annual dividend of $2.40 per share, a 6% dividend yield. Say the stock falls to 35, but dividends remain unchanged. At that price, the stock yields 6.86%, which may cause some investors to buy the stock. The dividend helps keep the price from falling too far. Stocks without dividends have no such life preserver: When they fall, they may fall harder and further.

Of course, "safer" is not necessarily better. It depends on your tolerance for risk. If you're retired, or soon to be, then most likely any stocks you buy should be dividend-paying ones.

This is not to imply that dividends are guaranteed. Even a perfect track record for the past 30 years doesn't guarantee you that a dividend will be paid next quarter. But certainly the track record for dividend payments should be taken into account.

► *Look at the trend in capital spending.* Capital spending means spending on new facilities, which can increase production or make production more efficient. A business that is putting its money into expanded facilities presumably thinks the outlook is good. A business that is cutting back on capital spending may be preparing to concede a growing share of a particular market to competitors.

There are several ways you may wish to analyze capital spending patterns. You can look at the raw dollar total and

122

compare it wtih competitors. You can look at the trend of capital expenditures by the company over the past few years. You can evaluate capital spending as a percentage of revenues and of earnings—and, to put these percentages in focus, compare them to what others in the industry are doing.

▶ *Check out the company's debt structure.* As you'll recall from Chapter 3, companies raise money from outside sources in two ways: by borrowing, and by issuing stock. If you contemplate becoming a stockholder, you must realize that all of the banks, institutions, and individuals who hold a company's bonds or other debts must be paid before you get a penny.

It behooves you, therefore, to check out how much the company owes on bank loans, bonds, notes, and commercial paper. What does the annual interest payment on this debt amount to? And how does that amount compare with the company's annual earnings?

One statistic often used by investors is a company's *debt-to-equity ratio,* which compares the amount of debt with the amount of capital generated by selling stock or plowing back earnings into the company. A company with a high ratio of debt to equity is said to be *highly leveraged.* What's high? It depends on the type of company. Utilities may have half or more of their capitalization in the form of debt. For most industrial corporations, if debt is 30% or more of total capital, the investor should check into the situation carefully.

When business is good, a highly leveraged company will have higher profits per share than a company with little debt. However, if business turns sour, a heavy debt can become an albatross, which may delay or prevent payment of dividends to shareholders.

While you're looking at debt, you may also find it revealing to see how Moody's and Standard & Poor's rate the

---

Some Sample Debt Ratios

Here are the ratios of debt to total capital for ten companies as of early 1981. Figures are rounded to the nearest
integer. Source: *Moody's Handbook of Common Stocks.*

Company	*Debt as % of Total Capital*
Duke Power	44%
Dun & Bradstreet	0
DuPont	15%
Duquesne Light	45%
Easco	28%
Eastern Air Lines	71%
Eastern Gas & Fuel	32%
Eastman Kodak	3%
Eckerd	2%
El Paso	55%

---

company's bonds. If the bonds aren't highly rated, it's a fair
guess that the stock involves a significant amount of risk.

▶ *Examine market share trends.* This information isn't
always available, but if you can get it, it can be revealing.
Perhaps the company you're looking at is one of three or
four that dominate an industry. In that case, market share
may be 25% to 50%, or even higher. In more broadly competitive industries, a market share as high as 10% would be
outstanding. What concerns you is not so much the size of
the slice of the pie, but whether that slice is growing or
shrinking.

▶ *Consider the company's governmental relations.* Whether
you applaud it or decry it, the fact is that government has
become entwined in the functioning of private enterprise.
Companies must deal with one or more federal regulatory
agencies (such as the Food and Drug Administration, Environmental Protection Administration, Federal Trade Com-

mission, and Occupational Safety and Health Administration), and often with a battery of state agencies as well. If the company whose stock you're considering has a history of adversary relationships with regulators, it's possible that regulatory tangles could dilute future earnings.

▶ *Consider the company's ethical standards.* Are the products it makes useful? Are they safe? Does the company treat its workers fairly? What is the company's record with regard to pollution?

There are two reasons why investors may want to consider questions of this kind. One reason has to do with the ethical stance of the investor. The other reason is that ethical considerations ultimately affect a company's profitability. A company may successfully merchandise a shabby product for a while. But there is a good chance consumers will eventually catch on. A company may cut costs for a while by neglecting product safety. But the marketplace is likely to wreak its vengeance eventually through product liability suits. A company may save money temporarily by treating workers poorly. But in the long run, such treatment makes for bad labor relations, absenteeism, inefficiency, and strikes. Pollution control can also be neglected for a while, with temporary savings. But the cost of catching up later may be heavy—and may be augmented by governmentally assessed penalties or private lawsuits.

▶ *Think twice before investing in companies with a high price-earnings multiple.* Companies with high multiples may be, and often are, excellent companies. That does not necessarily make them good buys. As we noted earlier, for you to make money in a high-multiple stock, the company must do even better than expected. Several studies have shown that stocks with comparatively low multiples offer a better potential for long-term appreciation.

▶ *Try to learn the stock's beta.* We discussed betas on

pages 112–119. If you plan to buy and hold for the long term, I generally favor stocks with an above-average beta. This is advice for people who are confident they will not be pressured into selling at a disadvantageous time. For further safety, I recommend that people who buy high-beta stocks be especially conscientious about diversifying.

It's important for investors to remember that beta is not synonymous with risk. Beta measures only one kind of risk—volatility in relation to general market movements. Other types of risk include the risk of adverse developments affecting the particular company, and the risk of adverse developments affecting the industry. (These risks, especially the first, are sometimes called *alpha*.) When you hear talk about a risky stock, it's probably these types of risk that are meant, not the stock's beta. To cite one example, gold stocks have low betas, but they are risky. The mere fact that a stock has a high beta does not tell you whether it is risky or not, in the comprehensive sense. Some high-beta stocks would properly be called speculations, others are companies with a solid record of earnings and dividend payments. In short, a high beta simply means that the stock tends to react more dramatically than the average stock does to upward and downward trends in the market.

For convenience, here's a summary of the 15 points we've just made about picking individual stocks.

Stock Picker's Checklist

1. Research the industry, not just the stock.
2. Look at sales.
3. Look at earnings.
4. Look at profit margins.
5. Look at cash flow.
6. Check the "extraordinary items."

7. Check for "qualifications."
8. Consider the dividend record.
9. Look at the trend in capital spending.
10. Check out the company's debt structure.
11. Examine market share trends.
12. Consider the company's governmental relations.
13. Consider the company's ethical standards.
14. Think twice before investing in a company with a high price-earnings multiple.
15. Try to learn the company's beta.

Where do you get all of this information? At your public library, and/or your broker's office. Many public libraries have extensive collections of investment reference material. I suggest using the *Business Periodicals Index* and the *Wall Street Journal Index*, to find useful articles in such business periodicals as *Forbes, Fortune, Business Week, Barron's, Financial World,* and the *Wall Street Journal.* Before making a decision on an individual stock, read the latest report issued on that stock by three major financial advisory services: Moody's, Standard & Poor's, and Value Line. Your public librarian or broker can usually help you find these reports.

Your stock portfolio.

Diversify. If you've read this far in this book, the word must be getting familiar. If you've read other investment books, you've probably heard it before. A lot of people recommend it. Not everyone practices it.

If you had a crystal ball, you would have no need to diversify. Each year, you would simply buy the one stock, among the 11,000 or so that are publicly owned, that was going to rack up the biggest gains. Diversifying would only lessen your total return.

It's certainly true that if you are fortunate enough to select a stock that dramatically outperforms the market, you do better by not diversifying. Unfortunately, minus a crystal ball, you have no way of knowing that you can do this. The hot stock you bought on a tip from your brother-in-law may rise 10 points, then drop 30. Most people can't afford to leave themselves exposed to this possibility. Diversifying lessens your risk.

But that's not all it does. It also gives you more chances to gain. *Forbes* Magazine pointed this out in trying to explain the success of its Dart-Board Fund, discussed earlier in this chapter. There were 28 stocks in the Dart-Board Fund. The value of the portfolio went from $28,000 in 1967 to $43,279 in 1979—a 55% gain during a period when the market averages hardly budged. Yet of those 28 stocks, 13 actually declined over that 12-year period.

The point is that, in a diversified portfolio, your losers can only lose 100% of their value, but your winners can gain much more. (In the case of the Forbes Dart-Board Fund, seven stocks gained more than 100%; one rose 848%.) The actual loss on *Forbes'* 13 losers was 17%, but even if those 13 companies had gone out of business, the portfolio would still have shown a profit.

The first basic principle of stock investing, then, is to diversify your holdings.

But how is this to be achieved? And how much diversification is enough? Value Line recommends that an individual investor's portfolio should consist of at least 15 stocks, drawn from at least 8 industries. I agree, that constitutes a well-diversified portfolio. But most individual investors can't accumulate such a portfolio overnight. For this reason, your first venture into the stock market should probably be through a mutual fund. (See Chapter 10.)

Next to diversification, the most important principle, in

my view, is to hold stocks for the long term. Attempting to make money in the stock market by frequent trading is extremely difficult, for three reasons.

First, the short-term trader does not get the income-tax advantages (60% tax deduction, as of 1981) that people who buy and hold for the longer term do.

Second, if you buy and sell a lot, you'll incur a lot of transaction costs. Say you buy 100 shares of a stock at $50 and sell 11 months later at $55. Your stock racked up an impressive 10% gain. But if you pay, say, $160 in commissions and another $160 in taxes (which you well might), your real gain is whittled down to 3.6%.

Third, and perhaps most important, you probably can't predict what a stock is going to do in the short run. A good deal of academic research has shown that, aside from the long-term upward trend, stock movements can be perfectly imitated by a computer using purely random processes. Princeton's Burton Malkiel had his students draw up stock charts based on the results of repeated coin flips. The charts looked convincing enough to fool a stock-market technical analyst.

Am I saying you can't make money in the stock market in the short term? Of course not. You can; perhaps you have; perhaps you know someone who has. What I'm saying is that the results of a strategy of frequent trading have been uniformly shown by studies to be inferior to the results of a strategy of buying and holding for the long term.

Incidentally, the Forbes Dart-Board Fund helped to convince the editors of *Forbes* that a buy-and-hold strategy makes sense. After reciting the history of the fund, the editors wrote (in 1979): "The moral? Stick with your picks. Your typical investor, professional or amateur, would have been tempted to take his profits early on the winners and so would have missed out on much of their gains. . . . The old rule is: Cut your losses and let your profits run. Our experience would lead us to rephrase that to: Let both your profits and your losses run."

The second basic principle of stock investing, then, is: Buy and hold. Pick your stocks carefully, and, once you've bought them, sell them only for the most compelling of reasons.*

Following this strategy makes considerations of timing less important than they are for the frequent trader. However, even the long-term investor should consider the proper timing for acquiring stocks. What you want to avoid is buying your whole portfolio, or a large chunk of it, at a market peak. If you do that, you may have to wait a long time indeed for any gains, since it frequently takes years for the market to regain a previously attained peak.

Unfortunately, market peaks are precisely the time when inexperienced investors may be most tempted to buy. When the Dow-Jones and other stock averages have been gaining for several months, when many stocks are selling at all-time highs, the mood on Wall Street is often euphoric. Prognosticators predict more of the same. Chartists (people who try to predict future price movements on the basis of charts of past movements) are full of talk of "breakouts" and "up-trends." Naturally, you might be filled with enthusiasm for the stock market. Yet this, chances are, is not the wise time to buy.

The wisest time to buy is when stock prices are sagging, the economy is chugging along on three cylinders, and the forecasts are gloomy. At such times, stocks sell for price-

* Examples of compelling reasons: 1. You're getting near retirement age, and want to shift to more conservative investments. 2. You need cash to buy a home, or for another genuinely pressing purpose. 3. The company you bought stock in is about to be merged out of existence. 4. You no longer feel the stock has good prospects; you expect it to go down, and you have identified another stock that you believe to be at least twice as good a value.

130

earnings multiples below normal. If you buy and hold for the long term, there's a good chance that both corporate earnings and multiples will increase, giving you a double chance to turn a profit.

What we are suggesting is that the ideal investor, in regard to timing, goes contrary to the conventional wisdom about the stock market at a given time. He or she is, in Wall Street jargon, a *contrarian*. There are, however, two problems with being a contrarian. One is that there are sometimes (as in the 1960s) long, relatively uninterrupted rises in stock prices. If you avoid buying at such times, you have to wait a long time to buy, and you miss out on some substantial profits. Second, and probably more important, the perfect contrarian owns a crystal ball, and you don't. How are you to know whether the market is peaking or still on the rise, bottoming out or still on the decline? It's not so easy, in practice, given the random zigzagging of stock prices. Sometimes it's not even easy to tell whether the market is in an uptrend or a downtrend. Given this state of uncertainty, the most practical way to avoid acquiring your portfolio at a market peak may be to acquire it a bit at a time, staggering your stock purchases over the months and years. Never keep 100% of your available money in the stock market. You should always keep a little "powder dry" to take advantage of market declines.

Once you have decided to embark on a program of stock purchases (and assuming you are keeping up your prerequisites for investment—your liquid fund, backup fund, insurance, and properly managed debt), you should probably keep going, investing something every year until you have a diversified portfolio. Whatever you do, don't skip investing one year because the stock market is down! That is precisely the best time to invest for the long haul.

The third basic principle of stock buying, then, is to time your acquisitions appropriately. That can mean either buying when price-earnings multiples are down, or staggering pur-chases over a period of time, to take advantage of market movements.

While we're discussing timing, let's take a moment to consider a fairly popular technique known as *dollar-cost averaging.* It consists of buying a fixed dollar amount of a certain stock (or mutual fund) at regularly spaced intervals. For example, you might buy $500 worth of Pan American World Airways stock every two months. Suppose that you do this, and that the prices of the stock on your first six acquisi-tion dates are $6, $5, $7, $6, $5, and $6. You will have in-vested, of course, $3,000. For that money, you will have acquired 520 shares (83, 100, 71, 83, 100, and 83 on the six occasions). At the end of the period, the value of your 520 shares is $3,120. You have a 4% capital gain, even though the price of the stock was unchanged during the pe-riod. Without dollar-cost averaging, you would have no gain at all. The principle behind the technique is that, by investing a fixed amount each time, you acquire more shares when the price is down, fewer when the price is up. Suppose the price pattern went: $6, $5, $4, $6, $5, $7. Then you'd wind up with 562 shares, and a profit of $934, compared with $500 if you didn't use dollar-cost averaging. Sounds good, doesn't it?

The trouble is, the technique doesn't always increase your profits; it can also backfire. Suppose the price series was $6, $5, $7, $9, $5, $7. Then dollar-cost averaging would pro-duce a profit of $360, but putting the whole $300 into the stock at the beginning would have produced a $500 profit.

What if the stock moves smartly upward? Let's say the price series was: $6, $8, $7, $9, $8, $10. In that case, dollar-cost averaging brings you a profit of $830. But investing the whole $3,000 at the start would have gained you $2,000.

It turns out that dollar-cost averaging, from the theoretical standpoint, tends to be advantageous when a stock trades within a narrow range. If the stock declines, you lose money, but less than you would ordinarily. If the stock does well, you gain money, but less than you would ordinarily.

In actual practice, dollar-cost averaging has some additional drawbacks. In most cases, you will have to pay brokerage commissions when you engage in securities transactions. The more frequent your transactions, the higher the commission cost. Another practical problem is the matter of nerve. It takes nerves of considerable firmness to consider making periodic investments in a stock when it's going down. However, if you don't do this, you incur the major disadvantage of dollar-cost averaging (higher commissions) while forfeiting most of the technique's advantages. Dollar-cost averaging may also tend to inhibit diversification by committing you in advance to putting available investment money into the selected stock. Thus, even though the technique does sometimes work, I don't recommend it.

Another practice brokers sometimes recommend might be considered as a simplified form of dollar-cost averaging. It's called *averaging out*. What that means, quite simply, is that if you've bought a stock and it goes down, you should buy some more. That may sound unwise at first blush, but it's not necessarily a bad idea. *If* the stock appeared to you when you bought it to be undervalued, and to have good prospects for long-term appreciation, and *if* subsequent events haven't changed your mind about the intrinsic merits of the stock, buying more could make sense. Perhaps the stock declined simply because the market as a whole declined, and price-earnings multiples are now lower. The stock could be more of a bargain now than when you first bought it.

The broker may point out that by buying more of the fallen stock, you lower your average cost per share of your holdings in that stock. This increases your chances of making a profit in that stock. That's true, but it misses the point of your investment program. You are not trying to maximize the number of winners you pick; you are trying to maximize the number of dollars you have. It isn't crucial whether you make a profit in a particular stock; it is important that you try to make your overall portfolio profitable.

Seen in this light, averaging out becomes an empty concept. You have a certain amount of money to invest at the moment. You may wish to put it in a stock you've bought before that's declined, if you still feel that stock represents an excellent value at the price. But you are equally free to select any other stock that currently seems undervalued. One advantage to picking a new stock is that it increases the diversification of your portfolio.

Let's now sum up what we've said in this section. Here are four basic principles for investing in stocks.

1. *Diversify*. Make your first purchase a mutual fund (see Chapter 12). In subsequent purchases, don't put all your eggs in one basket; invest in various companies in several industries, over time. The diversified stock portfolio you are building might ultimately include at least 15 companies from 8 different industries.

2. *Buy and hold*. It's likely that the market will head upward in the long run. What it will do in the short run is extremely hard to predict. Short-term trading also involves heavier brokerage costs and higher taxes.

3. *Time your stock purchases appropriately* by spreading your purchases over time, and by preferring bear markets to bull markets as a time for accumulating stocks to hold for the long term.

4. *In picking individual stocks, keep in mind the 15 suggestions on the Stock Picker's Checklist, pages 126–127.*

12

Mutual Funds

Almost any kind of investment can be made through a mutual fund. For small investors, it's an approach that makes a lot of sense—not because the fund will pick more wisely than you, but because its holdings are more diversified than yours would be.

Suppose you're just starting out in stocks. If you've got a limited stake, and don't want to pay a fortune in commissions, you'd end up buying only one or two stocks—and that can be dangerous. Through a mutual fund specializing in common stocks, you get instant diversification.

The same is true for bonds or money-market instruments. Through a bond fund or money market fund, you can quickly diversify your holdings. You want gold? Consider a gold fund. Instead of simply owning a few gold coins (and having to pay to insure them and store them), you can own a share of a diversified portfolio that may include bullion, coins, and gold-mining securities. These days funds are offering a wide variety of choices, including specialized ones. There are funds for investing in Eurodollars, foreign stocks, commodities, tax-exempt securities—you name it.

Most funds, however, invest principally in stocks. For that reason, and because I believe that common stocks are the average investor's best choice for the 1980s, this chapter is devoted mainly to common-stock mutual funds.

All of these funds are run by professional money managers (by definition, right?). This may give you some comfort, and, if so, fine. The truth is that the professionals who run the funds probably won't do much better in the long run than the overall market averages (or comparable yardsticks, for funds that invest in vehicles other than stocks). The reason to consider mutual funds is not that they'll necessarily do better than you could on your own. It's that they give you, at once, the kind of diversified portfolio it would otherwise take years to assemble.

For this reason, I suggest that most people's first investment or two in stocks (and most other risk-prone vehicles) should be made through a mutual fund.

What, exactly, is a mutual fund? It's an organization that pools the money of a large number of investors, and invests it in any of a large variety of ways. (The investment philosophy of a fund, and the type of investments it makes, are spelled out in its prospectus, and in some reference books described later in this chapter.) When you buy shares of a fund, you own a portion of that pool. A fund might, for example, have a $5 million portfolio including $100,000 worth of stock in each of 25 companies. If there were 25,000 shares of the fund in existence, the value of each share would be roughly $200. If you owned 10 shares, your holdings would be worth roughly $2,000.

I said "roughly" because the total value of the fund's portfolio is reduced slightly by the fund's operating expenses, and by the management fee imposed by the fund's managers. Subtract these from the total value of the portfolio and you have the *net asset value*. Divide that by the number of shares and you have the *net asset value per share,* which is what's printed every day in the newspapers. The good news is that expenses and management fee together usually amount to only 1% or less of the portfolio's total value. In the example above, if we assume a 1% difference between gross and net asset values, your net asset value per share would be $198.

When you achieve diversification, you accomplish two things. First, you limit your risk of a disaster from having all your eggs in one—spilled—basket. Second, you increase the chances that your portfolio's performance will approximate the norm. The fewer stocks you own, the more likely you are to do much better or much worse than the market averages. The more stocks you own, the more likely it is that your portfolio will perform about in line with the Dow Jones Industrials, Standard & Poor's 500, the New York Stock Exchange Index, or whatever yardstick you use to measure investment performance. The ultimate step in diversification is to buy an "index fund" that holds, for example, shares in each company in the Standard & Poor's 500.

Doing as well as the averages is nothing to sneeze at. In the 1979 edition of *Mutual Funds Almanac,* by Yale Hirsch, there is a chart titled "Stocks: The Perfect Long-Term Inflation Hedge." It points out that for any 25-year period between 1928–1953 and 1953–1978, an investment in stocks would have produced a real increase in assets relative to inflation. By contrast, a person who put money in a savings account would have lost money, in real terms, during 23 of the 26 periods under consideration. An adaptation of portions of that chart appears on page 138.

One thing the table dramatizes is the pernicious effect of inflation during the most recent 25 years. Even though the nominal return on a savings account for the period 1953–1978 was higher than in any previous period, in real terms the person who kept his or her money in a savings account during that period was losing money. The person who kept

HOW $1,000 GREW—OR SHRUNK

Value of Investment at End of 25 Years, if Money Is Put into Specified Investment

25-Year Period	Simple Total			Total Adjusted for Inflation		
	Mattress	Savings Account	Stocks	Mattress	Savings Account	Stocks
1928–1953	$1,000	$1,580	$2,472	$637	$1,006	$1,575
1933–1958	$1,000	$1,522	$13,993	$448	$682	$6,273
1938–1963	$1,000	$1,607	$11,408	$457	$737	$5,209
1943–1968	$1,000	$1,739	$15,047	$500	$889	$7,524
1948–1973	$1,000	$2,024	$10,043	$541	$1,094	$5,429
1953–1978	$1,000	$2,273	$5,835	$395	$898	$2,305

The figures in the table on return from savings accounts were based on passbook rates paid during the applicable periods by savings banks in the state of New York. The figures for return on stock investments were based on the Dow Jones average of 30 industrial stocks. Both sets of figures took into account income taxes (at a 23% rate); the figures for stocks did not include capital gains taxes, but did include a 2% charge for commissions. Dividends were assumed to be taxed and reinvested.

Source: *Mutual Funds Almanac*, 1979 edition.

his or her money in stocks came out ahead in real terms, but not so far ahead as in previous historical periods.

On balance, the figures suggest that holding a diversified portfolio of common stocks—even one that does no better than the market averages—has been, over the years, a good way to counter inflation and accumulate assets. The easiest and quickest way to get that sort of a portfolio is by proxy, through a mutual fund.

According to the Investment Company Institute (ICI), a trade group for mutual funds, $10,000 invested in the average mutual fund* in 1953 would have grown (assuming reinvestment of dividends) to $79,064 by the end of 1977. The average yearly rate of return over that 25-year period was calculated by the ICI at 8.6%—about in line with the 9% total return we talked about earlier as the average return on common stocks. (Don't compare that figure with today's bond yields—bond yields were a lot lower in 1953–1973.)

From mid-1974 to mid-1980, the average common-stock mutual fund went up about 115%, versus about 80% for the Standard & Poor's 500, and about 50% for the Dow Jones industrials. Does this mean that mutual-fund managers have learned the magic secret of beating the averages? It probably means no such thing. (In large part, it probably means that funds were holding more volatile stocks while the market was in an uptrend.) In the long run, I'd still expect the performance of the average mutual fund to be about equal to the broad market indicators. But that, to repeat, is nothing to sneeze at, particularly since the "av-

* The average of the 32 growth-and-income funds in existence during the period 1953–1977. The ICI tally assumed that the buyer paid 8½% of his or her initial investment as a sales commission. That practice was almost universal in 1953, but now there are many no-commission, or "no-load" funds.

erages" don't have to pay taxes or brokerage commissions.

Most funds disdain this book's advice to buy and hold. But then, they can better afford to trade frequently than you can. As large institutions, they negotiate much smaller brokerage commissions than the individual has to pay.

In sum, a mutual fund is a good starting place for an investment program in securities. After you've gotten started, and have a bit of diversification, you'll probably want to launch out on your own.

Types of mutual funds.

More than 700 mutual funds operate in the United States. There are funds that aim for income, funds that aim for capital gains, and funds that split up the two and let you take your pick. There are money market funds, gold funds, commodity funds. There are growth funds, performance funds, balanced funds. There are even "social-responsibility" funds. In short, there's a mutual fund to suit almost every taste.

Before we get into specifics, let's look at the large view for a moment. Mutual funds are distinguished from each other in two basic ways: according to their structure, and according to their financial objectives.

In terms of fund structure, the basic distinctions are between load funds and no-load funds, and between open- and closed-end funds.

▶ *Load versus no-load.* About two-thirds of all mutual funds are sold by salespeople, who are paid a commission by the fund. Some funds employ their own sales force, others sell through securities brokers. In either case, the commission is reflected in the price the buyer pays for shares of the fund.

The commission, or "load," is often 7½% to 8½% of the price of the shares; 8½% is the maximum, by order of the Securities and Exchange Commission (SEC). Thus, a load fund with a net asset value of $50 per share might cost you $54 a share to buy. That means the fund shares would have to increase in value 8% before you would begin to have any profit.

A no-load fund has no sales force. It simply waits for investors to request information or to buy shares. Investors may learn of its existence by word of mouth, through newspaper or magazine articles or ads, or by reading any of several reference books about mutual funds, described later in this chapter. The benefit of this arrangement is that the buyer pays no load, or sales fee. You do still pay the management fee, which typically amounts to less than 1% for both load and no-load funds. If you buy a no-load fund, you begin to make profits as soon as the net asset value per share increases.

Why would anyone, then, buy a load fund? The theoretical answer is that you might buy one if you expected it to have particularly good performance. And there may be a couple of load funds that might reasonably be bought on the basis of their track records. In the vast majority of cases, though, no-load funds are better. As a group, the no-load funds have not only performed as well as load funds, they have outperformed them—and by a margin considerably greater than the 8% or so attributable to the commission differential.

The practical answer to the question why anyone would buy a load fund is that in many cases the funds are more sold than bought. A skilled salesman may make a persuasive pitch for a particular fund (a load fund of course), and an investor may buy it, sometimes without fully understanding the differences between load and no-load funds. The public, however, has been catching on to the advantages of no-load funds. In 1979, no-load funds, though they accounted for only about a third of all funds, racked up more than 44% of all mutual-fund sales. That was up from about 23% in 1976, and only around 8% in 1967. It's clear that competitive pressures are pushing the mutual-fund industry toward dealing directly with the public, rather than selling through commissioned salespeople.

▶ *Open versus closed-end funds.* Strictly speaking, there's no such thing as a closed-end mutual fund. There are only closed-end investment companies. A mutual fund is open-ended if it will at all times accept new money for investment. When a new investor enters the pool, it has no immediate effect on the net asset value per share, because the assets and the number of shares outstanding rise in precisely the same proportion.

A closed-end investment company works differently. It has a fixed number of shares outstanding, and these shares are listed on one or more of the major stock exchanges. If you want to buy some shares, you buy them not from the investment company but through your broker; the shares you acquire come from a previous holder (except in the case of a brand-new closed-end investment company in which you are one of the initial investors). The price you pay for the shares will naturally rise or fall depending on how the investment company is doing with its investments. You might expect that the price you'd pay would be rather close to the net asset value per share, but in practice there are often considerable differences. The closed-end investment funds tend to rise and fall depending on investors' estimates of their probable future performance, and also depending on fluctuations in the stock market as a whole. At times, as in 1979 and 1980 for example, many closed-end investment company shares were priced at a substantial discount from net asset value. At other times, when investors are more optimistic, some closed-end investment company shares sell at a premium above net asset value.

When the time comes to sell your shares in an open-end mutual fund, you know that you can sell them back to the fund ("redeem" them) at the current net asset value per share. When you want to sell shares in a closed-end fund, you have to do it on the open market, and the price you'll get depends on what a willing buyer is then willing to pay.

Which type of fund, open or closed-end, is better for you? There are a number of pros and cons. When you buy a closed-end fund, you must pay a broker's commission. That's likely to be considerably smaller than the hefty sales commission on a load mutual fund, but of course it's greater than nothing, which is precisely the commission on a no-load fund. So, if everything else is equal, you're best off buying a regular, open-ended mutual fund of the no-load variety.

But everything else may not be equal. You might find a closed-end fund whose track record so captivated you that you were eager to invest in it. Or, more likely, you might be interested in a closed-end fund because it was selling at a substantial discount from net asset value.

Why do closed-end funds sometimes sell at discounts? Here are three possible reasons. 1. Their prices can get swept down in general downward movements of the market. 2. Their prices can reflect investors' anticipation of a downturn in the market. 3. They may suffer from lack of demand due to the fact that they aren't advertised or pushed by brokers. This last is the theory of Burton Malkiel, who points out that brokers make a much smaller commission selling a closed-end fund than selling a load fund. In his book *A Random Walk Down Wall Street,* Malkiel suggests you should buy closed-end fund shares when they're selling at a discount—particularly a discount deeper than is the historic norm for that particular investment company.

Buying closed-end shares at a discount gives you three chances to gain. First, your chosen closed-end investment company may invest well, pushing up the net asset value of the shares. Second, the discount may narrow, which would give you a capital gain. Third, as Malkiel points out, "Even if the discount does not narrow, you will tend to improve your return from closed-end companies, since for every dollar you put in you will have more than a dollar invested on which dividends can be earned. So if the fund just equals the market return, you will beat the averages."

Financial objectives.

At least as important as the structure of a mutual fund is the financial objective it pursues. Here's a breakdown, by investment objective, of the 524 mutual funds that reported to the Investment Company Institute (ICI) in 1979. (The figures represent the number of funds in existence of each type.)

142 Growth funds

 76 Growth and income funds

 76 Money market funds

 54 Bond funds

 54 Income funds

 50 Aggressive growth funds

 41 Municipal bond funds

 21 Balanced funds

 10 Options income funds

Let's take a look at how these funds work. We'll begin with the most conservative types of mutual funds, which invest in fixed-return vehicles. We'll then proceed to those that invest primarily in stocks, and close with a mention of some specialized or unusual types of mutual funds.

▶ *Money market funds* are discussed in Chapter 6. They invest, as we noted earlier, in short-term interest-bearing IOUs issued by corporations, banks, and the government. In the late 1970s and early 1980s, when short-term interest rates were extremely high, these funds—which came into being only a few years earlier—were the most popular type of mutual funds with individual investors. People have flocked to the money funds for a combination of safety, liquidity, and high yield. Eventually, as short-term interest rates decline, their appeal is likely to be less strong.

▶ *Corporate bond funds* are discussed in Chapter 8. They offer the individual investor a way to buy into a diversified bond portfolio. You might be able to get a higher total return (through a combination of current yield and capital gain) by buying a single bond on your own, but in doing so you're assuming more risk.

▶ *Municipal bond funds* are discussed in Chapter 9. They operate on the same principle as corporate bond funds, but are for higher-bracket investors interested in tax-sheltered income.

▶ *Income funds* typically hold a blend of bonds and high-yielding common stocks (such as utility stocks), and sometimes preferred stocks as well. As with a bond fund, the goal is a steady yield, not dramatic capital gains. In that case, you may ask, why not simply hold a bond fund if yield's your goal? One possible answer is that an income fund might provide you with greater flexibility. In times when interest rates are rising, bond funds will often show a decline in price per share, because the value of the underlying bonds declines (see Chapter 8). At such times, very high yields can often be found on some common stocks of major companies. Holding these stocks may provide some opportunity for capital gains. Over the past decade, income funds have shown great variation in their performance, some doing quite well, others poorly.

▶ *Balanced funds* are similar to income funds, but with a shade of difference. Income funds do not make it a stated objective to achieve long-term capital gains; balanced funds do. Still, the portfolios of both contain a mixture of stocks

145

and bonds, and the blend may change over time. If you're choosing between an income fund and a balanced fund, the line is fuzzy enough so that you should pay attention to the funds' actual investment results and portfolios, and ignore the nomenclature.

▶ *Growth and income funds.* These funds hold portfolios consisting primarily or exclusively of stocks, not bonds. They avoid stocks that pay no dividends, and try to strike a balance between attempting to achieve capital gains, and producing a steady flow of income for their investors. The yield on a growth and income fund will normally be lower than the yield on a bond fund, income fund, or balanced fund (in 1981, you might expect a yield of something like 4% on a growth and income fund), but the chance for capital gains will normally be greater.

▶ *Growth funds.* When you invest in a growth fund, you are deciding to place little importance on current income or yield, and to concentrate instead on achieving capital gains. Growth funds invest primarily or exclusively in stocks, without much regard to the size of dividends those stocks are currently paying. These funds tend to be more volatile in price than the funds we've discussed up to now. As the ICI breakdown makes clear, these are the single most common type of mutual fund. Within the broad category of growth fund, there may be found funds with varying investment philosophies regarding long- versus short-term growth, the selection of stocks, the percentage of assets (if any) to be put into money-market vehicles to reduce risk, and so on. You can become aware of some of these differences by studying comparisons of funds' performance, reading fund literature (including the prospectus of any fund you are particularly interested in), and checking the reference book *Investment Companies,* by Wiesenberger Services, Inc.

▶ *Aggressive growth funds,* sometimes known as per-

146

formance funds, are a further extension down the continuum of risk. They may magnify their profits and losses through the use of leverage, i.e., borrowing. They may invest in highly speculative stocks, small companies, or emerging technologies. The prices of aggressive growth funds tend to be even more volatile than those of ordinary growth funds: They may be on top of the charts one year, on the bottom the next. Often, they will pay no dividends, but will automatically invest any dividends or capital gains from the portfolio into the purchase of additional shares. (This may be true of ordinary growth funds, too.)

Since the market often tends to reward risk, aggressive growth funds can be a good purchase for certain investors. But consider these funds only if your portfolio also includes a reasonable proportion of less risky assets, and only if you have the staying power to shoot for gains over the long term. It would be a shame if you purchased an aggressive growth fund, only to find that a need for money forced you to sell it while it was in the down phase of a roller-coaster price path.

▶ *Options funds,* as their name implies, engage in buying and selling stock options (see Chapter 18). Since options trading is highly risky and often highly speculative, you might think these funds would be the same. To the contrary, most of them are actually *options income funds,* which use options in a conservative way—mainly by selling covered calls (explained in Chapter 18)—to augment dividend income. The track record of the options funds goes back only to 1977, so it may be too early to judge. But their record in the first couple of years has been uninspiring.

In addition to the types of funds catalogued by ICI, there are a couple of additional types worth mentioning here.

▶ *A hedge fund* is a variation on an aggressive growth fund. It usually shoots for short-term gains. Not only does it buy speculative stocks, it also sells short stocks it expects to decline (see Chapter 16).

▶ An *index fund* invests in a cross section of the stocks that compose one of the major stock averages, such as the Dow Jones average of 30 industrial stocks, or the Standard & Poor's 500. The idea is to allow the investor to ride with overall market movements and obtain broad diversification. When you buy an index fund, you don't expect to do better than "the market" as a whole, but neither do you have to fear doing much worse.

▶ A *multifund* has the same basic goal as an index fund— broad diversification, and performance approximating that of the market averages. A multifund achieves this aim simply by buying and holding shares of other mutual funds.

▶ A *social-conscience fund* attempts to invest in the stock of companies that have demonstrated an unusual degree of social responsibility. Probably the best known such fund is the Dreyfus Third Century Fund.

▶ A *dual-purpose fund* is one in which some investors get nothing but the capital gains (or losses) from the fund's portfolio, and other investors get nothing but the current income (dividends). The theory is that you get more bang for your investment dollar. Put in one dollar and you get close to two dollars' worth of either capital gains (or losses) or close to two dollars' worth of dividends. The theory is elegant, but results have been spotty. In the past decade, some dual-purpose funds have performed fairly well, others poorly. Generally, investors seeking income have fared better than those seeking capital gains. Most dual-purpose funds were founded in 1967, when the market was concluding a long-term upswing, and their investment performance has been a victim of this timing. Most dual-purpose funds are scheduled to dissolve between 1979 and 1985; whether new ones will be formed remains to be seen. The shares of most of these funds are traded on the New York Stock Exchange; some are traded over the counter.

▶ *Industry funds* specialize in the stocks of a particular industry grouping, like energy stocks, insurance stocks, or gold stocks. They may be a good addition to an existing investment portfolio, but I wouldn't suggest them for a first purchase. Not enough diversification.

▶ *Foreign funds* are vehicles designed to make it convenient (or, at any rate, possible) for U.S. citizens to invest in the stocks issued by corporations in other countries. There are only a few of these funds currently available, but some of them have been good investments during the past decade. In particular, the Japan Fund and Templeton Growth Fund of Canada have been outstanding investments, growing at compound annual rates of about 20% and about 17%, respectively. These rates of return look particularly good in contrast to the doldrums of the U.S. stock market during the past decade. (Interestingly, Templeton Growth Fund, which shifts funds from country to country according to its judgment as to where the best bargains are, shifted some 60% of its investments to the United States in 1979.)

One advantage to owning a fund for investing abroad is that it provides a further measure of diversification: One is investing not only in U.S. securities, but in the securities of other countries as well. Against this advantage may be weighed a couple of drawbacks: an extra measure of red tape, and some possible extra taxation, since you'll be paying taxes on your investment in more than one country.

Choosing a mutual fund.

Begin by thinking about the type of fund you want. Load or no-load? Open-ended or closed-end? A growth fund, bond fund, index fund? Further research may change your mind, but it helps to start with a concrete idea of the kind of fund you're after.

To narrow down your search to a few candidates, two sources of information may be particularly helpful. One is the Annual Mutual Fund Survey of *Forbes* Magazine, normally published in August. *Forbes* compares the performance of several hundred funds (652 in 1980) with the Standard & Poor's 500 stock average, and grades each fund (from A+ to F) for its performance during rising markets, and during falling markets. *Forbes* also provides figures for each fund on the latest 12-months' performance and (more important, in my view) 10-year average annual growth rate. To facilitate comparisons and investment decisions, *Forbes* clusters the funds into groupings. In 1980, the major groupings were stock funds, funds for investing abroad, balanced funds, bond and preferred stock funds, exchange funds,* dual-purpose funds, new funds, money market funds, and municipal bond funds. Some of these groupings were subdivided into load funds, no-load funds, and closed-end funds.

A second good resource for your initial research is *Mutual Funds Almanac* by Yale Hirsch, published annually by the Hirsch Organization, Inc., 6 Deer Trail, Old Tappan, N.J. 07675. As of 1980, the almanac cost $20. It provides a readable introduction to mutual funds and issues related to investing in mutual funds, plus year-by-year investment performance information on more than 600 funds. Of particular interest is a column that shows what a hypothetical investment of $10,000 would have grown to, over the past five years and over the past ten years, if invested in a particular

---

* Exchange funds are a tax-avoidance gimmick. They have been legal, illegal, legal again, and illegal again. No new ones can be started, but the old ones are allowed to continue.

The Forbes Honor Roll

Every year, *Forbes* Magazine selects, from hundreds of mutual funds, a few that it designates with "honor roll" status. In 1980, 19 funds were designated. Only funds that had been in existence since 1968, and had achieved an average total return of at least 8% from 1968 to 1980 were eligible. To make the list, a fund had to do well, consistently, in both up and down markets.

Shown below are the nine funds that were on the 1980 honor roll and had achieved an average annual return (from 1968 to 1980) of more than 10%.

		Ratings		Total
	Type	*Up Markets*	*Down Markets*	*Return*
ASA Limited	closed-end	B	A+	22.8%
International Investors	load	B	A+	21.0%
Templeton Growth Fund	load	A	A+	18.9%
Petroleum & Resources Corp.	closed-end	A+	B	13.1%
Charter Fund	load	A+	A	12.2%
Mutual Shares	no-load	B	A	12.1%
Over-the-Counter Securities Fund	load	B	A+	12.0%
20th Century Select Investors	no-load	A	A	11.0%
Founders Special Fund	no-load	A	A	10.7%

fund. The data on most funds are grouped together. Separate groupings are provided for closed-end funds, dual-purpose funds, and money market funds. The almanac also provides a list of the top 25 funds for each of the past 10 years, and of the top 50 funds, as ranked by total return over a 5-year and 10-year period.

Once you have narrowed down your search to just a few candidates, you can get more detailed information about each one by consulting an outstanding reference book called *Investment Companies,* published by Wiesenberger Services, Inc. (it is available at many libraries). You should also write each fund you're considering to obtain a prospectus. By studying the prospectus, you should be able to learn just about everything you want to know about a fund's organization, management, and track record.

Shown below are the names of some funds that have

	Sum that $10,000 Grew to over 10-year Period
Name of Fund	*1970–1979*
1. International Investors	$75,181
2. Templeton Growth	$55,840
3. 44 Wall Street	$48,110
4. Mutual Shares	$45,215
5. Pioneer II	$44,660
6. Twentieth-Century Growth	$39,139
7. Over-the-Counter Securities	$38,441
8. Twentieth-Century Select Investors	$38,129
9. Charter	$35,364
10. Founders Special	$31,500

**Top Funds by 10-Year Results
from *Mutual Funds Almanac*, 1980 edition**

showed up well in recent surveys by *Forbes* and by *Mutual Funds Almanac*.

The overlap between these two selected groups of funds is striking. Of the nine funds selected from the 1980 *Forbes* honor roll, seven also appear at the top of the *Mutual Funds Almanac* list. The two exceptions are two closed-end funds which weren't analyzed by *Mutual Funds Almanac*.

Two of the funds that did particularly well during the 1970s—ASA Limited and International Investors—are gold funds. I certainly didn't predict the dramatic rise in gold prices that occurred during the 1970s, so you may want to take my advice with a grain of salt. Here it is anyway. I don't think gold will do as well in the coming decade as it did in the one just past.* I'd stick to the stock funds. And among them, I'd give special attention to the ones that do well in the *Forbes* and *Mutual Funds Almanac* surveys.

---

* Between the time this was written and the time this book went to press, the price of gold dropped some 40%.

13

Tax Shelters

In the entire world, there are only three ways an investment can make money for you.

It can give you income—for example, dividends on stocks or interest on bonds.

It can bring you a capital gain: You sell the investment for more than you paid for it.

Or, it can give you tax shelter. Make no mistake about it, $1,000 chopped off your takes is every bit as good as $1,000 handed to you in cash.

Coincidentally, there are also three kinds of tax shelters. All three are nice—assuming you don't lose your money while trying to shelter it. But some are nicer than others. When anyone pitches you a tax shelter, be very sure you know which of the three types he's offering.

Tax deferral.

This is the most common type of shelter. You don't escape taxes, but you postpone the day of reckoning. Delaying your rendezvous with the IRS can often be very beneficial. If you can delay it long enough, you may be retired and in a lower tax bracket.

Shelter of income.

Here, the income an investment generates flows to you without producing any liability. If you're in the 25% tax bracket, tax-free income of $1,000 is worth as much as taxable income of $1,333. If you're in the 50% bracket, $1,000 of tax-free income is worth $2,000 of taxable income.

Shelter of capital.

This is the most powerful of all. It occurs when an investment actually lessens your tax liability. When you put $1,000 into a Keogh plan or an Individual Retirement Account (IRA), for example, your taxable income is reduced by $1,000. (Your actual taxes are reduced proportionately to your bracket.) When you receive a tax credit for depreciation on real estate, or for depletion of oil and gas-drilling properties, you again may achieve shelter of capital. Your taxes are reduced, based on a statistical assumption that the value of your investment is decreasing. Meanwhile, if things are going according to plan, the real value of the investment is not decreasing, but increasing.

There's nothing dishonest in claiming a tax deduction for depreciation (or depletion), even if your property isn't depreciating in actual fact. The federal government understands full well that your investment may be appreciating instead of depreciating. It has deliberately structured the tax laws this way in order to encourage selected activities like real-estate development and oil drilling. Congress has made a judgment about the social value of these activities, taking into account the fact that they are relatively risky investments, and that the return on them in many cases is delayed for years.

Most (though not all) tax shelters are risky. Most (though not all) tax shelters are illiquid. Keep that in mind. And never forget: It's easy to shelter your money by losing it. But that is not the aim toward which you have been striving all these years.

Always ask yourself (or your adviser), "Are the tax

benefits certain, or in dispute?" Always ask, "Stripped of any tax benefits, would this venture still make economic sense?"

An investment, if it's tax sheltered at all, may be so in one or a combination of the three ways described above. It may be totally tax sheltered, or only partially so. Because of the large number of investments that are at least partially tax sheltered, we can't discuss all of them here. However, here's a list of some tax-sheltered investments the average investor may be urged to try.

Some Tax Shelters

1. Home ownership
2. Pensions
3. Retirement Accounts (Keoghs and IRAs)
4. Tax-sheltered annuities
5. Cash-value life insurance
6. Real estate
7. Municipal and U.S. government bonds
8. Aggressive-growth stocks (capital gains)
9. Oil and gas drilling
10. Cattle raising

▶ *Home ownership* is discussed in Chapter 7. Its tax advantages are truly substantial. You can deduct your mortgage interest and your property-tax payments, neither of which a renter can do. In addition, up to $100,000 of capital gains can be completely tax free under the one-time, $100,-000 exclusion for people 55 years old or older.

▶ *Pensions.* The money your employer puts into a company pension plan is not taxed when it's put in. You do pay tax on it years later, when you start drawing the pension.

But then you're probably retired and in a lower bracket. Meanwhile, the money in the plan compounds faster than it would if subject to tax. Additional information on pensions is in Chapter 17.

▶ *Retirement Accounts.* Keogh plans, for self-employed people, let you put 15% of your income, up to $15,000 a year, into your account. Every dollar you put in comes straight off your taxable income. So, if you make $33,334 next year from self-employed ventures (after business expenses, but before taxes), you could put $5,000 into a Keogh plan and right away chop your taxable income down to $28,334. That's a first-class tax shelter.

In addition, the $5,000 you put in will grow tax free until you withdraw it—which means it will grow much faster than an ordinary investment. Suppose, for example, that you used the $5,000 to buy a corporate bond. (Buying a municipal bond would waste your money, since the yield would be lower and your income from the bond is already sheltered from tax by the Keogh.) In early 1981, it would have been easy to find a highly rated corporate bond paying 14% current income. Untaxed, your $5,000 would grow to $18,-500 in ten years. Taxed (at, say, 32%), the $5,000 would grow to only $12,400 in that time.

Individual Retirement Accounts (IRAs) work the same way as Keoghs, but the yearly limit is $2,000 instead of $15,000. IRAs used to be for people whose companies don't have a pension plan. Under the new (1981) tax law, however, anyone can have an IRA. Some people can have both an IRA and a Keogh. The tax advantages are the same: only the numbers are smaller.

You'll find some details on how to set up Keoghs and IRAs in Chapter 15.

► *Tax-sheltered annuities.* Annuities are discussed in Chapter 17. A deferred annuity can be set up so that the income you receive on it isn't taxed while it's accumulating, and is taxed only when you begin to receive payments, after retirement. The effect is to allow a faster accumulation of assets, and to transfer some income from your working years, when your tax bracket may be higher, to your retirement years, when your tax bracket may be lower. Competition has brought improvement in the returns on annuities, which used to be very poor investments. But see Chapter 17 for some important cautions. Commissions and management fees can chop the stated return drastically. You can often do better investing the money on your own.

► *Cash-value life insurance.* When you buy cash-value life insurance (the most common kinds are called "whole life," "straight life," and "ordinary life"), you get a fixed death benefit and a fixed annual premium. However, your risk of death is rising each year. To make possible the fixed annual premium, the company sets the premium higher than necessary to cover the risk of death in the early years. In turn, that allows the premium to be less than would otherwise be necessary to cover the risk of death in the later years.

It used to be that if you stopped paying premiums on a whole life policy, you simply forfeited your early overpayment. But in the nineteenth century, reformers crusaded for "nonforfeiture" legislation. The result: All such policies now have "cash values," which you get back if you drop a policy before you reach the policy's maturity date. The cash values start out low, but rise from year to year. At the maturity date, the cash value in a policy normally equals the policy's face amount (death benefit). So, if you live to age 100 or so, you can collect on your cash-value life insurance in full, without even bothering to die.

For a number of years, some agents selling cash-value life-insurance policies touted their investment merits. Actually, very few have much merit on investment grounds. To evaluate their investment merits, you have to compare what happens when you buy cash-value insurance with what happens when you "buy term and invest the difference."

Term insurance provides protection only—no savings—at a premium that starts out low but rises each year, or each few years, reflecting the rising chance of death. In the early years, the premium for term is far lower than for cash-value insurance. Eventually, the term premium will rise to meet and pass the cash-value premium. But meanwhile, the term policyholder has saved money that can be invested.

The key question: How good a return does the term policy holder need on his (her) savings to beat the cash-value policy? The answer: A return of 4% to 5% will suffice to beat most cash-value policies. The best cash-value policies usually offer an implicit return in the neighborhood of 6%.

That 6% is substantially tax-sheltered. You pay no tax on the cash value as it is building up. Once you cash in the policy, you pay tax on the cash value only to the extent that it exceeds the sum of the premiums you've paid over the years (minus the sum of any dividends that may have been paid to you along the way). Often, that means that you pay little or no tax.

To a person in the 50% tax bracket, that 6% return thus may equal a 12% return on a fully taxable investment. Moreover, the cash value in a life-insurance policy is fairly liquid, and the investment, if you're buying from a financially sound company, is extremely safe.

Still, for the average person, a 6% return, cash-sheltered or not, isn't anything to smile about. And remember, that's what the better policies pay.* The run-of-the-mill policy pays considerably less.

► *Real estate.* Your shelter here derives from tax deductions for depreciation and mortgage interest. While you gather these deductions, you hope that you will also achieve income from the property, and/or capital gains. (The depreciation is, you hope, a fiction.) Details in Chapter 14.

► *Municipal bonds.* The lure here is that the interest yield on most municipal bonds is not taxable by the federal government. In many cases, the interest will also be tax-exempt from state income tax in the state where the bond was issued. Municipal bonds were discussed in Chapter 9.

► *U.S. government bonds.* Some government bonds, like U.S. Savings Bonds, offer the advantage of tax deferral, allowing you to push interest income into a later year when you may be in a lower tax bracket. The highest-yielding government bonds don't offer this feature, however. With most U.S. government bonds, the only tax advantage is that the interest is exempt from state or local taxes.

► *Aggressive-growth stocks.* Stocks a tax shelter? Well, yes, to a degree. Dividends don't have much of a shield against taxes,† but capital gains do. You pay no tax until you cash in your stock, and even then, a substantial part of your gain isn't taxed. If you're in the 32% bracket, a $50,-000 long-term capital gain would cost you about $6,400 in

---

* The rate of return on a cash-value life-insurance policy is hypothetical, since to calculate it you have to do an analysis based on "buying term insurance and investing the difference." The number you get depends on what you assume the cost of the term insurance is. The figures I give in this book are based on a reasonable average of low-cost term-insurance prices.

† As of 1981, single people could exclude $200 of dividend income from their reportable income; married people filing jointly could exclude $400. A $4,000 to $8,000 savings account will provide enough interest to use up this deduction.

taxes; if you're in the 50% bracket, you'd still pay only $10,000. That's because 60% of long-term capital gains (i.e., gains on assets held more than a year) are excluded from your taxable income. There's some sentiment on Capitol Hill, as of 1981, for extending this deduction even further.

▶ *Oil and gas drilling.* The energy crisis has caused some investors to consider anew a longstanding tax shelter: oil and gas drilling. Drilling ventures, even in or near established fields, are always risky. For this reason, and because of tax considerations, experts often suggest that drilling ventures are a suitable investment only for people in the 50% tax bracket or above. Deals are normally structured as limited partnerships, and you should probably insist on this form, to make sure that your own personal liability is limited to the amount of your investment. Otherwise you might be financially liable for injuries or environmental damage caused by your drilling project, even if the amount of damages exceeded the amount of money you put in.

Most likely, there will be no income for two to three years after you put your money in. How soon you will begin to get income, and how likely it is that you'll get any at all, depends in part on what kind of drilling venture you go into. There are three basic kinds. *Exploratory drilling* is drilling for oil or gas in a location far from established producing wells. The organizers of the project may have geologic surveys or other reasons to expect there to be oil or gas in the area, and one venture may involve many drilling sites—but even so, there is still a significant chance that no oil or gas will be found, and your money will simply be lost. You shouldn't even consider exploratory drilling ventures unless you have enough capital to invest in more than one (under separate managements) and to absorb a potential total loss without feeling it too much.

Development drilling consists of sinking one or more new

wells in an area where there are already producing wells. It's more likely to produce some oil or gas than is exploratory drilling. But a dry hole is still possible, and even if oil or gas is found, the amount produced may not be enough to make the venture profitable.

The third kind of oil or gas venture involves using existing wells. You simply purchase all or a percentage of the future production of one or more wells that have already been drilled. It's called *production purchase,* or an *oil (or gas) income plan.* This is the least risky type of oil or gas venture, but it has fewer tax advantages than the others. And you may still have a loss, if production from the facility, for one reason or another, peters out, and your income isn't enough to recoup the amount of your initial investment.

The high risk you take when you invest in an exploratory or developmental drilling enterprise is rewarded by the government with substantial tax benefits. Not so with an oil or gas income plan, which doesn't significantly add to the nations recoverable oil reserves.

There are two kinds of tax shelter involved with the more risky plans. First, a large percentage of the money you put in is tax deductible. The percentage depends on the way the deal is structured, but traditionally runs between 70% and 100%. You should, of course, check with your tax adviser to learn of any recent revisions in tax law before considering this shelter. If the deal is structured so that your entire investment is sheltered, and you're in the 50% tax bracket, then a $10,000 investment really involves a risk of only $5,000 for you: The other $5,000 would have gone to pay taxes anyhow.

Unfortunately, some people become so mesmerized with the shelter aspect of such deals that they neglect to give the investment aspect the attention it deserves. If you pay the

$5,000 in taxes, and put the other $5,000 in a savings account, at the end of the year you'll have about $5,262. If you put it into an oil-drilling venture or other risky tax shelter, you could end the year with nothing.

Besides the shelter of capital just described, you can also expect a partial shelter of any income you get from the drilling venture. The primary tool for the shelter of income is the oil-depletion allowance; there are also some other tax wrinkles that come into play. We won't describe any of the technicalities here. Their net effect, in the late 1970s, was to shelter from taxes about 30% of the flow of income from drilling partnerships. Naturally, this benefit, too, is subject to change, and you need a good tax adviser to keep you up to date.

The amount of money you put into a drilling venture at first ($10,000 in our examples) is not necessarily the end of your investment. Many drilling partnership agreements specify that you can be charged additional assessments if the drilling proves costlier than anticipated. You should carefully check such provisions. Is there a limit of potential assessments? What rules apply if you are unable or unwilling to put up the assessment money? You should be very clear on the answers before going into any drilling venture. And the issue of assessments is an additional reason why oil and gas tax shelters should be considered only by people in high tax brackets.

▶ *Cattle raising.* Limited partnerships involving the breeding or feeding of cattle are probably the most commonly sold tax-shelter investments after real estate and oil or gas drilling. They are risky and speculative in the extreme. What's more, the tax benefits are uncertain.

The most common form of cattle tax shelter is a share in a cattle feeding operation. A cattle feeder buys calves when they are around 500 pounds and sells the full-grown cows or steers when they weigh 1,000 pounds or more. The profit, if any, comes when beef prices are high enough to more than offset the cost of the feed and care of the cattle.

As a business, cattle feeding is extremely chancy, subject to violent swings between profits and losses. Historically, prices for both feed grain and beef have fluctuated rapidly. So, if you invest, you are betting on which end of the teeter-totter will be up when the time comes to sell your cattle.

Your risk is heightened by the fact that a great deal of borrowed money is usually used in cattle feeding operations. With leverage in the 75% to 80% range, your potential gains—*and losses*—are greatly magnified. Your potential losses are not necessarily limited to the amount of money you put up initially, unless it says so in your contract.

The Internal Revenue Service allows deductions only for deals that you enter with a profit motive. If the outfit you invest with has never done anything but lose money, the IRS might well question whether you had a legitimate profit motive, or were just trying to escape taxes. If they conclude the latter, you might end up paying the taxes after all.

The tax benefits, as with oil drilling, can include a deduction at the time you make your initial investment, often amounting to from 70% to 100% of the amount you invest, depending on how the deal is structured. However, these tax savings may in some cases be subject to recapture provisions after you sell the cattle. So, you must consult carefully with your tax adviser to see if you are really achieving outright tax benefits, or merely deferring taxes.

As with real-estate syndications and oil or gas ventures, you must also pay close attention to the fees you will pay. Sales commissions, accounting costs, legal costs, and other fees can often eat up more than 10% of your initial investment.

Are tax shelters for you?

There are certain tax shelters that everyone should take advantage of who can. Home ownership, if you can afford it, is economically far more advantageous than renting (see Chapter 7). Almost everyone who's self-employed would benefit from a Keogh plan—not only for the tax advantages (which are huge) but also as a sensible beginning to the challenge of providing for the retirement years. If you're employed but don't have a pension plan where you work, the tax advantages of an IRA (like those of a Keogh) are simply too good to pass up. And I know of no one who's turned down company-financed pension benefits.

Beyond those items, I'd walk slowly into the thickets of tax shelters. Certainly, if you're in a high tax bracket, municipal bonds deserve consideration. (You can put your backup fund of three months' income in a municipal bond fund, and still retain substantial liquidity in most cases.) The more exotic shelters—oil drilling, cattle raising, and the like—should be approached extremely carefully, and generally are suitable only for truly wealthy people who can afford their large risks. It's better to give 40% of your income to Uncle Sam than to throw 100% of it down the shaft of a dry well.

14

Real Estate, Besides Your House

Real-estate salespeople like to quote Will Rogers: "Buy land, they ain't makin' any more of the stuff." It's a catchy slogan, but not a useful guide. Did Rogers have in mind a garbage dump in Denver, an empty lot in Hoboken, commercial space in Manhattan, or farmland in Iowa? Or did he think that all four were equal in investment value? Maybe you don't care what he thought. If so, that's fine, because you'll be making your own decisions, not letting a slogan make them for you.

During the 1970s, stock prices languished, while real-estate prices (in general, with many exceptions) moved briskly upward. The conventional wisdom became that real estate was more of a "sure thing" than stocks. But in investments, there are virtually no sure things. When people think something is a sure thing is precisely the time to look out: That particular investment may be near its peak, and ready to decline.

As you know from Chapter 7, owning your own house is an excellent investment. If you don't own a house (or condominium) and would like to, it certainly makes sense to save up for that goal. I would be hesitant, though, to buy when mortgage interest rates are at all-time peaks (as they were in early 1981).

Once you do own a home or condo, I'd be inclined to go slow for a while in making further real-estate investments. Chances are that your equity in your home constitutes a big slice of your net worth (see the chart, "Your Net Worth," in Chapter 2). If so, why not diversify some of your other investments outside the real-estate area? Diversification lessens your risks, and probably will increase your return on your total investment portfolio.

If you have enough assets so that your home equity doesn't already make up more than half your net worth, you may want to consider further investments in real estate. You can choose:

· Land
· Single-family residential property
· Rental property
· Commercial property (limited partnerships)
· Public syndications
· Real-estate investment trusts

Land.

Buying raw land is one of the simplest ways to invest in real estate. It's one of the most popular ways. And it's usually one of the worst ways.

Of the three possible ways to make money with an investment—current return, capital gains, and tax benefits—land offers you only one, capital gains. The other two are ruled out from the start. You get no income from raw land, unless you can rent it out as a campsite, or a balloon landing field. You get no tax benefits either, since you can't claim that the land is depreciating. In fact, it actually costs you money to own land. In all likelihood, you have to pay property taxes on it. You may also be paying interest on money you borrowed to buy the land.

Undeveloped land will gain in value only if it comes to be attractive for development and use. On the prospects of this happening, the last person whose word you should take is a developer's. Countless people have bought "homesites" that turned out to be miles away from the nearest road, utility line, or source of drinkable water. A fair number of times, the land turns out to be in a swamp or a desert. Don't laugh. At least, don't laugh until you have put your hand on a Bible and sworn that you will never buy land you haven't personally visited.

Some people get caught in land swindles coming and going. First, they buy land that turns out to be worthless. Then, along comes a fellow who promises—for a fee—to buy the land from them and take it off their hands. They pay the fee, and never see the "buyer" again.

Single-family residential property.

Some people have turned profits by buying a house, rehabilitating it, and then selling it. This generally requires a good knowledge of local real-estate trends—and the expenditure of a lot of time.

Some people buy a second home to use as a vacation home, but with the thought in mind that they may rent it out or resell it. If you're buying the home with investment considerations heavily in mind, here are a few caveats. Vacation homes are often in resort areas, the attractiveness of which may be diminished by changing tastes among vacationers, or by gasoline shortages. Resort-area properties often rise in price during prosperous times, but may be hard to sell when the economy's in a downtrend. The capital gains tax breaks that I described in Chapter 7 apply only to homes that are used as your principal residence.

Rental property.

Many real-estate experts believe that the best profit potential for individual investors who want to commit substantial assets to real estate lies in the ownership of small or medium-sized apartment buildings. The smaller the number of units, the more likely it is that you could afford the property. (Of course, you would need to put down only a fraction of the property's total value, obtaining mortgage financing for the remainder.) However, in a small building, one or two vacancies make a bigger dent in your rental return. It is essential that an individual investor considering any form of real-estate investment more sophisticated than simple home ownership obtain professional advice, both from a real-estate specialist and from an attorney. Among the items you should consider with these specialists are the following:

▶ *Is the neighborhood demand for housing stable?* Particularly unstable may be the demand for housing in areas where the majority of people are employed by a single large firm. In that sort of neighborhood, layoffs can precipitate a wave of moves and house sales. You would naturally want to look, also, at the trend in vacancy rates over a period of several years.

▶ *Is the condition of the building good?* The more intimately you know the building, the better insulated you are against unpleasant surprises and unexpected expenses. The cost of labor (and hence of repairs) has gone up substantially in recent years. The cost of fuel has soared even more dramatically, and may continue to skyrocket, so trying to project future heating costs for the building is important.

▶ *What are the applicable government regulations, and who enforces them?* Before undertaking to become a landlord, you should have some understanding of local legal requirements, building codes, and enforcement machinery. You should, of course, know whether there are any rent-control regulations in force or in prospect, and understand the impact of any such regulations on your potential profits. Further, you should try to assess how rapidly taxes are likely to rise, since tax payments are an important cost of rental property ownership.

▶ *Will you have a cushion against unexpected contingencies?* Among the expenses that may be difficult to predict are repair and maintenance costs, and tax payments. You should attempt to pin them down as best you can, with expert help. However, it is desirable that you have some cushion against unforeseen expenditures. To this end, your income from rentals should exceed by some margin your monthly payments of mortgage interest.

▶ *Will your profit margin be adequate?* Just how big a cushion you need is a difficult and technical question. Certainly not all your profit needs to come from rental income, for one of the primary advantages of real-estate ownership is the tax advantage. In brief, you are deducting depreciation costs from your taxes, while your property is, in fact (or at least you hope), appreciating. Thus, you may have a very worthwhile investment even if your rental income barely exceeds the cost of mortgage interest.

Your lawyer, accountant, or real-estate adviser, or some combination of the three, can help you work through the complex arithmetic, and choose the proper basis for calculating depreciation. In a book of this length, we can't go into this area in depth. We would suggest two guiding principles: First, you should fully understand the formulas by which your potential profits are calculated; and second, you should verify in a methodical, hard-nosed way, the realism of the numbers plugged into the formulas.

Before leaving the subject of rental property, a word

should be said about temperament. Not everyone is cut out to be a landlord. If you contemplate becoming one, you should be prepared to deal with tenant demands for services and tenant complaints, both legitimate and not-so-legitimate. If you plan to manage the building personally, you should realize that this is an extremely time-consuming chore, so that you may be trading a heavy investment of time for your monetary return. If you plan to hire a professional building manager and supervisor, you should find out what it costs to obtain competent ones, and be sure to include these costs in your financial plans.

What return should you expect? You should expect a return at least two to five percentage points above that prevailing on high-grade bonds, for the deal to be worth the candle. You are committing yourself to an investment that will probably involve a large time expenditure to maintain, and that is not nearly so liquid as securities investments. Furthermore, you are assuming a substantial amount of risk. For all these reasons, you should expect a substantial return if the venture is to be worth your risk, time, and effort.

Commercial property.

If you're a small investor, there's little chance you'd be considering an investment in commercial property. If you have substantial funds to commit, you might be solicited to join in a syndicate—usually a limited partnership—to finance construction of a shopping center, housing development, or other commercial property. In a limited partnership, your share of future profits is determined by your share of the initial investment capital, and your liability is legally limited to the amount of money you put in. The average investment in private limited partnerships is probably somewhere around $50,000.

Expect a long time lag before any profits begin to flow to

you. It may take two or three years for the organizers to obtain the necessary permits and bring construction to completion. More time elapses before the commercial building is fully rented to various businesses. So it's often years before there is any cash flow to you, and many more years before what you receive as your share of profits begins to offset or exceed what you put into the project in the first place.

During this long waiting period, all you get from your investment is a tax benefit. For this reason, investment in commercial real estate is generally suitable only for investors to whom tax considerations are highly important. Naturally, you and your attorney and financial adviser will want to be very sure that there is no question about the tax benefits before putting money into a venture of this kind. You will also want to look carefully at any recapture provisions in the tax code that could dilute the effect of these tax benefits.

Further, you will want to assure yourself that tax benefits are not the sole benefit of the enterprise. You will want to inquire about how similar commercial properties have fared, and about how the syndicate organizers have done in the past with their commercial real-estate ventures. You will want to obtain an independent appraisal about the market for commercial or office space in the vicinity, and gain some knowledge about what the trend in commercial rents has been in similar locations.

Last, you might wish to ask why this syndicate chose to rely on individual investors to furnish capital. Many large commercial real-estate ventures are financed largely by bank money or by money from other major financial institutions. Those institutions choose their locations and ventures based on professional advice. If major institutions have passed up the opportunity to invest in this venture, or weren't asked, you might want to ask yourself (and others) why. It may be that the project is sound, but too small for institutional investment. Or, the project may be unsound.

A private limited partnership is usually formed to invest in a real-estate project involving an investment of $2 million or less. Usually, most of the money will come from mortgage financing, and the balance (up to, say, $500,000) will be raised from individual investors, who become limited partners. Each investor may put up something in the range of $10,000 to $100,000, and the number of total investors in the private limited partnership will not exceed 35.

When more money must be raised, and the number of partners, therefore, exceeds 35, state and federal securities laws will probably require that the offering be registered with government authorities, and that a formal prospectus be issued. What results is called a *public partnership* or *public syndication*.

Public syndications.

In a public syndication, there can be a large number of limited partners—in some cases as many as 25,000. Each partner need put up only a moderate amount of money, often less than $10,000.

When you buy shares in a public partnership or syndication, you typically have less idea of where your money is going than you do with a private syndication. Public syndications typically invest in several projects, the nature of which is described in the prospectus.

Unlike a private limited partnership, a public one probably won't give you much tax shelter of capital. Reason: The available deductions (mortgage interest and depreciation) must be split among many parties.

The deductions often are sufficient to shelter all or a substantial part of your income from the investment in the limited partnership. In practice then, public syndications compete with municipal bonds for the investment dollars of people who want tax-sheltered cash flow. If you're in a tax bracket where that's what you need, public syndications are an alternative you may want to discuss with your financial adviser.

But public syndications have some drawbacks you should be aware of.

First, the cash flow you would receive is not guaranteed, as it is with a bond.

Second, the degree to which the cash flow is tax sheltered may in some cases be less than with a municipal bond; you should check to see.

Third, the organizers of public syndications often take a substantial chunk of profits for themselves, both directly (as a percentage of profits) and indirectly (through various fees). As a result, as much as 20% of your investment money may go to the organizers. When that's the case, you have to make a 20% "profit" just to break even.

The fourth drawback is a real killer. Some public syndicates invest in properties that have little long-term investment value, or pay excessive prices for the property they acquire. Some major real-estate owners try to fob off their inferior properties on public syndicates. And the public syndicates are sometimes only too willing to settle for less than the best, because the organizers make substantial profits whether the individual investors ever see a capital gain or not. Compounding the problem is the fact that, with rare exceptions, you don't know exactly what properties a public partnership will buy until *after* you've put your money down. And once you've done that, you may be locked in: A share in a public partnership may be hard to sell. Some sales pitches for shares in a public partnership include a suggestion that the syndicate would help you to find a buyer if you decide later that you want out. Such promises should be taken seriously only if the details are spelled out in writing.

Real-estate investment trusts (REITs).

An REIT is the real-estate equivalent of a mutual fund.* It issues a limited number of shares, which are traded in the Over the Counter (OTC) market, or, in the case of some big REITs, on the major stock exchanges. By government regulation, at least 90% of net income must be passed on to shareholders.

When you invest in a private limited partnership, you ordinarily know exactly what venture your money is going into. With a public syndication, you know in a more general way where your money will go. But when you buy shares in an REIT, you're really trusting the fund's managers to invest it wisely for you. The money is to be used at their discretion, with no advance commitment to you as to what projects they'll find worthwhile to pursue.

Ideally, an REIT can provide you with tax-sheltered current return, plus capital gains. The money you put in isn't sheltered from tax, but the money you get back should be, at least in part, as you're allotted a proportionate share of the REIT's expense for depreciation and mortgage interest.

REITs thus compete with municipal bonds. Compared to "munis," they offer less safety, but the possibility of more substantial capital gains.

So much for theory. Now for the blood-drenched historical record. The price of REIT shares has ridden a roller coaster since REITs first gained popularity during the 1960s. REITs grew rapidly from 1968 (when their assets totaled $350 million) to 1974 (when their assets totaled more than $21 billion). At their zenith, REITs accounted for about 20%

---

* If you want to be technical about it, it's the equivalent of a closed-end investment company (see Chapter 12).

of the nation's real-estate investment capital. Share prices rose rapidly until 1973, then plummeted. In 1974, 19 of the 20 biggest losers on the New York Stock Exchange were REITs. Shares of the average REIT lost about 83% of their value from 1973 to 1975. Recovery of share prices through early 1981 has been only modest. And in 1979, the Chase Manhattan Mortgage and Realty Trust, once the nation's largest REIT, filed for bankruptcy.

Among the factors that hurt the REITs were high interest rates, a heavily leveraged position that was disadvantageous when investments soured, poor choice of investments made during a period of rapid asset growth, and inflexibility caused by the requirement to pay 90% of net income to shareholders.

At depressed price levels, some people might reasonably consider REIT shares to be a bargain. As of 1981, some REITs seem to have learned from their past mistakes. They appear to be picking investments somewhat more carefully, and to be relying less on leverage than in the early 1970s. However, in light of their past track record, REITs must be considered extremely speculative. I recommend that you consider them, if at all, only for a small portion of your investment portfolio. Any investment should be made only after a very careful inspection of an REIT management's track record, and even then represents a trip to the high-risk end of the investment continuum.

15

Gold and Silver

From 1934 to 1971, the U.S. government fixed the official price of gold at $35 an ounce. That legal price was reasonable in light of prices in markets where gold was traded freely. As recently as 1970, gold could be bought in London or Zurich for $36 or $37 an ounce.

By 1973, the price of gold had tripled, to $112 an ounce. By mid-1979, at about $250 an ounce, it had doubled its 1973 value. And in early 1980, gold sold for more than $800 an ounce, having gone up more than twenty-fold in a decade.

What an investment! How could you lose by buying gold? Well, you could lose a lot. If you had put $10,000 into gold at its $875 peak on January 21, 1980, you would have had $5,954 left of your investment a year later, in January of 1981. (That's disregarding any commissions, insurance, or storage fees.) The price of gold had fallen back to about $500, and there seemed a good chance it would fall further.

Would you say gold is volatile? Would you say that gold is a speculative purchase? I thought so.

Frankly, I'm not keen on gold as an investment, though I think it's a reasonable purchase for wealthy people as one small part of a diversified investment portfolio. Gold tends to go up in price with inflation and with political turmoil. But if you look at gold over the long term, disregarding its great spurt upward from 1973–1980, the record isn't impressive. Roy Jastram of the University of California at Berkeley studied gold prices from 1560 to 1973. He concluded that the value of gold, in constant 1973 dollars, was essentially unchanged over the 413-year period.

Buying, selling, and owning gold can involve substantial transaction costs. When you buy, you typically pay a premium of 10% to 15% over the current selling price, so you need a substantial paper profit just to break even. You may have to pay a sales tax, in some cases. When you sell, you may have to pay a fee to have your gold assayed (evaluated for purity). While you own the gold, you may have to pay insurance and storage fees.

The price of gold isn't mainly determined by demand for it, either in jewelry or by industry. Rather, it's mainly determined by speculators, hoarders, and investors. These facts play a big part in producing the marked volatility of gold prices.

Like most tangible investments, gold produces no current income and relatively few tax advantages.

If you still want to buy gold—as a hedge against inflation, for diversification, or because you just plain like the idea of owning gold—there are several possible ways to invest in it. You can buy the metal outright, in the form of gold bars or gold coins. You can buy gold commodity futures. You can buy gold-mining stocks. Or you can buy shares in a gold mutual fund—which in turn will hold some combination of bullion, coins, and perhaps futures or mining stocks.

Recently, several major brokerage houses and banks have been taking steps to make it easier for their customers to buy gold. Merrill Lynch, for example, offers a plan with an initial minimum investment of only $100, and subsequent purchases as small as $50 at a crack. This sort of plan may save you money on commissions, compared to buying gold on your own. The gold is stored and insured for you, at no extra cost, and ordinarily there aren't sales taxes on its purchase.

Many of the plans offered by banks and brokerage houses are based on dollar-cost averaging. That is, you put in a fixed amount each month. When gold goes down in price, your dollars buy more of it. Over the long term, under most circumstances, you'll acquire your gold more cheaply this way than you otherwise would; the volatility of prices will tend to work in your favor. (Dollar-cost averaging isn't foolproof though. See Chapter 11.)

The silver shadow.

Silver prices tend to follow gold prices around like a shadow. The two usually rise or fall together, with rises most often accompanying political turmoil or expectations of high inflation. The price of silver typically is about $\frac{1}{32}$ the price of gold (e.g., silver $10, gold $320; or silver $20, gold $640), but this ratio is by no means fixed. When silver drops to a smaller fraction of the price of gold, it may be a sign that silver's undervalued, but it certainly isn't sufficient evidence to base an investment decision on.

Partisans of investing in silver like to note that silver, unlike gold, is much used in industrial applications. The single biggest user is the photographic industry. Eastman Kodak alone often accounts for a third of U.S. silver consumption. While film is the mainstay of industrial use, there's also flatware and some electronic equipment. Put all this together, it's said, and silver has a dependable base to fall back on, which should prevent its price from plunging like the price of gold occasionally does.

Nice theory. Doesn't work, though. Take early 1980, for example. Riding a tide of speculation (much of it by the Hunt family), and moving, as usual, in tandem with gold, silver had soared to more than $50 an ounce, from $6 an ounce in late 1978. Industrial users rebelled, and found substitutes for silver in film, flatware, and electronics. Consumption of silver by industry fell about 40% between early 1979 and early 1980.

The price of silver plummeted, too. Not only did industry cut back, but consumers starting selling silver like crazy, increasing the available supply considerably. Margin calls against the Hunt family holdings, and technical rule changes on the commodity exchanges accelerated the downfall. The price didn't stop going down until it hit about $10. (In early 1981 it was about $18.)

So, if you'd put $10,000 into silver at the beginning of 1980, you could easily have been left with only $2,000 of your investment a few months later. Like gold, silver is extremely volatile, and should only be bought, in my opinion, by people who have large portfolios, are looking for diversity, and can withstand a sizeable loss without flinching.

Like gold, silver can be bought in several forms: 1. bars; 2. coins; 3. commodity futures; 4. mining stocks; or 5. mutual funds or similar pools. As with gold, some major banks and brokerage houses have recently formed plans to help small investors partake of the goodies. For example, Bache Halsey Stuart Shields markets Citibank Silver Certificates with a minimum initial purchase of $1,000 and subsequent purchases as small as $100. The maximum commission is 3%. Storage is free for a year; after that it's covered by an administrative fee of ½% of the silver's value each year. The selling fee is 1%. If you want to take physical possession of your silver, it would cost you another 1%.

16

Collecting for Profit

From French Impressionist paintings to Chinese porcelain, from beer cans to barbed wire, collectibles have been enjoying a major vogue in recent years. Collecting provides the dual satisfaction of a hobby and an investment. As a hobby, it's great. As an investment, it's iffy.

"Tangible" investments outperformed stocks and bonds during the 1970s. A breakdown by the research department of Salomon Brothers, published annually since 1977, is getting to be quite well known. The breakdown released in 1980 is shown on page 182.

How can I look at a chart like that, and then proceed to recommend that you seriously consider stocks, while going relatively easy on collectibles as an investment? In a nutshell, I think many stocks are conservatively valued, while many tangibles have been flying high and are due for a fall. Some, in fact, had already begun to fall between mid-1980 and early 1981. Gold was down 40% from its peak, and falling. Silver was down 60% from its peak. Housing prices edged down a shade in 1980, after ten years in which they did nothing but rise. Tangibles and collectibles deserve a place in a well-diversified investment portfolio. But I wouldn't make that place disproportionately large. And if I were starting an investment program, I'd begin with stocks and mutual funds, not with collectibles.

Item	Average Annual Increase, June 1, 1970 to June 1, 1980
Gold	31.6%
Oil	31.6%
Silver	23.7%
U.S. stamps	21.8%
Chinese ceramics	18.8%
Rare books	16.1%
U.S. coins	16.0%
Diamonds	15.1%
Old Masters	13.4%
U.S. farmland	12.6%
Housing	10.2%
Consumer Price Index	7.7%
Foreign currency	7.5%
Stocks	6.8%
Bonds	6.4%

Many people think differently. In fact, the rise in value of tangible assets has caused some people to begin a radical rethinking of what it means to invest. For example, in 1979 the state of Alaska made headlines when it asked Congressional approval to put state pension money into investments in gold, foreign currency, and real estate. State officials said that Alaska's traditional investments in stocks, bonds, money-market instruments, and mortgages were producing only an 8% annual return, and that such a return simply wasn't enough to protect the purchasing power of future state pension recipients.

Such a request, which raised eyebrows even in 1979, would have been unheard of a few years before. Public trust funds (and private ones, for that matter) are supposed to act according to a standard of prudence. Traditionally, investments in real property—collectibles, precious objects, and precious metals—were regarded as speculative.

They still should be. Here are a few of the drawbacks of investing in real property, which must be balanced against the advantages.

· With most real property investments, the standard of value is totally subjective. As we saw in Chapter 8, the value of bonds is pegged closely to their interest yields. As we saw in Chapter 11, the value of stocks is tethered, somewhat more loosely, to the earnings per share of the issuing company. But against what standard is the value of a Chinese vase measured? There is no intrinsic yardstick; there is only what someone was willing to pay last year, and what someone is willing to pay today. That can go up rapidly, when a particular sort of collectible is in vogue. But it can also go down rapidly, when the fad passes. Buy at the peak, and you're likely to lose a lot of money. And estimating future movements in public tastes is a tricky undertaking.

· Expertise is at a premium. You might reply that this is true also with securities and other investment vehicles. So it is, but to a lesser extent. It doesn't take much expertise to see that you can get a higher return by purchasing a 30-month certificate of deposit than by leaving your money in a passbook savings account. Nor does it take a great deal of special knowledge to pick out a high-grade corporate bond offering a good yield. In the realm of common stocks, the individual investor probably has about as good a chance to make money as does the expert, due to the efficient-market theory (see Chapter 9) and the tendency of stocks to rise over the long term.

In the realm of collectibles and real property, there is less of an overall trend to ride. Profit opportunities depend to a great extent on expertise in a particular type of item (be it Colonial American furniture, nineteenth-century coins, or whatever) and to spot the undervalued item. Unless you are a professional dealer, you are most likely to acquire such expertise gradually, over a period of years, while you collect some item as a hobby. Thus, paradoxically, it is people who don't have profit uppermost in mind who are most likely to make a profit!

· Real property is not a liquid investment. If you own 1,000 shares of common stock, you can sell them at a moment's notice, and receive your money within a week or two. If you own 1,000 vintage comic books, or a roomful of limited-edition prints, turning your collection into cash is a much more complex matter.

· Collectibles and precious metals offer only one way to make money—capital gains. There is no stream of current income, as there is with stock dividends, bond interest, or rental property. In this respect, collectibles are like stock options, commodity futures, or raw land. If the price goes up, you win. If it doesn't, you lose. It may also be noted that investing in precious objects or metals provides no significant tax advantages, at least in the short term. If you are fortunate enough to make a profit, however, your profit is taxed at capital-gains rates, which are relatively favorable.

· You can't be assured that the recent price boom will continue. It's difficult to predict how long the recent upswing in prices for real property will last, partly because, as noted earlier, there is no intrinsic standard of value. Historical information on real property values is not collected and published as regularly and completely as information about securities, so you may have only a sketchy or intuitive notion about what current price trends are, or what the historical record has been. Authorities even disagree as to whether, historically, the prices of collectibles kept pace with inflation before the late 1960s.

Once anything becomes highly popular, it runs the danger

of becoming overpriced, and there is some evidence that this may have happened with certain forms of real property. For example, in 1978, Tiffany & Company, the famous jewelry firm, publicly stated its opinion that speculation had pushed retail prices for diamonds beyond what it considered reasonable levels.

One spokesman for the view that collectibles do not currently represent a good investment value is John Train, a New York investment counselor. He wrote in *Forbes* Magazine, "While investors have recently relearned the old lesson about realism and 'value' in securities, with the other half of their brain, so to speak, they have discarded prudence and experience in a rush to accumulate antique cars, Tiffany glass, Old West objects, Art Deco, bric-a-brac, primitive statues, militaria, timepieces, tea boxes, Judaica, folk art, comic books, tarot packs, old bottles, quilts, toys, and 'limited editions' of coins, ceramics, and medals. . . . All are of unascertainable value, unlike a security, where you can try to calculate how long it takes to recover your investment out of income; all are being bought because they are 'going up'. . . . Contrary to general belief, art objects and collectibles in general do *not* tend to increase in value in real terms; they tend to decline in real terms from the moment they are first sold until they finally disappear altogether."

Train also urged investors to consider the transaction costs involved in collecting. "You buy an object from a dealer for $1,000. He keeps 40%, say, after which the sales tax and various charges leaves $500 or so for the original seller. Suppose in five years the market triples over what the seller got, from $500 to $1,500, and the object is sold at auction. The house takes its commission of about $300 and sends you a check for $1,200. After all this you're down to a 20% profit in five years—less than inflation. Yet how often will an object rise more than 300% in that time?"

Obviously, Train is a partisan of securities investments, and is not entirely disinterested. Nevertheless, his cautions have merit. Investing in art, precious objects, metals, or collectibles must be viewed as speculative. If you're doing it as an investment, rather than a hobby, I suggest you limit collectibles to no more than about 20% of your investment portfolio.

We can't go into detail here on the many types of collectibles, from baseball cards to postal memorabilia, in which you could put some of your money. For that, get thee to a library and read up—in detail. Here, however, are a few observations on some of the most common types of collectible investment vehicles: gems, antique furniture, stamps, coins, rare books, and art.

Gems.

We'll talk chiefly about diamonds in this section because diamonds are the most popular form of gem purchase, accounting for about 75% of all gem purchases each year. Much of what we say about diamonds also applies to other precious stones.

The arguments for buying diamonds are similar to those for buying gold. Their purchase may provide a hedge against inflation. They are accepted as valuable in almost every corner of the world. And their track record for appreciation during the 1970s was outstanding. In 1970, a top-quality, clear, one-carat diamond could be purchased wholesale for about $1,375. The same diamond might have cost more than $7,000 wholesale in 1978.

The drawbacks to investing in diamonds also tend to parallel those for gold. First, the upsurge may have petered out. In 1978, the South African diamond-mining giant, De-Beers, issued a public warning that speculation might have pushed retail diamond prices above sustainable levels. Tiffany & Company echoed the warning, taking the unusual step of placing an ad in *The New York Times* to warn potential diamond buyers, "Look before you leap." Since 1978, diamond prices have fluctuated erratically, but the trend has still been upward. In early 1981, though, prices were falling rather rapidly.

Second, as with almost any commodity, there is a potential for volatility. Diamond prices have not shown as pronounced a zig-zag pattern as gold prices have. However, one can imagine situations in which they could. The world diamond supply is currently controlled in large part by DeBeers, which in the past has used its monopoly power to keep markets smooth. A change in corporate policy, a radical change in South African politics, or the emergence of new, Third-World diamond suppliers (in Sierra Leone, for example) might make for a much more volatile market than has existed in the past.

Third, recent skyrocketing prices haven't been the long-term trend. As recently as 1968–1971, diamonds were rising in value at only 2.6% a year.

Fourth, you must consider the transaction costs. These are even more important with diamonds than they are with gold, because the retailer's markup is much greater in the case of diamonds. A markup of 100% is not unusual. Even if you shop around carefully and negotiate at length with reputable dealers, you are likely to pay at least 30% above the wholesale price. And when you go to sell your diamonds a few years later, you will probably get less than the then-prevailing wholesale price.

Let's suppose, then, that the wholesale price of a diamond you buy goes from $8,000 to $16,000 in just five years. That would certainly represent a substantial increase in diamond prices—14.9% a year! But what would your profit be? Let's say you bought 30% above wholesale, and sold 20% below.

187

You would then have paid $10,400 for your gem and received $12,800, for a gross profit of $2,400, or about 4.2% a year! You could do better than that in a passbook savings account.

What's more, your gross profit may be further diminished by the cost of storing the diamonds and insuring them.

One expert, New York diamond dealer Jack B. Backer, has said that you need to be able to invest $100,000 in diamonds to make them worthwhile as an investment. When you invest smaller amounts, he told the *Wall Street Journal,* you have to pay too much in commissions to make it worth the candle.

Fifth, you must be alert for possible fraud when buying gems. Gems of lower quality may be substituted for those advertised. In some cases, an altogether different gem (or even nonprecious stone) may be substituted—for example, a zircon for a diamond. To protect yourself against fraud or bad deals, you can do four things. 1. Read up on gems, particularly those you contemplate buying. 2. Deal only with established, reputable jewelers—not from people who peddle gems by mail, by telephone, or through high-pressure "seminars." 3. Be sure to get in writing from the jeweler/dealer the specifications of the gems you are buying. 4. Consider spending a bit extra to have the gems appraised by an independent appraiser certified by the Gemological Institute of America.

Diamonds are graded according to four qualities: color, carat, clarity, and cut. While genuine colored diamonds can be extremely valuable, they are also extremely expensive, and usually less easy to sell than clear diamonds. Most buyers will want a diamond that is clear, and the clearer the better. The Gemological Institute of America has a uniform grading system for clarity, with letter grades running from D (clearest) through I (least clear). Investment advisers sometimes suggest that investors stick with diamonds graded D through G.

There is also a uniform grading system for the presence or absence of flaws. A diamond qualifies as "flawless" if an experienced observer can detect no cracks or spots on it under a 10-power magnifying lens. The next highest grades are "very, very slightly flawed" (VVS) and "very slightly flawed" (VS); these diamonds may also be suitable as investments.

A sixth drawback of diamonds, as of gold, is that much of its price upswing during the 1970s was triggered by speculation, hoarding, and emotional buying, not by buying for economic use. Price rises fueled by emotional factors may later unravel in price declines. Diamonds also share the seventh disadvantage discussed for gold, namely, that profits must come, if at all, through capital gains, with no hope for current income.

My overall judgment about the purchase of diamonds is similar to that for gold. I think diamonds should be considered chiefly as a defensive, diversifying investment by people who already have substantial investment portfolios.

Less wealthy individuals who may want to consider gems as a diversification move and speculation (for the high-risk segment of their portfolios) might do well to consider a variety of other precious and semiprecious gems, which have not shot up in price as much as diamonds have during the 1970s. Any such investments should be undertaken only after some serious study of the gem in question, its suppliers, its markets, and its price history. Any gem investment should be made through a reputable dealer, with details of gem quality clearly spelled out in writing. An independent appraisal may also be a good idea.

We will close this section with a warning that should be

unnecessary. Never buy gems that you have not personally seen and inspected. Unfortunately, many otherwise sophisticated people have in recent years fallen for pitches in which they purchase a sealed container of gems, allegedly of fine quality. The sellers in this racket claim that they will buy back the gems after a specified period has passed; some even claim that they will guarantee a profit. They tell buyers that the containers must remain sealed (good luck resisting that temptation!) in order to assure that lesser-quality gems won't be substituted before the buy-back date arrives. However, by the time the day comes, the seller has usually vanished, and the buyer, upon opening the container, finds that the gems were of poor quality all along.

Antique furniture.

I won't give you advice on what periods are currently "in." The fads can change within a year or two. If you intend to invest seriously in antiques, you can do your own market research by buying books on the subject, subscribing to antiques periodicals, and saving useful material to build up your own reference library.

One advantage to the purchase of antique furniture is that the furniture, unlike most investments, can be used and enjoyed. What's more, antique furniture may often cost less than new furniture of comparable quality, so it can represent a bargain if you were shopping for furniture anyway. If you buy new furniture and then decide to sell it when you move two years later, you would probably take a big loss. If you had bought antique furniture, you might have a gain.

Strictly speaking, the word "antique" refers to items more than a century old. In common practice, however, the word is used loosely as a synonym for old. Something made as recently as the 1940s or 1950s may be touted as an "antique."

190

If your interest in antiques is heavily influenced by investment considerations, you may do better to stick with genuine antiques, dating back at least one hundred years. The market for these is likely to be less subject to fluctuations of whim and fad.

However, even with antique furniture dating back two centuries or more, you can expect price fluctuations over time as popular interest in a particular period waxes or wanes. Experienced antique collectors and investors suggest that you buy only what you genuinely like and want to have in your house. That way, you will be less despondent if your furniture's period goes out of favor.

With antique furniture, as with many collectibles, fraud is a problem. Signatures can be faked; newer furniture can be sold as older; cracks and defects can be hidden. The best solution to these problems is to study antiques in detail before buying, and to deal only with reputable dealers and appraisers. If you don't have time to check on a dealer's reputation, don't buy an antique from him—at least not with any thought of investment in mind. Dealers and appraisers can be checked out with the Better Business Bureau, and, if possible, with other collectors, with major auction houses, or even museums.

If your prospective purchase or sale of antiques involves more than $1,000, you may well want the services of an appraiser. (For lesser amounts, the appraiser's fee usually isn't worthwhile.) Some people double as dealers and appraisers. But you should remember that this involves a potential conflict of interest. A dealer who wants to buy your collection may undervalue it; one who wants to sell you an antique may overvalue it. It's best to use for appraisals someone who does nothing but appraising—or at the very least, someone who will not be involved in the particular transaction being appraised.

Appraisers' fees may be hourly, or by the piece. In evaluating hourly fees, you should find out in advance whether you will be charged only for time spent inspecting the antiques, or also for time spent in office work connected with the appraisal. In evaluating fees by the piece, you should find out in advance how a "piece" is defined. Is a table with four chairs one piece or five? What about a set of eight coffee cups?

Speaking of sets, antiques experts often suggest that a set of furniture from a single period is worth more than a polyglot of pieces from various periods. Thus, it makes sense for the collector to specialize. (It makes sense in terms of home decor, too.) However, by specializing in one period, you render yourself more vulnerable to the risk of that period going out of favor. This is one reason why this form of investment is speculative.

Stamps.

Stamp collecting has always been popular as a hobby, but only recently has it been taken seriously as an investment. A few rare stamps now command prices in the range of $100,000 and up.

Before you run to your attic and get ready to buy a yacht, however, it's worth remembering that such stamps are *extremely* rare. Most stamps issued in the past 30 or 40 years are worth precisely the amount they say on their face. In other words, they're worth more for mailing a letter than they are as investments.

A number of factors influence the value of a stamp. First, there's *rarity*. The older a stamp is, the more likely it is to be rare, but there are many exceptions. Stamps with typographical errors are generally rare, and as such are worth much more than conventional stamps. However, stamps can be doctored to simulate such errors. So, before investing in a stamp alleged to have a typographical error, you should have the stamp authenticated by a disinterested expert.

A second factor influencing a stamp's value is its condition. Holes, wrinkles, tears, and "thins" (places where a stamp is thin from having been torn off an envelope) diminish a stamp's value. So does a cancellation mark, as a rule. However, some cancelled stamps, attached to envelopes, can be worth a good deal of money.

To evaluate factors of condition and authenticity, you need either to be an expert, or to employ one. Four useful sources of information about stamps as an investment are:

· Scott Publishing Company, 3 East 57th St., New York, N.Y. 10022.
· American Philatelic Society, P. O. Box 800, State College, PA 16801.
· The Philatelic Foundation, 99 Park Ave., New York, N.Y. 10016.
· American Stamp Dealers Association, 595 Madison Ave., New York, N.Y. 10022.

The first two can provide useful information; the Philatelic Foundation provides authentication services; and the American Stamp Dealers Association may be able to help you check on a dealer's reputation.

A stamp collection has more value when it's a coherent set—best of all, a complete set. By specializing in a particular time period, geographical location, or genre within the field of stamp collecting, you can boost your chances of acquiring a collection that is complete or outstanding. A friend of mine, for example, has quite a valuable collection of postal memorabilia from Germany during the Allied occupation just after World War II. Another friend's father specializes in United Nations stamps. Such collections have far more value than a random accretion of stamps from various areas and periods.

In considering stamps as a potential investment, keep in mind that the transaction costs can be extremely high. Most collectors must buy stamps at their official book value. But when it's time to sell, they often will get only about 50% of book value from a dealer. That means that if your stamps increase in value from, say, $2,000 to $6,000 over 12 years, your actual profit might be only $1,000. In that case, your compound annual return would be only about 3½%. However, you might sell an extremely valuable collection not through a dealer, but at auction. In that case, your transaction cost would be much lower—perhaps in the neighborhood of 10%.

Coins.

Like stamp collecting, coin collecting has recently begun to be viewed as more than just a hobby. A handful of banks will now even accept retirement accounts consisting of coin collections.

Most U.S. coins, like most stamps, are worth exactly their face value. A penny that's 20 or 30 years old will ordinarily be worth more as currency than as a collector's item. As currency, it will buy you 12 minutes on a parking meter, or maybe a piece of bubble gum. As a collector's item, it is worth only a fraction of a cent.

The things that can make a particular coin valuable are similar to those that can make a stamp valuable. Rarity is important. But some rarities are worth much more than others, because they are well-known or popular. Greater collector demand means a higher price. Age plays a part. But an old coin is not necessarily a valuable coin. Anomalies or mistakes can heighten the value of a coin. But, as with stamps, these can be faked, and the investor should proceed only with caution—and an independent appraisal. Condition plays a part, too. But don't try to clean coins yourself unless you are an expert. If you have a valuable coin, your attempt to clean it could make it worth less rather than more.

As with most investments in collectibles, the transaction costs can be sizeable. In general, you're better off buying fewer, more expensive coins rather than many moderately priced ones. Dealers' markups are usually the greatest on the least expensive coins.

However, the mere fact that a coin is offered at a high price doesn't make it investment grade. Many worthless or near-worthless coins are sold at high prices in expensive leather or velvet cases. If you buy them the case might turn out to be as good (or bad) an investment as the coins. Be particularly wary of coins sold as investments through the mail. And watch out for "limited edition" commemorative coins minted by private firms. Often, the edition is "limited" only by how many of the things the firm can sell. Even if an edition is truly limited, that does not necessarily mean that the coins will be in demand or will increase in value. It's best to buy coins through a reputable dealer whose reputation you've checked, and who offers you a guarantee to buy back from you at full price any coin that proves to be fake.

As with stamps, a collection that is specialized usually has more value than one that is scattered over various time periods, locales, or types of coins. And a complete collection within a certain coin genre may have a value somewhat greater than the sum of its parts.

Two books that offer extensive information about coin collecting, both as a hobby and as an investment, are:
· *A Guidebook of United States Coins* by R. S. Yeoman, Western Publishing Co., 1220 Mound Ave., Racine, WI 53404.
· *Coin World Almanac* by Amos Press, Inc., P. O. Box 150, Sidney, OH 45367.

A final note. When collecting money, some people may be

tempted to put a bit too much emphasis on the difference between a coin's face value and its current value. Fifty dollars of confederate currency recently sold for about $1,000. That may create the impression that the currency is rocketing upward in value. But people sometimes forget the effect of compound interest. The confederate money in question was 118 years old. If you took $50 and invested it conservatively in a passbook savings account, you would have, 118 years later, not merely $1,000 but more than $15,000.

Rare books.

It's easy to find dealers in rare books who will tell you that rare books have been appreciating in value in recent years at an annual rate of 20% or more. Books, said the head of one well-known auction house, have "little or no downside risk."

A sure thing, then? As usual, not. The only thing you can be almost certain of in the world of investing is that there are no sure things. A first-edition book by John Galsworthy, published in 1906, is today worth half of what it was worth in 1930. In fact, many rare books have never regained the price heights scaled during a great rare-book fad of the 1920s.

That doesn't mean you might not make money in rare books. People who collected the autographed or first-edition works of Ernest Hemingway, F. Scott Fitzgerald, Karl Marx, or even Joseph Heller have multiplied their initial investments several times over. And book collecting also has a charm and mystique that many people don't attach to other forms of investing.

For the true book lover, however, a problem intrudes. The books that are worth most are those in "fine" condition —in other words, virtually untouched. Most lovers of books,

196

like lovers of any kind, prefer to touch and interact with their love objects. So the bibliophile in you and the investor in you have a potential conflict of interest.

One advantage of collecting rare books, compared to some other forms of investing in collectibles, is that your initial investment can often be fairly modest. You may be able to pick up a high-quality vintage book for $100 or $200.

The hierarchy of values in book collecting generally assigns the highest prices to manuscripts or galleys, next highest to first editions. Autographs or other handwritten notations by the author will always enhance the item's value.

If you decide to collect rare books, most experts advise you to specialize in a particular period, subject, or author. Specialization offers you a couple of advantages. You get to know the field, enabling you better to spot values. Your items become a collection, the whole of which may well be worth more than the sum of its parts.

If and when you decide to part with a portion of your collection, it's often suggested that an auction is the setting where you'll get the best price. Absent an auction, selling rare books is a time-consuming task that requires great patience, since it may take a long time to find a willing buyer.

The advice is different for buying. As a buyer, you'll often do best to avoid auctions, where competition and bidding excitement may push up your investment price. Rather, you may want to do your shopping in bookstores and in dealer's catalogues. As with any form of collectibles investment, you should take pains—and time—to make sure you deal with a reputable dealer.

Art.

Paintings, sculpture, ceramics, and other art objects can combine aesthetic pleasure with investment value. The art lover, unlike the collector of rare books, is free to display and enjoy his or her treasures.

In purely investment terms, art is a highly speculative investment. Many collections have doubled or tripled in value; many others have not appreciated at all. People who bought, say, the paintings of English water colorists or the photographs of Ansel Adams at the height of their price curves found that they ended up with a large negative return on their investments. The key to profits lies not necessarily in the intrinsic quality of the work, but in anticipating popular tastes. That is partly a matter of skill, partly intuition, partly luck.

As with furniture, there is less price volatility among older works than newer ones. Modern artists can go in and out of vogue quickly, making their works rise and plunge in price. A genuine old masterwork, by contrast, is likely to continue a fairly steady rise in price, partly because the supply is inherently limited.

The need to have an art work's authenticity verified by a professional can hardly be overstressed. Forgeries have been a fly in the art world's ointment for centuries, yet unwitting buyers continue to be fooled.

A recent development is the rise of art-investment syndications, somewhat parallel to real-estate syndications, though without the tax advantages. The early track record of such syndicates is less than promising. As with real-estate syndicates, the organizers can often profit whether or not investors do; hence, they may be less than careful about the quality of works purchased for the syndicate's portfolio. Some syndicates reportedly have been careless about authentication. Since the number of partners is typically small, problems may also arise if one of the members wishes to sell and others don't have the ready cash to buy him or her out. A syndicate probably shouldn't be your art-investment adviser.

If you do deal with a syndicate, check out the credentials of the organizers extremely carefully.

Hobby or investment?

Is collecting a hobby or an investment? Clearly, it's some of both. But, as we noted early in the chapter, the people who stand the best chance of turning a profit are those who enter a collecting field primarily out of love for the field, rather than out of a desire for gain. Unless you really enjoy your collecting specialty, you're unlikely to acquire the in-depth knowledge that may enhance your chance for an unusual and valuable collection.

If you love playing with your coin collection, if you have a pantry wall that would look terrific decorated with a set of Christmas plates, if you'd rather spend Saturday afternoon haunting art galleries than going to baseball games, by all means go ahead with what gives you pleasure. In those moments when you view your collection as an investment, keep in mind that it's relatively illiquid, that your transaction costs are probably high, and your chances for appreciation uncertain. Have fun; buy the best items you can afford, in a way that forms a cohesive pattern. Become knowledgeable. Some day you might make some money this way—if you can ever bear to part with your collection.

17

Retirement Accounts, Pensions, and Annuities

Individual Retirement Accounts (IRAs) and Keogh Plans are about the best deal an individual investor can get. And yet, amazingly, the Federal Trade Commission estimated a couple of years ago that only 10% of people eligible to start one had done it. In 1981, the law was changed so that anyone can have an IRA. Nearly everyone should.

In this chapter, you'll find out why IRAs and Keoghs are such good deals, and how to go about setting up the plan or plans for which you're eligible. We'll also discuss two other investments designed to help you save up money for retirement—pension plans and annuities.

All of these investments operate on the same basic principle. You set aside money during your income-producing years, putting it into some kind of fund. The interest income or capital gains you receive on that fund—unlike the return on ordinary investments—is not immediately taxed. That allows your fund to grow much more rapidly than it normally would. When you retire, you withdraw the money, usually in installments. Some or all of the money you withdraw is now taxable. However, you have gained two advantages. First, as a retiree you're in a lower tax bracket than you were while you were working. So you get to keep a higher percentage of the money. Second, there's more money to keep. Your retirement fund has grown to a more substantial sum than it would have had it been taxed all along.

Pension plans.

Companies are not required to offer pension plans. When a company chooses to offer one, however, the Employee Retirement Income Security Act of 1974 (ERISA) requires it to meet certain standards. One concern workers have always had is, "What if I work for the company for years, and then leave? Do I forfeit all of the money that had built up in my pension fund?" For years, the answer was all too often that, yes, the money went right down the tubes. Since 1974, the situation is improved. ERISA prescribes standards for "vesting" of pension benefits. Your benefits are vested if you're guaranteed to receive them, even if you leave the company. Benefits can be 100% vested or partially vested. If you have vested benefits and you leave your job, your company will usually offer you the option of a lump-sum settlement. (You can take this lump sum and "roll it over" into an IRA without paying taxes on it. The usual $2,000 per year limit on IRA contributions doesn't apply to rollovers.) However, the company isn't obliged to offer you the lump sum when you leave. If it wants (and your pension plan so provides), it can wait and pay you the stipulated monthly benefits when you reach retirement age.

ERISA imposes what I call a "minimum-speed limit" on companies for vesting. It lets employers choose from three formulas. An employer can offer quicker vesting than stipulated under the formulas, but it can't go slower; it must meet the terms of at least one of them. Your company must: 1. provide full vesting when you've had 10 years on the job; or 2. provide gradual vesting, starting with 25% after 5 years

201

on the job, and increasing to 100% vesting after 15 years; or
3. provide gradual vesting under the "rule of 45," which calls
for 50% vesting in the year when the sum of an employee's
age and years of service total 45. Under this option, vesting
rights increase at least 10% a year after the "trigger" year,
so that you would have your pension fully vested 5 years
after the year in which the rule of 45 was activated.

Take a little time to get acquainted with the pension benefits you have coming to you at work. Find out the vesting
formula—and don't leave your job when you're just about
to cross a vesting threshold.* Find out what percentage of
your total compensation is going into the pension plan, and
how much your employer is contributing each year.

Here are some other questions to ask. How does the company calculate your length of service? If you work intermit-
tently, do you lose credit for some time worked? If you
leave the job before retirement age, what happens to your
pension money? Are there any age requirements, union
membership requirements, or other requirements for the re-
ceipt of pension money? How is your benefit calculated, and
will it be paid as a lump sum, or in installments?

The benefits manager where you work should be able to
give you clear answers to these questions. If you believe
that your employer isn't dealing fairly with you in regard to
a pension, won't provide answers to your questions, or isn't
following the rules under ERISA, you can seek help from the
nearest office of the U.S. Department of Labor.

Individual Retirement Accounts (IRAs).

These are do-it-yourself pension plans for everyone. Until
1981, IRAs were only for people who didn't participate in

* Unless someone makes you an offer you can't refuse. In that case,
your new employer should be willing to compensate you for the pension rights you're losing by leaving your old job.

a pension plan at work. Starting January 1, 1982, you may have an IRA whether you have a pension plan on the job or not. Into your IRA, you may put up to $2,000 a year, regardless of what your income was for the year before. (Before the 1981 tax law was passed, you could put only 15 percent of your income into an IRA.) By letting everyone have an IRA—and by giving IRAs generous tax advantages, the government is encouraging you to save for the long term.

Let's suppose that your gross income for a year was $20,000. If you put $1,500 into an IRA, you would pay taxes only on $18,500. Supposing you were in the 25% bracket, this would save you $375 right off the bat. Furthermore, your $375 (along with the rest of the $1,500) would stay in the IRA, earning interest. You are not taxed on the interest as it accumulates. In that way an IRA is unlike a conventional savings account.

Suppose you invested $1,500 each year in an IRA paying 8% interest. (In early 1981, it's a cinch to get a higher rate than that, but 8% is probably realistic for the long term.) After 30 years, you would have accumulated more than $183,000 in your IRA.*

By contrast, if you didn't set up an IRA, that $1,500 would be taxable each year. If you're in the 25% bracket, you'd have only $1,125 of it left to invest. And if you earned 8% (the same rate we assumed for the IRA), taxes would clip it to 6%. As a result, you'd accumulate only about $94,500. If you were in the 32% bracket, you'd accumulate only about $78,000 without the IRA. The net result is that you're likely to accumulate from 50% to 100% more with an IRA than without one.

* When you withdraw this after you retire, it's taxable. If you're in the 20% bracket after you retire, the after-tax value of your IRA fund would be roughly $146,000.

The wider the spread between your tax bracket when you're working and your tax bracket when you retire, the more value an IRA (or other tax-deferred investment plan) is to you. When I say you're 50% to 100% better off with an IRA, I'm assuming only a modest spread (5% to 12%) between your pre- and post-retirement tax brackets. If you're in a high bracket now, or will be in a very low bracket when you retire, a tax-deferred retirement plan is an even better deal.

The most obvious, and the most popular place to start an IRA is at the bank or savings institution where you keep your savings account. Insurance companies, brokerage houses, mutual funds, and certain other financial institutions also sponsor IRAs. That means you can have an IRA with the assets in the form of cash, stocks, bonds, money market funds, certificates of deposit, or a variety of other vehicles. Most people prefer to invest their retirement money conservatively, so they pick a conservative vehicle like certificates of deposit.

Once you've put money into an IRA, you can't get it out before age 59½ without incurring a rather stiff penalty of 10% of the amount withdrawn. You must also include the full amount you withdrew in your taxable income for the year you withdrew it. So if you live from paycheck to paycheck, you may not be in a position to establish an IRA. If you possibly can adjust your budget, though, to allow you to put the money away for the long term, the financial advantage to you is huge.

The earlier you start your IRA, the better off you'll be. Reason: You'll have compound interest working for you, tax free, over a longer period. For example, if you contribute $1,500 a year to an IRA starting at age 25 and retire at 65, you will have accumulated (assuming 8% interest) $366,-000. If you do the same, but wait until age 30 to begin, the accumulation is $279,000. If you wait until age 35, it's $183,000; if you wait until age 40, it's $108,000; and if you wait until age 45, your accumulation would be only $73,000.

One important thing to know about IRAs is that you can put into them any lump sum dispersements you get from a pension plan. Let's say you were working for the Zebra Corporation, which had a pension plan, but then left to work for the Anvil Corporation, which doesn't. You might receive a lump-sum dispersement from Zebra. Ordinarily, this dispersement would be taxable at regular income-tax rates. However, if you act within 60 days to set up an IRA and "roll over" this pension money into the IRA, you can usually defer any tax due on it, and the money will continue to earn tax-deferred interest in your IRA. Money from such rollovers is usually exempt from the $2,000 annual limit.

Another, and smaller, exception to the limit: If you and your spouse are both working, and neither one of you has a pension at work, you can contribute up to $2,250 a year.

One of the most important aspects of choosing an IRA is to pay attention to any commissions, management fees, or other charges connected with it. These can sometimes cut into your effective return considerably. If there are any such charges, check them carefully. Are they one-time fees or recurring charges? You may have to probe to find out the impact of these fees: Some IRA trustees inadequately disclose the fact that not all of your deposit will be producing income for you. You should take all such charges into account in deciding where to place your IRA.

Joe A. Mintz, who has studied IRAs and written a shopper's guide about them, suggests that you ask any prospective IRA trustee for a copy of a completed IRA Internal Revenue Service Disclosure Statement, showing (among other things) how an annual deposit of $1,000 would grow *after* all fees. This form can be a useful comparison-shopping tool. It doesn't matter much whether a particular IRA claims a rate of 8.49% or 9.11%. What matters, ultimately, is how much money you will accumulate in your account. Methods of compounding interest, and varying ways of computing your balance, as well as fees, can make the stated yield and the effective yield to you two different things.

If you decide to put your IRA money into certificates of deposit, you should be aware of one possible pitfall. Some banks or savings institutions will automatically reinvest your money in a new certificate when a given certificate expires. The new one may be for the same term you selected originally, or for the longest term then available. The problem is that a renewal may come shortly before you retire, which means that you might be locked into a long-term certificate and be unable to collect your retirement funds without paying a penalty. If you contemplate setting up an IRA using certificates of deposit, or if you already have such a plan, you'd be wise to check on this detail.

If you establish an IRA using a brokerage firm as trustee, the assets in it will normally consist in large part of stocks or bonds. Nevertheless, you may wish at times to have some of your holdings in the form of cash, whether as a hedging measure or because the near-term outlook for the stock and bond markets looks poor to you. So, before establishing an IRA with a brokerage firm, you should check to see what rules govern cash holdings, and what interest rate is paid on them. In addition, you should check carefully any and all management fees, and realize that these are in addition to the firm's regular commission charges for any buying and selling of securities.

No matter what type of IRA you contemplate setting up, check what happens if you decide to transfer your funds to a different trustee. Federal laws, which originally made it rather difficult to change trustees, have been liberalized so that you can do so once a year, if you wish. Frequent switches shouldn't be necessary, if you choose wisely. But it's prudent to find out in advance what contractual provisions apply if you do decide to switch.

If you already have an IRA, but are dissatisfied with it, you'll find it's not too hard to determine whether a switch is justified. Ask an official of your current plan to provide an accurate statement of what's in your account, and a written description of how it will grow over a specified number of years, after deducting all fees. Then find out what you'd lose, if anything, by transferring to a new trustee. Ask the prospective new trustee for a similar written estimate of how your account would grow, starting from the amount you would be able to roll over. Then compare the results.

Since you have freedom to switch, there is no reason why you shouldn't seek terms advantageous to you. And there are major differences among plans administered by various trustees. For example, in March of 1979, *The New York Times* reported that one New York bank was paying only 5% interest on IRAs with balances below $5,000, while some others were paying what was then the maximum allowable rate of 8%. A 1978 survey by the Federal Reserve Board suggested that only a third of commercial banks were paying the maximum allowable rates on IRAs.

Joe Mintz cited another example of the importance of shopping around for a retirement account. He took the case of two insurance company plans, in each of which an individual deposited $1,000 annually. At the end of a year, one plan would have a balance of $870 (a negative return because of various fees) while the other would have a balance of at least $1,060. After 25 years of deposits, the first plan would have a guaranteed sum of $34,390 in it; the second plan would have a guaranteed sum of $44,062. The estimated sums in the two plans (which were not guaranteed) were $59,960 for the first plan, $75,952 for the second. The difference: about 26%, and more than $15,000.

As mentioned, an IRS Disclosure Statement can be a valuable comparison-shopping tool. Trustees are required to provide you one on request. Unfortunately, they are allowed to give it to you as late as the time your contract documents are delivered. After that, you have a seven-day right to cancel. I think you should be able to examine the disclosure statements first, at your leisure, and then decide which plan to choose. While the law doesn't require it, I see no reason why you can't make it a personal requirement that you must receive the disclosure statement in advance, before you'll consider a particular trustee. Reluctance to provide the statement should be viewed as a negative sign.

A decision that comes later is the question of when to start taking money out of an IRA. Under current law, you can't withdraw funds before age 59½, and you have to start withdrawing them by age 70½. The longer you can afford to wait, the longer you have a tax-deferred accumulation working for you.

All of the considerations discussed here are important, but none matters a whit if you don't start an IRA. The effort to investigate potential trustees and set up an account is well worth your while. It might well have more effect on the health of your finances at retirement time than any other single piece of advice in this book.

Keogh Plans.

Almost everything I've said about IRAs applies—often with redoubled force—to Keogh Plans. While IRAs are now available to anyone who is smart enough to start one, Keogh Plans are for self-employed people. The maximum annual contribution is $15,000, vastly above the $2,000 annual lid on an IRA. (With the Keogh Plan, there's also a limit of

15% of your annual income.)

The financial power of a Keogh Plan can be formidable. If you have a net pretax income of $40,000, for example, you can deposit $6,000 in a Keogh Plan and deduct that $6,000 from your taxable income. For some people, this can result in additional tax savings by pushing them into a lower tax bracket. Best of all, the $6,000 earns compound interest for years with no obligation to pay any tax on the interest until after retirement.

Let's say you deposited $6,000 a year in a Keogh Plan starting at age 35, until you were 65. If your money earned an 8% return, you would have accumulated a retirement fund of $732,000 (while actually putting in $180,000 over 30 years). The money, of course, would be taxed when you withdrew it.

Naturally, you want to choose the trustee for a Keogh Plan with care. As with IRAs, the possibilities include banks, savings institutions, insurance companies, brokerage firms, and mutual funds. Another possibility, present with both Keoghs and IRAs but making more sense in the case of Keoghs (because of the larger amount of money at stake), is the use of a flexible trustee. The advantage is that you maintain discretion to switch your funds among various investments, including some unusual ones not normally available in conventional plans. A possible disadvantage is that a flexible trustee may charge management fees larger than the norm.

If you have employees, starting a Keogh Plan for yourself also obligates you to set up one for your employees, and to make certain minimum contributions to it. We won't provide details here, but the potential trustees you deal with can fill you in. If you have one or more partners, similar rules apply, and the partnership is the entity that should set up the plan.

If you are self-employed now, but think you might be on a payroll again some day, that's no reason not to set up a Keogh Plan. In fact, it's an excellent reason to start one. If you become an employee, you won't be allowed to make further contributions to the plan, but the money you put in earlier will remain in the plan, accumulating interest tax-deferred.

If you're self-employed only part time, you can still have a Keogh. You can put into it 15% of your income from everything from writing novels to mowing lawns, from painting to tending bar. What's more, the 15% limit doesn't apply to the first $750 you put in; you can put in 100% of your self-employment earnings up to $750.

Annuities.

Some people find annuities difficult to understand. But many of the same people understand perfectly well the dynamics of a simple bank loan. The bank lends you money because it expects to get the money back with interest. When you buy an annuity, you are in effect loaning someone (usually an insurance company) money, and you expect to get it back later with interest. The company issuing the annuity finds the deal worthwhile because it can turn around and lend your money at higher rates to various commercial ventures.

The possible variations are many, but they all fall within the principles of common sense. The money you pay to the issuing company may be paid in a lump sum (a *single premium* annuity), in a series of fixed installments (a *fixed premium* annuity), or in a series of installments the size of which are at your discretion (a *variable premium* annuity).

The money you get back is normally paid in monthly installments. (Most annuities also give you the option of a lump sum.) But annuities vary in how long, and to whom, these installments are paid. Some annuities pay while you live (*lifetime* annuities) and cease all payments when you die. Some pay only for a certain specified period (e.g., ten years certain). Some pay while you live, and also guarantee continued payments to a beneficiary for a specified period if you die prematurely (e.g., lifetime annuity, ten years certain). Some pay as long as either you or your spouse is alive.

No matter which set of benefits you select, you may be certain of one thing: The lunch isn't free. The more inclusive the benefits you select, the higher your premiums will be, or, alternatively, the lower will be the amount of the monthly benefits.

Annuities also vary in when the payments start. You can buy an annuity and have payments start immediately. Or you can buy an annuity at one time with the arrangement that payments will start sometime later, such as when you reach retirement age. The latter is called a *deferred annuity*. When you buy a deferred annuity, your premium is less than if you buy one involving immediate payment. But that doesn't mean that deferred annuities are necessarily cheaper, in a real sense. During the period before payments to you begin, the issuing company has your money to earn interest on, and you don't.

An important distinction is one between *fixed-dollar* annuities and *variable* annuities. When you buy a fixed-dollar annuity, you know from the moment you purchase it exactly what your monthly benefits will be. When you buy a variable annuity, you don't. Instead, you buy a certain number of "units," the value of which may fluctuate from month to month. The company which issues a variable annuity typically invests much of the premium proceeds in stocks or other risk-prone investments. Thus, buying units of a variable annuity is much like buying shares of a mutual fund. However, with the annuity, the proceeds are normally paid out in monthly installments.

Many annuities sold nowadays are not strictly fixed dollar or purely variable. Rather, they are variable, but with certain minimum benefits guaranteed. If you find yourself shopping for an annuity, pay close attention to the guaranteed benefits, not just the estimated ones. Talk is cheap; so are estimates. In any case, not all companies use the same statistical assumptions in making their estimates, so the estimated figures should be taken with a few grains of salt.

The guarantees also merit careful scrutiny. Quite often, a certain rate of return is stated and prominently advertised, but this rate of return is guaranteed only for a limited period, such as two years, or six months, or even ninety days. After that the guaranteed rate of return may go down in step fashion, or it may simply drop off steeply. So be sure to check the guaranteed rates of return for various durations, including long-term ones.

The next question to ask is, "On what base is that rate of return calculated?" Too often, an honest answer would be, "On the pittance that's left after we deduct our sales commissions and management fees." The Federal Trade Commission in 1978 published a study that contained some pungent cautionary examples, involving fixed-premium annuities with premiums of $1,000 a year. In the plan offered by one major insurance company, the cash value of the annuity was only $178 at the end of the first year. With another company, five years' contributions (totaling $5,000, disregarding interest) left the annuitant with a cash value of $3,895. Moral: Watch those fees.

Sales charges or management fees sometimes run about 15% the first year and 7% in subsequent years. Fees of that magnitude can put quite a dent in your potential return. When someone takes a 7% charge out of your deposit, and then pays you "9% interest" on it, your effective interest rate for the year is about 1.01%. And that's not the worst possible case. For years, one giant insurance company charged a first-year sales commission exceeding 25%, and subsequent other fees that often totaled 12% per year!

One of the best ways to avoid pitfalls is to pick a series of target years. For example, you might pick the end of years number 2, 10, 20, and 30. Find out what the value of your annuity would be (both in lump-sum terms and in terms of monthly installments) if you were to withdraw the money at those points. You can use these figures as checkpoints of comparison, both for comparing one annuity against another, and for comparing annuities against other investment alternatives like certificates of deposit or bonds.

Deferred annuities can be tax sheltered so that you pay no taxes on the interest as it accumulates. When you eventually withdraw the money after you retire, you must pay tax on that portion of it that represents your investment return.

Sales presentations for tax-sheltered annuities sometimes conveniently forget to take into account the fact that the money you eventually receive is taxable. Watch out for this little trick, and remember that annuities may sometimes be a tax-deferred investment, but are rarely a tax-exempt one.

The money you put into an annuity is (under ordinary circumstances) not tax deductible. In this respect, an annuity is not as good as an IRA or a Keogh Plan. Of course, you can if you wish buy an annuity under your IRA or Keogh umbrella; then you'd get the full tax deduction.

In recent years, brokerage houses as well as insurance companies have been selling annuities, and the competition has helped push interest rates up from levels that were historically quite low compared with alternative investments. Even so, proceed with caution before buying any annuity. You can often do better investing the same amount of money on your own.

18

Getting Fancy:
Margin, Short Selling, Options,
Convertibles, and Commodities

This chapter will tell you how to understand some of the fancier footwork in investing. It will familiarize you with buying on margin, selling short, buying or selling options, convertible bonds, and commodities.

It will also tell you why you probably shouldn't do any of these things.

So, if you have no desire to fool around with any of these advanced—and in most cases, speculative—techniques, you can skip ahead to the next chapter. If you *are* tempted to try some of the hotter stuff, welcome aboard and here we go.

Leverage.

Leverage is a concept crucial to understanding many of the more sophisticated investments you'll be invited to partake of. As you may already know, leverage is the magnification of investment profit or loss through the use of borrowed money. The average person is most likely to see the effects of leverage through ownership of a home. Say you put $50,000 into a house. If the value of your house goes up 20% you have gained $10,000. But if you *leveraged* your investment by borrowing half of the initial cost, you would put up $25,000, and the bank $25,000. Then a 20% increase in the value of the house (to $60,000), would give you a $10,000 gain, or a 40% return on your initial $25,-000 stake! (Minus, of course, whatever interest you pay on the loan.) People who bought their homes during the 1960s or early 1970s have been very pleased with that effect, indeed.

Leverage, then, is swell . . . *if* the value of the investment goes up. But leverage also magnifies losses. Suppose the house you bought for $50,000 declined in value to $40,000. That's a 20% loss, ordinarily. But if you leveraged your initial investment by borrowing half the money to make it, your percentage loss is doubled. If you borowed $25,000 for the $50,000 house, the 20% loss equals $10,000, which is 40% of your $25,000 stake. And you still have to pay back the loan, plus interest. As you see, leverage is a two-edged razor blade. The way it worked in the example of a house is the way it can work—for you or against you—in many investment situations.

Consider this: If your odds of winning or losing were even, leverage would obviously be a bad idea. The interest you pay tilts the balance against you. For example, no rational person would borrow money in order to bet on an honest flip of a coin.

The concept of leverage will come up several times in this chapter, so if you're not sure you've got it, please reread the last few paragraphs before proceeding.

Buying stock on margin.

Buying on margin is a leveraged way to buy stocks (or bonds). It's used by only about 10% of people who own stocks. To buy stocks on margin simply means buying them, in part, with borrowed money. The lender is your broker.

The *margin* is the amount of your own cash (or other assets) you have to provide in the transaction. If you buy stocks on 50% margin, you are borrowing half the purchase money from your broker. If you buy stocks on 60% margin, you are borrowing 40% of the purchase money.

To engage in margin buying, you first need to set up a *margin account* at a brokerage office. There is a minimum amount of cash required, which may vary from broker to broker and from time to time. There may be a check on your credit status, since, in effect, the broker is extending you a line of credit.

In the 1920s, you could buy stocks on 10% margin—in other words, borrowing 90% of the funds. In a rising market, this made for great fun. Put $1,000 into a stock selling at $5, on 10% margin, and you can control not a mere 200 shares, but 2,000. If the stock goes to $6, you make a profit of $2,000 on a $1,000 investment—a 200% profit on a 20% rise in the stock. It worked beautifully, so long as stocks were rising.

When stocks began falling in 1929, however, the mechanism accelerated their downfall. When the price of a stock declines, a broker may need to ask the customer for additional margin. (If that $5 stock fell to $4, the broker no longer had enough collateral for his $9,000 loan.) So in 1929, brokers made a large number of *margin calls*—demands that customers put up additional money. If a customer fails to meet a margin call (that is, fails to put up the money), a broker is free to sell as much of the stock as necessary to satisfy margin requirements. Of course, a customer faced with a margin call may also decide on his own to sell stock to raise the needed money. During the market crash of 1929, margin calls precipitated selling, and selling drove down stock prices, and declining prices caused more margin calls, and so on. It was a vicious downward spiral—and a bloody mess.

Never again, vowed the federal government. And so, since 1934, there have been regulations governing the buying of stock on margin. The Federal Reserve Board is empowered to set minimum margin requirements, and no broker may extend more credit than the Fed permits. As of 1981, the margin requirement was 50%, and had not been changed since 1974. The lowest the Fed has set the margin requirement is 40% (from late 1937 through early 1945). The highest was 100%—in other words, no margin trading at all—from early 1946 to early 1947. The requirement was 90% from late 1958 to mid-1960, and 80% from mid-1968 to mid-1970. When the stock market is zooming upward, and people may be tempted to overuse margin, the Fed is likely to throw a wet blanket on the fire by raising the margin requirement*

The Fed is not the only organization that lays down rules for margin accounts. The major stock exchanges and individual brokerage firms impose additional rules. For example, the New York Stock Exchange requires that anyone who buys NYSE-listed securities through a margin account must deposit at least $2,000 in cash (or equivalent in securities) when opening the account.

The NYSE and the other stock exchanges also have—and use—the power to impose extra margin requirements for any listed stock, when speculative trading in that stock seems to be getting out of hand.

Furthermore, the exchanges, mainly the NYSE, set rules that determine how much additional money you must put up if the stock you bought on margin falls. The NYSE's basic *margin maintenance* rule amounts to this: Your broker *must*

* When the Fed raises the margin requirement, only new purchases are immediately affected. If you have a margin account, you don't have to put up additional collateral on stocks you've already bought. However, when you sell these stocks, you may be able to withdraw only part of the proceeds.

require you to put up more money when the value of the stocks in your margin account falls below 1.33 times the amount of your loan. The practical effect of the rule is this: If you buy a stock on 50% margin, it can drop up to 33% in price before you're asked for more margin.

Just as the NYSE's rules are superimposed on those of the Fed, so individual brokerage firms can add their own rules to those of the NYSE—so long as the additional rules are more restrictive of credit, rather than less.

Margin calls, of course, may come at inconvenient times. The stock market may turn sour just after you needed a new car, your little girl needed braces, and your garage roof collapsed under a pile of snow. The margin call may come at a time when it's hard for you to scrape up loose assets. It *always* comes at a time when you don't want to sell stock to raise cash, because margin calls only happen when your stocks have been going down.

The person getting a margin call, then, may find himself stuck between a rock and a hard place. He doesn't really want to put up more margin, nor does he want to sell the stock. However, if he doesn't meet the call, the broker has the right to sell some of the stock anyway—enough to meet the firm's margin maintenance requirements. Margin calls aren't pleasant for anyone. For the person with plenty of assets in reserve, they're a nuisance and a disappointment. For the person whose assets are less plentiful, they can be a disaster.

Besides the margin-call menace, consider also the interest cost. What your broker will charge you depends on interest rates generally; the brokerage house borrows the money itself, then lends it to you at a higher rate. Figure out how big a bite the interest charges would take out of any potential profits. For example, if you buy on 50% margin, and are charged 12% on the loan, your stock has to go up 6% just for you to break even, and it has to go up about 9% just for you to do as well as you would by putting your money in a savings account. Under the same circumstances, suppose your stock drops 20% (not even enough to trigger a margin call). Your loss (including interest charges) would then be a lip-biting 52%. As I said, leverage cuts both ways.

My advice to most people who are thinking of buying stocks on margin: Forget it.

Short selling.

Selling a stock short means selling it when you don't own it. How can you do this? Simple—you borrow the stock in order to sell it.

The idea is to make money off a stock's decline. Say you think the stock of General Gizmo, now selling for $60 a share, will drop drastically. You arrange with your broker to sell General Gizmo short at $60. You sell 100 shares (which you don't own) for $6,000. Sure enough, your prediction comes true. In the next six months, General Gizmo drops to $40. You now *cover your short position* by buying 100 shares. This allows your broker to return the 100 shares you borrowed to whomever he borrowed them from. The cost of buying 100 shares at $40—disregarding commissions—was $4,000. Your gross profit: $2,000.

To sell short, you need a margin account. In practice, almost all short selling is done on margin, anyway. When you sell short your 100 shares of General Gizmo, you put up $3,000 in cash, your broker does likewise, and the $6,000 goes into the account of the person from whom the stock was borrowed. Your account is credited with $6,000—which, however, you cannot withdraw until you have covered your short position.

The warnings I gave about buying on margin apply with equal force to short selling. Again, you have to pay interest to your broker. Again, you're subject to a possible margin call—only this time the call would come if the stock goes *up* too much.

The advantage of selling short is that it's a way you might be able to make a profit, even a dramatic profit, during a down market. But I think the disadvantages drown out the advantages. Start with interest cost, and the danger of margin calls. Next, consider that there is no limit on your potential loss when you sell short. That's not the case when you buy a stock on margin, because a stock can fall only so far (to zero). There's no ceiling on how high a stock can go, so theoretically there's no limit on how much you lose by short selling.

Keep in mind, too, that short selling is essentially a short-run tactic, a tool for active traders and speculators. But the short-term course of stock prices is precisely the hardest to predict. In fact, as we saw earlier in the book, a fair amount of convincing academic research has shown that short-term market movements are unpredictable, and can be perfectly simulated by chance.

On top of that, any profits you make from selling short are fully taxable, no matter how long you maintained your short position (even if it's more than a year). Some traders think that's unfair. I don't, because short sales do not serve the same capital-formation purpose that ordinary stock purchases do. In any case, fair or not, it's a fact.

To cap it all off, there are potential hassles involved in the process of borrowing the stock. You may be assessed some money to compensate the stock's owner for lost dividends. In some rare cases, you might be forced to cover your position when you don't want to because the owner wants it back.

When you pile these various disadvantages together, it's hardly surprising that short sales are only about 7% of all transactions on the major exchanges. Most of that 7% reflects the activity of professional traders (chiefly the "specialists" who make markets in particular stocks on the exchange floor).

If you think stock prices are going to go down, don't sell short. Either ride it out or just sell.

Options.

Buying an option gives you a crack at a big gain, with a small initial investment. It also gives you a large chance of losing that initial investment entirely.

There are options to buy stock—*call* options. And there are options to sell stock—*put* options. Both can be bought and sold. The most common interest of the average investor is in buying call options.

Buying one call option gives you the right to purchase, at any time before the date specified in the option, 100 shares of a given stock, at a given price. That price is called the *striking price*. The cost of the option is called the *premium*.

If the current price of the stock is right around the striking price, then what you're paying for is the chance to make a profit if the price goes up further. When the current and striking prices are the same or almost the same, what you've got is an *on-the-money* option. Roughly, it'll cost you from 10% to 20% of what it would cost you to buy the stock, depending on whether the option is for three months, six months, or nine months. The longer the option the more it costs, because you get a longer time for the price of the stock to go up.

Let's say you buy an on-the-money option giving you the right to buy Docile Industries at $50 a share (exactly the current price) any time in the next six months. The option costs you $750 (15% of the value of 100 shares). If Docile rises to $70 a share, you could get a $1,250 profit by exercising the option. (That's $7,000 for the risen value of the stock, minus the $5,000 you'd have to pay for it, minus the $750 you paid for the option. It's a 66% profit, before taxes and commissions.) Or, you could get a commensurate profit by selling the option itself.

An *in-the-money* option is one where the market price of the stock is already higher than the striking price. Naturally, it costs more than an on-the-money option.

An *out-of-the-money* option is one where the market price of the stock is lower than the striking price. Naturally, it costs less to buy than an on-the-money option. It gives you a chance to make a tremendous profit. But it also poses odds against your making any profit at all.

Options offer one of the advantages of leverage—the chance of a big gain from a modest stake—while limiting the size of your loss on any given transaction. However, if you trade options very much, you'll probably have a lot of small losses that can add up to a big loss pretty quick. Here are seven reasons why you shouldn't buy options.

1. When you buy a call, you're making a double bet. You're claiming that you not only know which stock will go up, but *when* it will go up (i.e., before the option expires). That's asking too much of any mortal.

2. When you buy a stock, a loss need not be a total loss. If you buy 100 shares at $62 and they drop to $40, of course you're very disappointed. But you still have $4,000, and a chance for recovery. When you buy an option and it doesn't pan out, you lose every dollar.

3. Stocks pay dividends. Options don't.

4. Brokerage costs tend to be higher for options trading than for stock trading.

5. For the stockholder, any increase in the stock's price is good news. For the option holder, only an increase that makes it likely the striking price will be reached affects the

value of the option. When time is running out on an option, it sometimes happens that the option drops in value even while the underlying stock price is rising.

6. Even if the stock reaches the striking price, the option buyer doesn't necessarily make a profit. The stock price has to rise enough to cover the cost of the option, plus commissions, plus taxes.

7. Since almost all options are written for less than a year, gains are taxable as ordinary income.

Never have I seen a study that tells what percentage of investors make a profit in options. I would guess the percentage is minuscule, but there doesn't seem to be any data on the point. Said a spokesperson for the Chicago Board Options Exchange (the largest trading place for options): "If there is such a study out there, I'm unaware of it."

Your broker has two strong economic incentives to want you to trade options. One is those high commissions; the other is that option traders are usually active traders—which means a lot of commissions. Given these incentives, it's only human for your broker to convince himself that options trading may be just the thing for you. However, it might only be just the thing for him.

In some cases, brokers have acted irresponsibly. For example, in 1979 the Securities and Exchange Commission accused one well-known brokerage firm and 16 of its employees with inducing certain customers to trade options without a sufficient explanation of the risks involved, and causing excessive trading in those customers' accounts. The charges involved brokers in several cities, including New York, New Orleans, Fort Worth, and Chicago. The complaint stated that 83 customers had lost $907,000 through options trading, while generating $548,000 in commissions for their brokers, over a two-and-a-half-year period from 1975 to

1978. The company and 13 of the employees settled the case by accepting censure or sanctions, without admitting guilt. This case was not an isolated incident: The SEC had previously brought similar cases against two other major brokerage firms in 1978 and 1979.

At this point, someone is sure to object that I've been talking as if buying calls was the only element in the options game. In fact, there are several other ways to trade in options, some of them rather conservative.

The most obvious example is writing covered calls. Don't panic. "Writing" just means selling. "Covered" means that you own the underlying stock on which you sell a call. An increasing number of wealthy, fairly conservative investors are using this strategy. It's sensible, because instead of having the premium working against you, you have it working for you. If the stock rises dramatically, you get only a part of the gain you'd otherwise have had. (Everything up to the striking price is yours; beyond that, the gains will go to the foolhardy fellow who bought the call.) But the combination of dividends, modest capital gains, and premium income is enough to keep some investors happy. It works best when you do it systematically on a large and diversified portfolio.

You can also use options for hedging. For example, suppose you'd got a big gain in Speculative Industries, which you bought at $3.75 a share and which now is selling for $30. You think it might take a dive, but you can't bring yourself to sell the stock. You could buy a put, giving you the right to sell 100 shares (or 10 puts, giving you the right to sell 1,000 shares) at $25 or $30. If the stock goes up further, the money you wasted on the put at least bought you peace of mind. If the stock goes down, that put was relatively cheap insurance against a big loss.

The only trouble with using options for hedging is, how do you know when to hedge? If you hedge all the time, you spend a lot of money on options and commissions, which eats into your basic investment profits.

Convertibles.

Besides being a rather romantic kind of car, a convertible is a type of security. It's a security that, under some conditions, can be converted to the issuing company's common stock. The two types of convertible securities you may encounter are *convertible bonds* and *convertible preferred stock*. Bonds and preferred stock were discussed in Chapters 8 and 10. You'll recall that the chief attraction of bonds is a combination of a relatively high interest rate with a fair degree of security. The attractions of preferred stock, for ordinary investors, are essentially nonexistent. Therefore, we'll confine our discussion here to convertible bonds.

A *convertible bond* pays interest like a bond, but can be exchanged for a set number of shares of the company's common stock. (The chart on page 228 provides a few examples.) At the time a convertible bond is issued, the exchange rate will be such that it won't be worth an investor's while to trade the bond for stock. However, an investor has the hope that the stock price will rise, allowing the possibility of a significant capital gain. For example, Fledgling Industries might issue a $1,000 bond convertible to 100 shares of stock, at a time when the stock sold for $7 a share. No one would want to convert at that price, since the proceeds would be only $700 worth of stock. However, if the stock price surged, over the next few years, to $14 a share, the bondholder could convert, and get a 40% capital gain.

Pending conversion—which, of course, may never come—the bondholder gets interest. The interest rate, however, is below that paid on conventional bonds issued by the same company, or by other companies of similar financial standing.

The convertible bond is, then, a hybrid, a compromise. The person who might buy stock, but finds that to be a little bit too risky, can have the relative security of a bond and still some hope for dramatic gains. The person who might buy bonds, but finds them a shade too tame, can have the hope of stock ownership at the end of the rainbow, but steady income until then. The buyer, in accepting this compromise, gives up some of the interest he or she would normally get on a bond, in hopes of a stock payoff that might or might not develop.

From the point of view of the issuing company, a convertible bond's most obvious advantage is that it allows the company to raise money at a lower cost. However, if the bonds are converted, this will have the effect of increasing the number of stockholders, and diluting the company's earnings per share.

It should be noted, by the way, that convertible bonds are rarely secured; they are almost always unsecured, or debenture bonds. So, besides giving up some interest, the bond buyer who chooses convertibles may be giving up a bit of safety, too. Convertible bonds, like conventional ones, are rated for financial stability by the major ratings services (Moody's and Standard & Poor's). A buyer should of course pay careful heed to a bond's rating before considering purchase.

The price fluctuations of a convertible bond are subject to two kinds of pushes and pulls—those that move all bonds, and those that move the issuing company's stock. Which factors predominate depends on how big is the *conversion premium*—that is, how far the bond is priced above the value of the stock to which it entitles the holder. In the example above, the conversion premium was 42.8%, because the stock was worth $700 while the bond was priced at $1,000. That's a rather high conversion premium.

When the conversion premium is high, the bond tends to move up or down in price according to how its interest rate compares with that of other fixed-return investments. A bond with a high conversion premium and a coupon rate of 6% might be priced at around $666 at a time when straight bonds were commonly offering a 9% yield.

When the conversion premium narrows, because of a rise in the price of the stock, then a convertible bond begins to resemble a call option on a stock. The closer the prices approach *parity* (the point where the value of the stock option equals the face value of bond), the more the bond's price will be determined, not by bond-market factors, but by movements in the price of the company's stock.

The chart on pages 228–229 shows some of these factors for a small sampling of convertible bonds in 1979.

The figures in the chart show how the principles we've just described apply. If you look, for example, at the convertible bonds issued by Hilton Hotels or Digital Equipment, you'll see that these bonds are behaving very much like stocks. The current yield is modest, the chance for capital gains substantial. If you look, by contrast, at the convertibles issued by Chase Manhattan or Lockheed, you can see that they have been priced so that their yield was close to that available at the time on conventional bonds: Investors had more or less given up hope that a rise in the price of the stock would make the bonds worth converting.

For three of the bonds shown (Allied Artists, Caterpillar Tractor, and Hilton Hotels), the price of the company's stock had already risen to the point where someone who had held the bond from the outset could have made a capital gain by converting it to stock. You might wonder, then, why these bonds were still on the market. Why hadn't they been converted? There are several answers, several reasons why you might prefer to hold onto a convertible bond even after

CONVERTIBLE BONDS — Some Examples

Company	Yield* (current return)	Number of Shares to Which Bond Can Be Converted
Alaska Airlines	7.83%	153.37
Allied Artists	6.25%	444.44
Bally Manufacturing	7.36%	16.13
Baxter Travenol Laboratories	4.70%	21.33
Caterpillar Tractor	4.58%	19.80
Chase Manhattan Corp.	8.78%	17.39
Digital Equipment	4.09%	17.54
Eastern Airlines	8.60%	29.41
Federated Department Stores	5.00%	24.39
Hilton Hotels	3.69%	65.57
Lockheed	7.94%	13.79
Reynolds Metals	6.62%	16.91
Zapata Corp.	7.54%	45.79

* Data as of year-end 1978. Source: *Standard & Poor's Bond Guide.*

the stock price had risen enough to make conversion feasible. For one thing, the stock might go back down again. If you were holding, say, the Caterpillar Tractor convertibles, you would be in a position to sit back and wait until the year 2,000 if you wished, and then see where the stock was before deciding to sell. (Of course, you could miss out on profit this way, if the stock rose and fell. But if you were planning to hold the stock for the long term anyway, it makes little difference whether you hold it *as* stock, or in the form of a convertible bond.) Another possible advantage of holding the bond is that the interest rate on the bond might be higher than the company's dividend on common stock. (In

Expiration Date of Conversion Privilege	Stock Price Above Which Conversion Produces a Gain**	Stock Price (Actual Value)*	Approximate Cost of Bond	Conversion Premium
1986	$6.52	$4.88	$830	34%
1990	$2.25	$3.12	$1,400	1%
1998	$62.00	$41.38	$815	50%
2001	$46.88	$41.00	$1,010	14%
2000	$50.50	$58.75	$1,200	3%
1996	$57.50	$29.38	$740	96%
2002	$57.00	$53.62	$1,100	6%
1993	$34.00	$8.50	$552	300%
1985	$41.00	$32.00	$900	28%
1995	$15.25	$22.38	$1,490	2%
1992	$72.50	$19.50	$535	272%
1991	$59.14	$32.62	$680	81%
1988	$21.84	$11.12	$630	96%

** For buyer who paid par value ($1,000) for the bond.

the case of Caterpillar Tractor in 1979, the bond was paying about $55 a year in interest, while the common stock dividend the bondholder would get by converting was about $42.) A futher incentive to hold the bond is that the interest payment on the bond is guaranteed, while the amount of the dividend can go up or down, depending on how the company is doing in any given year. For all these reasons, a person may wish to hold a convertible even after the underlying stock price has risen enough to make conversion feasible. It isn't necessary to convert the bond at all in order to make a capital gain, since the bond itself rises in price and can be sold.

You'll notice that even on a bond that is already a candidate for conversion, there still is a conversion premium. In the chart on page 228, the conversion premium on such bonds was about 1% for Allied Artists, 2% for Hilton Hotels, and 3% for Caterpillar Tractor. The person who buys the Caterpillar convertible at $1,200, for example, was essentially paying about $1,163 for the value of the underlying stock, and about $37 for the chance to receive a guaranteed interest payment while awaiting further developments.

▶ *Picking convertible bonds.* Recognize that if you decide to invest in convertibles, you are likely to be sacrificing something. You will sacrifice some interest, compared to buying a straight bond. If you view your investment as an indirect way of buying stock, recognize that you are often starting off behind the eight ball—that is, that the actual price of the stock underlying most convertibles is well below the conversion point, and may stay there forever.

If you are unfazed by these considerations, and want to invest in convertibles, you then need to think about how much of a conversion premium you are willing to pay. I suggest you consider confining yourself to convertibles on which the conversion premium is less than 25%. Otherwise, you may be giving up current yield on the hope of a dramatic stock-price rise that will never materialize.

Second, you need to consider how much current yield you expect to get. I think you should expect a return at least equal to that offered by many common stocks and not too far below passbook savings rates—in other words, at least 4% to 5%. The percentages may change from year to year, as interest rates change.

Third, since part of what you are buying is safety, by all means check the ratings given by the bond-rating services. You may want to accept a higher degree of risk than you would on a straight bond, since if you wanted more substantial safety, you'd be buying a straight bond in the first place. Indeed, you'll *have* to accept a lower rating, since it's very rare for a convertible issue to be rated higher than single-A. However, I suggest you steer clear of convertible bonds that are rated in the C range or below, and also of ones that are unrated.

Commodities.

If you raise corn, wheat, soybeans, cattle, or hogs, if you own a copper mine, or a tin mine, or a silver mine, you have a logical reason to be intensely interested in the commodities market. If you are an individual investor, you don't.

The farmer who grows a crop of wheat must inevitably assume a number of risks. One, of course, is the risk that the crop won't grow, a risk he does his best to minimize through skill and technology, but which remains present nonetheless. Another risk, which the commodities market enables him to do something about, is the risk that prices will be too low when the crop is harvested. To guarantee himself a certain price, the farmer can sign an agreement to deliver his wheat at an agreed price on an agreed date. This gives him some protection, although it limits his potential profit if the price of wheat soars.

The person who buys a futures contract (say, to accept delivery of 5,000 bushels of wheat in June) takes over the price risk. If the price goes up, he makes money on the speculation. If the price goes down, he loses. For example, if you were inclined to speculate in commodities, you could have purchased on margin, in January of 1981, a contract on September wheat for about $2,425. (The price was $4.85 a bushel on the Chicago Board of Trade, one of 13 commodities exchanges in the U.S. The standard contract is for purchase of 5,000 bushels, and margin is often 10%. If you want to increase your investment, you could buy two contracts for about $4,850 or three for about $7,275. If you want to decrease your investment, you'd have to pick a cheaper commodity, since commodities are traded only in standard contracts for fixed amounts.)

Naturally, you wouldn't expect to take physical possession of 5,000 bushels of wheat. What you would hope for would be that the price would rise so that you could resell your contract later at a profit. The ultimate buyer would be a grain-trading company or some company that had a direct use for the wheat, such as a cereal manufacturer.

If the price of wheat rose to $6.00 a bushel by August, you would have a profit on a single contract of about $5,750. Because commodities trading is done on remarkably low margin, you might have put up only $2,425 or so in cash. This would work out to a profit of about 137% (before commissions and taxes), earned over a seven-month period. However, if the price of wheat fell to $3.50 a bushel, you'd have a loss of about $6,750, or 278%, plus commissions. You can see why trading in commodities is called speculating.

Is it for you? Probably not. Even brokerage firms that promote commodities trading often issue strict cautions about who should become involved, and to what extent. For example, Merrill Lynch, the nation's largest brokerage firm, solicits new commodities clients with the following caveats: 1. The individual who is considering speculating in commodities (and speculation is the only kind of investment available here) should have at least $75,000 in liquid assets, *excluding* the value of his or her home, and the cash value of life insurance. 2. The would-be commodities speculator should have at least $10,000 in risk capital, including at least $5,000 in cash. 3. The speculator should not put more than 10% of his or her liquid assets into commodities speculation.

The lure of commodities speculation is the possibility of spectacular profits. And the profits can be spectacular indeed. One reason for this is that the commodities speculator has the kind of immense leverage that prevailed in the stock market before 1929. You can buy commodities futures contracts on 10% margin—indeed, that's the normal way to buy them. Sometimes the margin is only 5%. With that kind of leverage, a $5,000 investment can control $50,000 to $100,000 worth of goods, and a 10% upswing in the value of the goods can return a profit of 100% to 200%. A 50% upswing in the value of the commodity can return a profit of 500% to 1,000%, in other words a $25,000 to $50,000 profit on a $5,000 investment—all this in a matter of weeks.

Why, then, do I discourage the purchase of commodity futures contracts? For several reasons, chief of which is that the risks are savage. When you buy on margin, you are subject to the possibility of margin calls. When the margin is 5% or 10%, the pyramiding effects of margin calls can be brutal. You could, for example, lose $25,000 on a $5,000 investment.

The standard advice in commodities trading is to cut your losses (in other words, sell as soon as you see that the price is declining) while letting your winnings run. In this way, the theory goes, you'll have a few big winnings that will outweigh a number of small losses. Even if you try to follow this advice, you can run into a problem. On any given day, you might not be able to execute a trade. That is because, to maintain some stability in the marketplace, authorities have set maximum amounts by which the price can change in a day. On the Chicago Board of Trade, for example, the daily limit for wheat trading is 20 cents a bushel. If wheat closed the previous day at $3.50 a bushel, and moves to $3.70, it is "up the limit," and no trades at prices above $3.70 are permitted that day. If it goes to $3.30, it is "down the limit," and no trades at lower prices are permitted for the rest of the day. This does not mean that trading is officially halted. However, it might just as well be, for in a downtrend buyers may prefer to wait until the next day, and in an uptrend, sellers may prefer to do so.

Suppose, then, that you hold a contract on wheat when some major news that will depress the price comes out. (Perhaps the government has announced huge imports of wheat from Canada or banned exports to the Soviet Union.) Chances are, wheat will go down the limit. You, wishing to cut your losses, may try to sell, but you may not be able to find a buyer. The same thing could happen the next day, and the next. In one case, sugar was down the limit for nine days straight. Such occurrences are rare, but they can happen.

The risk of a very large loss, then, is the first and most important reason why I discourage individual investors from trading commodities. A second reason is the *probability* of loss. A number of surveys, government and private, have been made of people's experience in the commodities market. A common finding is that from 75% to 90% of people who try to trade commodities lose money.

A third reason is that, in this marketplace, the individual is up against competitors with superior expertise, information, and resources. You might at first blush think that this goes for the stock market, too. However, as we saw in Chapter 9, there are several reasons why in the stock market a skilled amateur may be able to do as well as a professional. Not so in the commodities market. Here there is no long term, and short-term moves depend on a flow of vital information about weather conditions, political movements, government actions, and so on. Under these circumstances, it is unlikely that your information and expertise in the wheat market will match that of, say, Kellogg, or that your grasp of developments in the platinum market will exceed that of the person who trades in platinum for, say, General Motors.

Let me sum up this chapter very briefly. Here's what you should do if you feel like buying on margin, if you feel like selling short, if you feel like buying calls, if you feel like speculating in commodities, and yes, probably even if you feel like purchasing convertible bonds: Go to a discount department store. Find the section where games are sold. Pick out an exciting board game with lots of play money and fast action. Indulge.

The money you spend on that game may be the best capital-preservation investment you ever made.

19

Brokers and Financial Advisers

The term sounds imposing, impressive: "financial adviser." Henry Kissinger was an adviser; so was Bernard Baruch. "Financial consultant" sounds perhaps equally impressive.

But the labels really carry little weight. Stripped to the rudiments, anyone who gives you advice about money is, ipso facto, a financial adviser. If you take things this literally, the tout at the race track and the tipsy occupant of the seat adjoining yours on the bus probably qualify.

In a more practical sense, to whom might you turn for financial advice? Let's run through a few of the major possibilities.

Types of financial advisers.

▶ *Accountants.* A fair number of people with a substantial income employ accountants, particularly to help with taxes. One possible drawback of using an accountant as your principle financial adviser is that his or her advice may be too tax-oriented, perhaps distorting your overall financial planning a bit in an attempt to minimize your tax burden.

▶ *Lawyers.* Some people who regularly consult an attorney carry over the habit of consultation into financial

236

matters. This may or may not be wise, depending on the background and expertise of the attorney.

▶ *Bankers.* Many banks and savings institutions employ a person with the title financial counselor. Depending on the size of the bank, this may be a specialized function, or it may be part of the job of a loan officer or a branch manager. In cases where you know your local bank personnel, you may have established a degree of trust and rapport that can enhance a banker's value as a financial adviser. However, you might also wish to reflect that the bank's interests and yours may not always coincide. Banks make money by attracting deposits, and have an incentive to urge you to keep money in the bank rather than in other investments. Too, banks make money by issuing loans, and may be therefore at times a bit prone to see a loan as the cure for whatever ails you, financially speaking.

▶ *Insurance agents.* When he calls or writes to ask for a chance to come talk with you in your home, he's a "financial planner," or perhaps an "estate planner." When he gets there, lo and behold, he wants to sell you some insurance. Nevertheless, hundreds of insurance agents have every right to call themselves Certified Financial Planners, in the sense that they've earned a C.F.P. degree from the College of Financial Planning run by the International Association of Financial Planners. I don't think you should regard the C.F.P. designation as an important distinction.

▶ *Mutual-fund salespersons.* Here, the same comment applies as with insurance agents. They will indeed help you draft your financial plans. But coincidentally, their recommendations often seem to include purchase of their products.

▶ *Brokers.* A stock broker is a traditional choice as a financial adviser. Some brokers have a good command of the workings of the securities industry, and a working knowledge of other investment alternatives as well. However, you can't assume that every broker does. Some rely heavily on canned research reports prepared by their home offices; some rely on charm and a confident manner; some don't know which end is up.

Even supposing you find a knowledgeable broker with whom you can communicate well, there is still a consideration to remember: Your interests and those of the brokerage firm may diverge. To cite the most obvious example, you may be better off holding investments for the long term. Your broker is undoubtedly better off when you buy and sell rather often. The extreme case, in which a broker unscrupulously encourages excessive trading, is called "churning." But leaving the extreme aside, it's natural for your broker to see frequent trading as wise; he or she has a built-in economic and emotional incentive to think so.

Another example is that a broker may urge you to buy shares of a new stock offering, or a bond from a just-issued bond offering. This may in fact be a good deal for you, since your commissions may be reduced or eliminated. However, when a brokerage firm participates in underwriting or bringing out a stock or bond issue, the firm often has an economic incentive to see that the issue sells out rapidly. Your broker is part of his firm, and, in response to subtle or unsubtle pressure, may be more concerned with getting the issue sold than with making sure that it is an investment perfectly suited to your circumstances.

Since much of this book is concerned with securities investments, we'll have more to say about brokers later in this chapter.

▶ *Independent financial counselors.* A small but growing number of firms and individuals offer investment counseling for a fee, unconnected with the sale of any other product or service. The removal of any source of potential bias is a plus, but there's a hitch. While advisers who sell you something else often throw in the advice for free, advisers who sell only advice often charge stiff rates. A detailed financial analysis from an independent consultant is likely to cost you at least several hundred dollars, and more likely $2,000 or more. Unless you have a net worth in the six-figure range, and are in a tax bracket around 50%, you're likely to conclude that this kind of advice costs more than you can afford.

One type of independent financial consultant manages your assets for you. The adviser, not you, decides when and what to buy, when and what to sell. You give the adviser free rein —subject to three rather important checks. First off, you and the adviser will normally have agreed in writing on some general guidelines regarding how much risk you wish to assume in your investment program. A professional consultant violates these guidelines only at risk of a lawsuit. Second, the adviser serves at your pleasure. If a consultant makes choices of which you disapprove, he (or she) knows that you are likely to terminate the contract forthwith. Third, you are protected in some measure against churning of your account by the nature of the compensation arrangement. Normally, an independent consultant receives no brokerage fees from you. (Those commissions are received by a broker, who may be specified either by the consulting firm or by you, depending on your arrangement.) Instead, the consultant receives annually a small percentage of the actual value of the assets being managed (2% would be a fairly common provision). This obviously gives the consultant a direct stake in increasing the value of your portfolio: He gains by your gain, and suffers by your loss. Excessive trading would drain assets from the portfolio and lessen his fee. This sort of asset management service may be available through a bank trust de-

239

partment, a special branch of certain brokerage firms, or a completely independent firm or individual.

Before you give any individual or corporation carte blanche to make investment decisions for you, give careful thought to a few questions. How do you rate your own aptitude for financial management? Do you have the temperament for it, and the inclination to spend time managing your money? Would you reasonably expect a professional adviser to achieve results sufficiently superior to your own to justify the fee? Last, but most important, have you carefully checked out the qualifications, track record, character, and references of the financial consultant you plan to use? This might seem like a tall order, but if you are really to forfeit decision-making powers you owe yourself no less.

Another, quite different, sort of financial advisory arrangement is one in which the independent financial counselor does not make the final decisions about what to buy and sell, but merely prepares detailed recommendations for your own actions. This sort of arrangement might better meet the needs of most investors. Unfortunately, it is priced out of reach of most investors. One major consulting firm, for example, charges from about $1,500 to about $15,000 in return for an "integrated financial analysis" that may culminate in a 75-page report. The firm, Oakland Financial Group of Aptos, California, employs a team of accountants, lawyers, tax experts, and investment analysts to process information gained from an initial interview that lasts two or three hours. According to Tom Kuhr, the firm's president, a relatively simple financial review involving tax planning and investments would usually cost $1,500 to $2,500 (as of 1981). To be a suitable client, Kuhr said, a person would need an annual income of at least $60,000, and a net worth of at least $200,000. A more complex review, including estate planning as well as taxes and investment planning, would probably be offered to a client with annual earnings of $100,000 and up, and a net worth exceeding $500,000. The cost of that sort of review might range from $4,000 to $20,000.

▶ *Financial publications.* If you manage your own assets, you can find a great deal of valuable information at relatively low cost through periodicals devoted to business and investing. The *Wall Street Journal, The New York Times,* and other daily newspapers carry extensive business and financial coverage. *Forbes, Financial World, Fortune, Business Week,* and *Barron's* are among the magazines that many investors read for insights into investment possibilities, market conditions, industry developments, and the investment process. *Changing Times* and *Money* magazines contain useful articles written for the lay person.

More expensive, and more specialized, are the materials put out by the major investment advisory services. The three largest such firms are Moody's, Standard & Poor's, and Value Line. Each publishes stock-market reports on a regular basis, covering from several hundred to several thousand stocks. Prices for these publications, on an annual basis, range roughly from $90 to $400. You can go to a large public library and look for copies of such publications as *The Value Line Investment Survey, Moody's Handbook of Common Stocks, Standard & Poor's Stock Reports* (eleven volumes); or *The Outlook.* If you are particularly interested in bonds, you may want to look at such publications as *Fixed Income Investor* or *Moody's Bond Survey.*

In addition to these well-known investment publications, there are an estimated 1,000 investment newsletters, written by people whose qualifications range from the excellent to the abysmal. In evaluating the worth of any such publication, it is well to view with some skepticism advertising claims regarding remarkable successes or uncanny predictions by the author of the newsletter. Only a long-term batting average for successful recommendations is germane, and advertising copy isn't a reliable indicator of this. Some newsletter authors maintain a fixed viewpoint toward investing (e.g., sell short, or buy gold) and come out right whenever conditions come around to match the pre-set advice. Others change their advice with the winds of fashion, but are often a bit too late to do investors reading the advice much good. Best are those who sometimes predict in advance the winds of change—but no one can do this all the time. In trying to decide whether to subscribe to an investment newsletter, your best guide is your own judgment of the writer's judgment. It may also be helpful to discuss the newsletter's value with your personal financial adviser—if you have one!

▶ *The conglomerate approach.* The ideal situation for each investor would be to have a trusted, personal investment adviser, whose advice was independent, disinterested, and wise, and whose fees were low. Sadly, the arrival of such an individual in your life may be no more likely than your chance of inheriting $1 million.

What you will probably end up doing, therefore, is taking smatterings of advice from a number of sources, and making the ultimate decisions yourself. You may, at various times, listen to an accountant, a lawyer, a banker, an insurance agent, a mutual-fund salesperson, or a broker. In each case, you will try to discount the element of self-interest in what the person suggests; you may wish to put special value on that advice that goes against the apparent self-interest of the adviser. You can supplement what you learn from these sources with additional information gained through your reading of financial publications or investment literature. You'll then proceed to factor in the information you know better than any adviser: your own situation, financial standing, temperament, and tolerance for risk.

Brokers.

If you're reading this book, it's likely that you have at least some interest in securities. And if you buy or sell securities, you are almost certain (the exception being if you deal only in mutual funds) to use the services of a broker. As the person who executes your securities transactions, a broker is likely to be a particularly important figure in your financial picture.

How do you pick a good broker? Should you use a full-service broker or a discount broker? What should you do if you encounter problems with the broker you've selected?

Throughout this book, I've stressed that in making any investment you should take into account the transaction costs. When you're buying or selling securities, transaction costs usually translate as brokerage commissions. Until 1975, investors had little reason to shop for low commission rates. All major brokers charged about the same fees. The New York Stock Exchange, scene of most stock transactions, long maintained a rigid minimum-rate schedule specifying what brokers should charge. (The fee depended, then as now, on how many shares you were trading, and on the price of each share.) In 1975, the Securities and Exchange Commission (SEC) abolished the minimum-rate schedule and declared that rates would be subject to negotiation between brokers and investors. The idea was to establish a competitive rate structure.

When the SEC action was under consideration, some observers hoped that abolition of fixed rates would mean lower prices for all. Others predicted that it would be a matter of bargaining muscle. Big traders such as bank trust departments and insurance companies, they said, would demand and get hefty discounts from the old, fixed rates. Individual investors would probably end up paying more than they did under the fixed-rate system. That, in fact, is what ended up happening.

At a major brokerage house, you, as an individual, are likely to pay a commission of at least 50 cents a share (on an average-priced stock), while a large institution is likely to pay only about 8 or 9 cents a share.

One way you can whittle down your commission cost is to use a discount broker. A discount brokerage office is in essence a bare-bones operation: no fancy furniture, no research analysts or research reports, no newsletters, no phone calls bearing the latest tips. A discount broker simply buys or sells what you tell him (her) to.

The discounts can be quite substantial in percentage terms, often between 25% and 75%. *Consumer Reports* Magazine published a survey in June of 1979 comparing the brokerage charges for several sample trades. For buying or selling 50 shares of a $30 stock, all of the large brokerage houses surveyed (Merrill Lynch, Bache, Dean Witter Reynolds, and E. F. Hutton) charged between $40 and $42. Discounters (such as Source Securities, Quick & Reilly, and Charles Schwab & Co.) charged from $24 to $32.

If you trade stocks frequently, that magnitude of a difference is well worth pursuing. But if, as I urge, you follow a buy-and-hold strategy, the commission difference, though large in percentage terms, isn't really very important. More important is the financial standing of the brokerage house; its ability to execute your trades at a favorable price, given a particular day's bid-and-asked spread; and its ability to handle the paperwork connected with your account efficiently. These factors, more than price, should determine your choice if you're an average small investor who doesn't trade securities frequently. The best way to check on many of these points is to check with friends or acquaintances on their experience with local brokerage houses.

Another point worth checking is the treatment of limit orders. A limit order is a conditional order to buy or sell securities—e.g., "buy at any price below $40 a share" or "sell at any price above $42." Some brokers charge extra for processing limit orders, some charge their standard rates.

Not all discount brokers will handle all transactions. Some want only active accounts, and will discourage customers who don't intend to do a lot of trading. To this end, some discount brokers have minimum commissions that aren't too different from the minimums imposed by the large full-service brokerage houses. You get major savings only when you're trading above the minimum levels.

A final factor in your choice of brokerage houses is the question of how much advice you want from your broker. Many full-service brokers provide advice on request; some provide it whether you want it or not. Discount brokers, as we've seen, just execute trades. Which way has more beauty is in the eye of the beholder.

If you have friends or relatives who own securities, listening to their experiences and recommendations is a good place to start. Find out from these sources how accessible a particular broker is, what sort of advice he or she gives, and whether the broker has urged speculative trading or frequent buying and selling.

One information source that won't help you is advertising, particularly television advertising. It's almost all image and fluff. Pay attention to the ads and you'll learn that Merrill Lynch is bullish on America, that Bache works hard for its brokers so that they can work hard for you, and that when E. F. Hutton talks, people listen. You'll learn, in short, nothing.

Before you open an account with any brokerage house, make a personal visit to the office. Talk with the broker a bit about your financial situation, your investment objectives. Ask him what type of investment strategy, in general terms, he would be urging you to pursue. If some of his ideas are different from yours, that's okay—another perspective can be useful. But he should lay out his reasoning candidly for you to consider. If he pressures you, it's a bad sign.

For many investors, a broker can be a valuable counselor. Just keep in mind that your interests and his don't always coincide. "Where," goes an old Wall Street adage, "are the *customer's* yachts?" And don't expect your broker's advice to be tinged with any special magic. Remember, even the best-paid professional money managers usually don't beat the market averages in the long run.

Now that we've talked about how to find the right broker, let's also consider what happens if he turns out, after all, to have been the wrong one. By that I don't mean that his recommended stocks drooped instead of soaring—that, alas, could happen to everyone. If you decide a broker is giving you inferior investment advice, your recourse is simply to find another broker or adviser. But there are some forms of poor performance in a broker that merit stronger measures.

For example, a broker might:
· buy stock for your account that is obviously unsuitable, based upon the instructions you have given him;
· buy or sell the wrong stock by mistake;
· fail to pass on dividends to you;
· fail to pass on to you within a reasonable time the cash from proceeds of selling stock;
· urge you to buy a stock while concealing important facts about it or about his company's relationship with the issuing company;

246

- misrepresent an investment;
- churn your account, making excessive trades to line his own pockets with commissions;
- fail to execute a trade, or execute it so late or so poorly as to cause you loss of income.

If you encounter what seems to you to be a serious abuse along these or similar lines, you have five potential avenues of recourse.

Recourse #1. Complain to the broker directly. If you state your complaint not abusively but clearly, directly, and firmly, your broker may see the light. He may perceive that you're serious about pursuing the matter, and that it's better to settle it now than later.

Recourse #2. Complain to the brokerage firm. Begin with the branch manager. If that produces no satisfaction, write to top officials at the firm's home office. At this point, all complaints should be made in writing, though you may wish in addition to follow up by telephone. Your complaint should state clearly how you were harmed, what abuse you believe your broker was guilty of, and all relevant factual information, such as dates and sums of money involved.

Recourse #3. Complain to the Securities and Exchange Commission. The SEC may write back to the brokerage firm to attempt a resolution, but that's all right: An inquiry from the SEC probably carries more clout than your original complaint did. Address your correspondence to Office of Consumer Affairs, Securities and Exchange Commission, 500 N. Capitol Street, Washington, D.C. 20549.

Recourse #4. Arbitrate your claim. The major stock exchanges have formal procedures for resolving disputes through arbitration. These are in all cases faster, less cumbersome, and less costly than going to court. However, if a substantial sum is involved, you might be better off going to court. You should decide only after consulting a lawyer.

(Keep in mind that the lawyer's fee for an arbitration will usually be much less than for a court proceeding.)

You should understand that if you agree to resolve a dispute by arbitration, you are giving up your right to go to court on the matter. However, you cannot legally be forced to give up this right in advance. In 1979, the SEC ruled that brokerage firms would have to stop using forms in which customers flatly agreed in advance to send any and all disputes to arbitration.

Arbitration is a procedure less formal than a courtroom hearing, but otherwise similar. In cases involving $2,500 or less, the major stock exchanges follow a procedure approved by the SEC in 1978. A single arbitrator decides the case. That arbitrator is usually a knowledgeable person not directly employed by the securities industry. But an insider may be used if arbitrators are in short supply. When less than $2,500 is at stake, you need not be present in person to submit your case to arbitration. You can present your case through a letter.

Addresses of the major arbitrating organizations are:
- Investor/Broker Liaison, New York Stock Exchange, 55 Water Street, New York, N.Y. 10041.
- Rulings and Inquiries Department, American Stock Exchange, 86 Trinity Place, New York, N.Y. 10006.
- American Arbitration Association, 140 W. 51st Street, New York, N.Y. 10020.

Which forum you use depends on which stock exchange was involved in the disputed transactions, and on which brokerage firm you were doing business with. The fee for arbitration in cases involving $2,500 or less is only about $15.

When $2,500–$10,000 is involved, there are normally three arbitrators (the majority of whom are supposed to be drawn from outside the securities industry, strictly defined), and your fee would usually amount to about $180. When still larger amounts are at stake, five arbitrators are usually used, and the fee would normally be $240 (in cases involving $10,000–$20,000) or $350 (in the largest cases).

When only a relatively small sum of money is at stake, it may not be necessary, or financially wise, for you to hire a lawyer, even if you choose to appear in person at the arbitration hearing. When larger amounts are at issue, a lawyer may well be helpful. But you can expect legal fees to dwarf the cost of the arbitration itself. A lawyer taking on a case will usually charge either a contingency fee consisting of a percentage (such as 33%) of any award won, or a fee based on hefty hourly rates ranging from $50 to $200 an hour. These rates are, of course, negotiable.

One advantage to using arbitration is that it consumes less of a lawyer's costly time than a court case would. Also, you can expect results from an arbitration within weeks or months. Court cases often take years.

Recourse #5. File a lawsuit. In cases where a major sum is at stake, this is sometimes the best course, expenses and complications notwithstanding. If you prevail, you might be awarded all or part of the cost of your legal fees, in addition to the basic award. Also, some brokerage firms that would not budge in response to lesser measures will offer to settle a dispute out of court once they see that someone is serious and persistent enough to institute a suit.

I hope you will have to use none of these methods of recourse. If you do run into a serious dispute, your knowledge of your rights and remedies may help to achieve a speedy resolution.

The more care you take in making your investments, and the more of your personal care and attention you give to them, the less likely it is that you'll find yourself involved in a bitter dispute over investments gone awry.

Saving or Investing for a Specific Goal

Often you'll want to save money for something specific—a car, a vacation, a college education for your child (see Appendix II). If you know about how much the item will cost, you can see the chart below to figure out how much you need to put away each year. This chart assumes (conservatively) that your return will be 5% per year, after taxes.

Years Until Fund Is Needed	Amount to be Saved or Invested Each Year to Accumulate to a $1,000 Fund (at 5%)
1	$952
2	$465
3	$302
4	$220
5	$172
6	$140
7	$117
8	$100
9	$86
10	$76
12	$60
14	$49
16	$40
18	$34
20	$29
25	$20
30	$15
35	$11
40	$08

For every $1,000 needed, multiply the figure in the right-hand column accordingly. For example, to accumulate a $40,000 fund in 7 years requires an annual saving or investment of 40 times $117, or $4,680. To accumulate a $200,000 fund in 25 years requires an annual saving or investment of $4,000 (200 times $20).

Accumulating a College Fund

If you have children, and expect to finance their college education, you'll need to start saving or investing for this purpose well in advance. Costs (including tuition, room, and board) recently averaged around $8,600 for four years at a state school, and around $20,700 for four years at a private college or university. Obviously, costs can vary from these averages depending on how far a child must commute, how high are living costs in the chosen city, and how high are the fees charged by the individual school your child attends.

Less obviously, costs are affected by inflation. Assuming that education costs inflate at 7% a year (the recent average), the 1980–81 costs can be extrapolated as follows.

Year*	Average cost, state college or university (4 years)	Average cost, private college or university (4 years)
1981	$8,628	$20,680
1983	$9,878	$23,677
1985	$11,310	$27,107
1987	$12,948	$31,035
1990	$15,862	$38,019
1995	$22,248	$53,324
2000	$31,203	$74,790

* Select a year that approximates your child's third year of college.

252

These are frightening figures, but based on present trends they have to be viewed as realistic. Your child might have a portion of the cost defrayed by a scholarship or some other form of financial aid. A wide variety of scholarships are available, with eligibility usually based either on merit (academic or athletic) or financial need. Some scholarships, however, are based on more recondite criteria: There are scholarships for people with certain names, people from certain ethnic groups, people whose parents (or other relatives) are members of certain occupations, and so on. Two organizations may be useful in helping parents discover possible sources of financial aid for college expenses. One is Scholarship Search, 1775 Broadway, New York, N.Y. 10019, which for a fee furnishes a computer printout showing possible sources of scholarships for a particular applicant. Another is Student College Aid, 3641 Deal Street, Houston, Texas 77025, a newer firm that provides a similar service. Recent fees were $67 for Scholarship Search, $45 for Student College Aid.

Once you have an idea what the cost will be, you can use Appendix I to figure out how much you need to set aside each year to meet it.

You may have noticed that I've assumed college costs will inflate 7% a year, but have credited you (in Appendix I) with only a 5% yearly after-tax return on your savings or investments. That's conservative. If you do better than that with your investments, I'm confident you will be able to find plenty of places to plug in the extra money.

Accumulating a Retirement Fund

The worksheet in this appendix is adapted from a similar worksheet I developed for the New York State Consumer Protection Board, which appears in the board's publication *Getting Ready for Retirement*. It is used here with permission.

How much money do I need to retire? That's a question people often ask themselves. But they end up shrugging, not knowing how to prepare any reasonable estimate. This worksheet is designed to help you figure out how much money you'll need in your retirement fund, and also how much money you'll have to save each year to accumulate that size a fund.

The calculations here arbitrarily assume that the long-term inflation rate will be 5%, and that you can earn 5% after taxes on your savings and investments. Inflation may be higher than that, but if so, your return on savings and investments might well also be higher.

1. What is your current annual income after taxes?

   _____

2. Estimate the amount you now spend for child care, commuting to work, savings, and other needs that will be eliminated after retirement.

   _____

3. Subtract step #2 from step #1.

   _____

4. Multiply your step #3 total by 20, because 20 years' income should provide an ample retirement fund.

---

5. Adjust this total for inflation, choosing a factor for the number of years until you're 75. (Age 75 comes roughly in the middle of your retirement period.)

Years Until You're 75	Inflation Factor
5	1.3
10	1.6
15	2.1
20	2.7
25	3.4
30	4.3
35	5.5
40	7.0

Multiply your step #4 total by the inflation factor you selected. The result is your total need for retirement funds.

---

6. Figure out about how much money you'll be earning per year just before you retire. To do this, take your current salary and adjust it for inflation.

Years Until You Retire	Inflation Factor
5	1.3
10	1.6
15	2.1
20	2.7
25	3.4
30	4.3

Multiply your current earnings by the inflation factor.

———————

7. Now figure out about what percentage of your preretirement earnings will be replaced by Social Security retirement benefits. To make an educated guess, use the chart below.

Present Yearly Earnings	Probable % of Earnings Replaced
$10,000	38%
$15,000	34%
$20,000	28%
$25,000	24%
$30,000	20%
$35,000	17%
$40,000	15%
$45,000	13%
$50,000	12%

Based on the chart estimate what percentage of your own earnings are likely to be replaced by Social Security: _____%

8. Multiply your step #6 total by the percentage in step #7. This tells you roughly how much income you can expect per year from Social Security.

———————

9. Multiply your step #8 total by 33, reflecting the fact that Social Security retirement benefits are adjusted for inflation yearly. (The factor of 33 is based on the assumption that you'll collect these benefits for about 20 years.) This tells you about how much money you can expect to collect from Social Security retirement benefits throughout your retirement period.

———————

10. Ask your company benefits manager to help you estimate your yearly income from a company pension, at current benefit rates.

_____

11. Multiply the step #10 total by an inflation factor, since company benefits will probably rise roughly in step with inflation.

Years Until You Retire	Inflation Factor
5	1.3
10	1.6
15	2.1
20	2.7
25	3.4
30	4.3

This tells you about what your pension benefit will be per year at the time you retire.

_____

12. Multiply the step #11 total by 20. This reflects the assumption that you'll collect benefits for about 20 years. The total isn't adjusted for inflation this time around, because company pensions, unlike Social Security, are almost never adjusted for inflation once a person retires. (If your employer is one of the rare exceptions, multiply by 33 instead of 20.) This gives you a rough total of what your pension benefits will amount to throughout your retirement period.

_____

257

13. Now subtract from your total need the portion that will be provided by Social Security and by your company pension.

Total need (step #5): _____

— Social Security (step #9): _____

— Company Pension (step #12): _____

= Amount you must provide through savings and investments: _____

14. Figure out how much you've already saved up for retirement.

_____

15. Subtract step #14 from step #13. This tells you how much more money you need to accumulate in your retirement fund. _____

16. Use the chart below to see how much you need to invest to save each year to reach your retirement-fund goal.

If You Will Retire in This Many Years	Divide Your Step #15 Total by This Amount
5	5.7
10	12.9
15	22.1
20	33.9
25	48.9
30	68.1

This bit of division gives you the average amount you would need to save each year from now until you retire to preserve roughly the same standard of living you currently have.

_____ per year

Suggested Further Reading

Books

A Random Walk Down Wall Street by Burton G. Malkiel. New York: W. W. Norton & Co., second paperback edit., 1981.

The Inflation Beater's Investment Guide by Burton G. Malkiel. New York: W. W. Norton & Co., 1980.

How to Make Money in Wall Street by Louis Rukeyser. New York: Doubleday & Co., 1974, 1976.

The Only Investment Guide You'll Ever Need by Andrew Tobias. New York: Harcourt Brace Jovanovich, 1978.

Magazines

The following are magazines that you might want to subscribe to. They're listed in order of my personal preference.

Forbes

Financial World

Fortune

Business Week

Barron's

Advisory Services

Most of these services are expensive, and are best used, at least initially, at the library.

The Value Line Investment Survey

Standard & Poor's Stock Reports

Moody's Handbook of Common Stocks

Twenty Investment Rules
in a Nutshell

1. Try to invest 15% of your after-tax income.
2. Keep three months' income in a NOW account or savings account.
3. Keep another three months' income in either a certificate of deposit or a money market fund.
4. Don't invest until you have enough insurance.
5. Don't invest until your debts are under control.
6. Keep at least 20% of your investment money in investments that involve some risk.
7. Don't put more than 80% of your investment portfolio into risky vehicles.
8. Use an Individual Retirement Account (IRA) or a Keogh Plan if you're eligible to.
9. If you can afford it, own your home.
10. If you're going to buy a bond, consider high-quality discounted corporate bonds or municipals.
11. Buy stocks when they're undervalued.
12. Hold stocks for the long term.
13. Prefer stocks with low price-earnings ratios.
14. Diversify your holdings.
15. In buying a mutual fund, look for consistency.
16. Tax shelters should be evaluated as straight investments first, tax dodges second.
17. Go light on investments in gold, silver, and collectibles.
18. Use leverage sparingly.
19. Avoid entirely short selling, options trading, and commodities speculating.
20. In getting advice, consider the source.

Index

Accountants, 236
Aggressive growth funds, 144, 146–147
Aggressive growth stocks, 156, 160–161
Alaska, 182
Annuities, 210–213
 charges and fees, 212–213
 deferred, 211
 fixed-dollar, 211
 fixed-premium, 210, 212
 lifetime, 211
 single-premium, 210
 tax sheltered, 156, 158, 213
 variable premium, 210, 212
Antiques, 183, 190–192
Apartment buildings, 169–171
Appraisers, 191–192
Arbitration, 248–249
Arrearage, 89
Art, 182, 197–199
Art-investment syndicates, 198–199
ASA Limited, 151, 153
Assessment bonds, 85
Auditors, 121
Averaging out, 133–134

Backer, Jack B., 188
Balance, 33–35

Balanced funds, 140, 144, 145–146
Bankers, 237
Bankruptcy, 63, 77
Banks, choosing, 33
Barron's, 127, 241
Beta figures, 112–119, 125–126
Bills. *See* Treasury bills
Bonds, 30, 48, 135, 182
 assessment, 85
 callable, 73–75
 collateral trust, 76
 convertible, 72–73, 225–231
 corporate, 61–79
 debenture, 226
 discounted, 72, 75, 78
 full faith and credit, 85
 funds, 54
 income, 76–77
 issue, 62, 77–78
 rating services, 64–66, 84, 85, 226, 230–231
 refunding, 74
 yields, 70–72, 84, 85, 139
Books, rare, 182, 196–197
Borrowing to buy goods, 16
Borrowing to invest, 10, 16
Brokers and brokerage firms, 31, 51, 62, 103, 237–238, 243–249

Brokers and brokerage
firms (*cont.*)
  commissions, 9, 23, 28, 133,
    243–244
  discount, 244
  disputes with and claims
    against, 246–249
Budgeting, 4, 17
Bullion, 135, 178
Business Periodicals Index, 127
Business Week, 97, 127, 241
Buying on margin, 215–219

Callability, 73, 85
Capital gains, 8, 57–60, 62, 72,
    77, 84, 95–98
  and collectibles, 184
  tax on, 97–98
Cash-value life insurance, 156,
    158–160
Cattle raising, 156, 163–164, 165
Certificates of deposit (CDs),
    7, 14, 23–24, 38–47
  choosing, 45–47
  jumbo, 43–44, 48, 51
  penalties, 44–46
  six-month, 39–41, 50
  tax-sheltered, 44
  thirty-month, 41
  time deposit, 43
Certified Financial Planner, 237
Changing Times magazine, 241
Chase Manhattan Mortgage and
    Realty Trust, 176
Checking account, 12, 33
Chicago Board Options
    Exchange, 223
Chicago Board of Trade, 231,
    233
Chrysler Corporation, 22, 63
Coins, 135, 178, 180, 183, 194–
    196
Collateral trust bonds, 76

Collectibles, 6, 10, 29, 181–199
College fund, 252–253
Commercial paper, 48, 50–51, 52
Commodities, 11, 135, 231–235
  funds, 140
Common stocks. *See* Stocks
Companies:
  price-earnings multiples, 103–
    112, 125, 130–131, 132
  researching of, 119–127
Compounding of interest, 35
Condominiums. *See* Home
    ownership
Consumer Price Index, 182
Consumer Reports, 244
*Consumers Union Report on
    Life Insurance, The,* 15
Convertible bonds, 72–73, 225–
    231
  choosing, 230–231
  conversion premium, 226–227,
    230
  interest, 225
  sample chart, 228
Convertible preferred stock, 225
Corporate bonds, 8, 21–22, 61–
    79, 81
  callability, 73–75
  funds, 78–79, 145
  rating of, 64–66
  risk, 63–64
  security for repayment, 75–76
  yields, 70–72
Coupon rate, 62, 70, 71, 75, 84
Credit cards, 16
Current yields, 70, 71, 84

Day-of-deposit to day-of-
    withdrawal, 33–34, 36
Dead days, 35
Debentures, 76
Debt management, 12, 16–19
Debt securities, 87

Debt-to-equity ratio, 123–124
Dependents, 24
Diamonds, 182, 185, 186–190
Disability insurance, 14–15
Diversification, 10, 20, 27–29
 stock portfolio, 9–10, 28, 118–
  119, 126–128, 134, 136, 137,
  139, 140
Dividends, 92–95
Dollar-cost averaging, 132–133
Dow Jones Industrial Average,
  27*n.*, 30, 98, 130, 137, 148
Dreyfus Third Century Fund,
  148
Dual-purpose fund, 148–149

Education costs, 4, 252–253
Efficient-market theory, 101–102
Emergency, financial, 13
Employee Retirement Income
  Security Act (ERISA), 201,
  202
Eurodollars, 135

Fama, Eugene, 100
"Fannie Maes," 87
Farmland, 182
Federal Deposit Insurance
  Corporation, 39
Federal National Mortgage
  Association (FNMA), 87
Federal Reserve Bank, 49, 86
Federal Reserve Board, 207, 217
Federal Savings and Loan
  Insurance Corporation, 39
Federal Trade Commission, 7,
  124–125, 200, 212
Financial advisors, 4
 brokers, 237–238, 243–249
 types of, 236–243
Financial analysts, 103
Financial planners, 237

Financial publications, 241–242
Financial records, 20, 29
Financial World, 127, 241
Fitch Investors Service, 50
Fixed Income Investor, 241
Fixed-income securities, 49
Fixed-return investments, 49
Food and Drug Administration,
  124
Forbes Dart Board Fund, 100,
  128, 129
Forbes magazine, 10, 58, 59, 99,
  100, 113, 127
 Annual Mutual Fund Survey,
  150–153
Foreign currency, 182
Foreign funds, 149
Fortune magazine, 127, 241
Free-lancers, 13
Full faith and credit bonds, 85
Furniture, antique, 183, 190–192
Futures contracts, 231

Gas-drilling, and tax shelters,
  155, 156, 161–163, 165
Gemological Institute of
  America, 188–189
Gems, 186–190
General Motors, 107, 108, 109
General obligation bonds, 85
Getting Ready for Retirement,
  254
"Ginnie Maes," 87–88
Gold, 10, 29, 30, 177–179, 181,
  182
 funds, 135, 140, 153
Government bonds, 73, 77, 80–
  88
Government National Mortgage
  Association (GNMA), 87–
  88
Grace days, 35

Growth funds, 140, 144, 146
Growth and income funds, 144, 146

Health insurance, 14, 15
Health-maintenance organization (HMO), 15
Hedge fund, 147–148
Hirsch, Yale, 137, 150
Home insurance, 14, 15–16
Home ownership, 8, 27, 55–60, 166–167
  and leverage, 214–215
  as tax shelter, 156, 165
Hooker Chemical, 107, 108
House. *See* Home
Housing market, 182
Hunt family, 179, 180

IBM, 108, 109
Income:
  amount to invest or save, 3–6, 32
  fluctuations in, 13
Income bond, 76–77
Income funds, 144, 145
Income tax, 57, 60, 72, 80, 81, 97–98
Independent financial counselors, 238–241
Index fund, 137, 148
Individual Retirement Account (IRA), 7, 155, 157, 165, 200, 202–208, 213
  trustees, 206–207, 208
Industries:
  price-earnings multiples, 110
  researching of, 119–120
Industry funds, 149
Inflation, 4, 16, 96, 137, 254
Insurance, 14–16
Insurance agents, 237

Insurance program, 12, 14–16
Interest, 69
  balance method, 33–35
  ceilings, 31, 44
  compounding, 35
  grace days, 35
  tax on, 72, 97
Interest rates:
  coupon rate, 62, 70, 71, 75
  current yield, 70, 71
  shocks, 53
Internal Revenue Service (IRS), 29, 42, 57, 164
  Disclosure Statement, 205–206, 208
International Investors, 151, 153
Investing, for specific goals, 251
Investment(s):
  average family, 3
  basics, 20–29
  diversification of, 9–10, 20, 27–29
  liquidity, 12, 20, 22–23, 24
  portfolio chart, 26–27
  records, 29
  risk, 20–22, 24, 25, 28
  rules, 3–11, 260
  size, 20, 23
Investment advisory services, 113, 241
Investment bankers, 51
Investment certificates. *See* Certificates of deposit
Investment Companies, 54, 146, 152
Investment Company Institute (ICI), 139, 146
Investment officers, 103

Japan Fund, 149
Jastram, Roy, 178
Jumbo certificate, 43–44, 48, 51
Junk bond fund, 79

Keogh plan, 7, 155, 157, 165, 200, 208–210, 213
  trustees, 209
Kirkpatrick, Charles, 58–59
Kuhr, Tom, 240

Land, 167–168
Lawyers, 236–237
Leverage, 214–215, 233
Life insurance, 14, 15
  cash-value, 156, 158–160
Liquidity, 12, 20, 22, 23, 24, 38, 56
Loans, 16, 18
  low-interest, 14
  mortgage, 17

McDonald's Corporation, 109
McIntyre, Thomas, 100
McMoRan, 107, 108
Malkiel, Burton, 103, 129, 143
Margin account, 216, 219
Margin buying, 215–219
Margin calls, 216, 218, 220, 233
Market share trends, 124
Martin, Jackie Pinson, 34
Maturity, 49
Merrill Lynch, 178, 232
Mining stocks, 178, 180
Mintz, Joe A., 205, 207
Modified pass-through certificate, 87
Money magazine, 241
Money market funds, 7, 14, 24, 30, 31, 41, 48–54, 69–70, 140, 144–145
  instruments, 48–51, 135
  mutual fund, 51–54
Monthly-payment test, 17, 18
Moody's Bond Survey, 241
Moody's Handbook of Common Stocks, 124, 241

Moody's Investors Service, 50, 64–66, 84, 85, 123, 226, 241
Morse, Richard, 34 and *n.*
Mortgage(s), 16–18, 56, 59
  bonds, 75, 87
  interest, 8, 87
Multifund, 148
Municipal bonds, 8, 73, 77, 80, 81, 175
  funds, 88, 144, 145
  as tax shelters, 156, 160, 165
  yields, 81
Mutual funds, 10, 28, 135–153
  choosing, 149–153
  commissions, 143
  discounted closed-end shares, 143–144
  financial objectives, 144–149
  gold, 178
  index fund, 137, 148
  load vs. no-load, 140–142
  management fee, 136, 137, 141
  net asset value, 135
  net asset value per share, 135, 141
  open vs. closed-end, 142–144
  operating expenses, 136, 137
  performance, 99–101
  salespersons, 237
  silver, 180
  types, 140–149

Nabisco, 107, 108
Net-worth test, 17, 19
New York Stock Exchange, 217, 243
  Index, 98, 137, 149
  margin requirements, 217–218
New York Times, The, 54, 100, 207, 241
Notes. *See* Treasury notes

NOW account, 12–13, 14, 21, 23, 24, 30–32, 33, 36

Oakland Financial Group, 240
Occupation, 24
Occupational Safety and Health Administration (OSHA), 125
Oil drilling, 155, 156, 161–163, 165, 182
Options, 11, 221–225
funds, 144, 147
Outlook, The, 241
Over the Counter (OTC) market, 175

Paintings. *See* Art
Passbook savings account, 20
Pensions, 7, 200, 201–202, 257, 258
as tax shelters, 156–157
Performance funds, 140
Pinson pattern, 34
Preferred stock, 89–90, 225
Premiums, 74
Price-earnings multiples, 103–112, 125, 130–131, 132
Price-earnings ratios, 8, 9
Prime rate, 21
Princeton University Financial Research Center, 103
Property tax, 8, 60

Random Walk Down Wall Street, A (Malkiel), 143
Random-walk theory, 100, 102
Reagan, Ronald, 80
Real estate, 6, 27, 29, 30, 55–60. *See also* Home ownership
commercial property, 167, 171–173

depreciation, 155
land, 167–168
public syndications, 167, 173–175
rental property, 167, 169–171
single-family residential property, 167, 168
as tax shelters, 156, 160
taxes, 8, 60
Real-estate investment trusts (REITs), 167, 175–176
Real property, 184
Records of transactions, 29
Refunding, 74
Regulatory agencies, 124–125
Rental property, 167, 169–171
Renting of home or apartment, 8, 59–60
Retirement, 4, 24, 25, 122
accounts, 155–157
funds, 254–258
Revenue bonds, 85
Risk, 7, 20–22, 25, 28
and age, 24
Rosenberg, Barr, 113

Salary, 32, 80. *See also* Income
Saloman Brothers, 181
Samuelson, Paul, 100
Saving(s), 3
average family, 3
cushion, 12–14, 30–32
for specific goals, 251
Savings account, 12, 20, 21, 23, 24, 30, 137
checklist, 36–37
closing prematurely, 35
excess withdrawals, 35
interest ceilings, 31
vs. CDs, 38
Savings bonds, 86–87
Saving certificates. *See* Certificates of deposit

Securities, 149
  analysts, 103
  convertible bonds, 225–231
  dealers, 62
  tax exempt, 135
Securities and Exchange Com-
  mission (SEC), 140, 223,
  224, 243
Senate Banking and Currency
  Committee, 100
Short selling, 11, 219–221
Silver, 10, 30, 179–180, 181, 182
Six-month certificates of deposit,
  39–41, 50
Social-conscience fund, 140, 148
Social Security benefits, 15, 256,
  258
Speculation, 126, 232
  commodities, 231–235
Stamps, 182, 192–194
Standard & Poor's, 50, 64–66, 84,
  85, 109–111, 123, 226, 241
Standard & Poor's 500, 98, 99,
  137, 148, 150
*Standard and Poor's Stock
  Reports,* 241
Stocks, 6, 23–30, 61–62, 66, 75,
  182
  alpha figures, 126
  average returns, 96
  averaging out, 133–134
  beta figures, 112–119, 125–126
  buying on margin, 215–219
  buying undervalued, 8–9
  checklist for choosing, 126–
  127
  choosing, 119–127
  common, 91–134
  dividends, 103–106, 122
  dollar-cost averaging, 132–133
  estimated earnings, 106 *n.*
  foreign, 135
  mutual funds specializing in,
  135–153

portfolio, 127–134
portfolio diversification, 9–10,
  28, 118–119, 126, 127–128,
  134, 136, 137, 139, 140
preferred, 89–90, 225
price-earnings multiples, 103–
  112, 125, 130–131, 132
short-term vs. long-term, 9,
  111, 129, 130, 131, 134, 140
short selling, 219–221
staggering of purchases, 131,
  132, 134
as tax shelters, 156, 160–161
volatility, 112–119
yield, 92–98
Stock market:
  averages, 98–103, 130
  crash of 1929, 216
  indexes, 27 and *n.*
  peaks, 130, 131
Subordinated debentures, 76

Tax benefit, and commercial
  property, 172
Tax bracket, 7, 8, 80, 81, 84,
  203, 204
  chart, 82
Tax credit, 155
Tax deductions, 8
Tax deferral, 154, 160
  IRAs, 155, 157, 165, 200,
  202–208
Tax exempt bonds, 80–84, 88
  chart, 83
Tax-sheltered certificates, 44
Tax shelters, 10, 154–165
  tax deferral, 154, 160
  shelter of capital, 155–165
  shelter of income, 154–155
Taxes, 42, 56–57
  income, 57, 60, 72, 80, 81,
  97–98
  property, 167

Templeton Growth Fund, 149
Thirty-month certificates of
    deposit, 41
Time deposits. *See* Certificates
    of deposit
Train, John, 185–186
Treasury bills, 39–40, 49–50, 86
Treasury bonds, 86
Treasury notes, 48, 49, 86
Truth in Savings legislation,
    34 *n.*

Unit investment trust, 79
U.S. Department of Labor, 202
U.S. government bonds, 85–88.
    See also Government bonds
    as tax shelters, 156, 160

U.S. Savings bonds, 86–87
U.S. Treasury. *See* Treasury

Value Line, 128, 241
*Value Line Investment Survey,
    The,* 24

Wall Street, 130
Wall Street Journal, 54, 127,
    188, 241
Wall Street Journal Index, 127
Wilshire Associates, 114
Withdrawals, 35

Yield curve, 40, 42
Yield to maturity, 71, 72, 84
Yields, bond, 70–72, 84, 85, 139

John Dorfman, formerly chief securities writer for the Associated Press, is the author of a half-dozen books, including *A Consumer's Arsenal, Consumer Tactics Manual,* and *Consumer Survival Kit,* which was named one of the fifty best books of 1976 by *Library Journal.* He has also written a syndicated newspaper column, "Count Your Change," and his articles on consumer and financial affairs have appeared in *Money, Consumer Reports, Playboy,* and other magazines. He was born in Chicago in 1947, and received his B.A. from Princeton and an M.F.A. from Columbia University. He now lives in Westchester County, New York, with his wife and two daughters.